LUFTWAFFE IN COMBAT

DER ADLER

THE OFFICIAL NAZI LUFTWAFFE MAGAZINE

THE ENGLISH LANGUAGE EDITIONS

Pen & Sword
AVIATION

This edition published in 2013 by
Pen & Sword Aviation
An imprint of Pen & Sword Books Ltd, 47 Church Street, Barnsley, South Yorkshire S70 2AS

First published in Great Britain in 2011 in digital format by Coda Books Ltd.

Copyright © Coda Books Ltd, 2011

Published under licence by Pen & Sword Books Ltd.

ISBN 978 1 78159 140 6

A CIP catalogue record for this book is available from the British Library

Printed and bound in India by Replika Press Pvt. Ltd.

Pen & Sword Books Ltd incorporates the Imprints of Pen & Sword Aviation, Pen & Sword Family History, Pen & Sword Maritime, Pen & Sword Military, Pen & Sword Discovery, Pen & Sword Politics, Pen & Sword Atlas, Pen & Sword Archaeology, Wharncliffe Local History, Wharncliffe True Crime, Wharncliffe Transport, Pen & Sword Select, Pen & Sword Military Classics, Leo Cooper, The Praetorian Press, Claymore Press, Remember When, Seaforth Publishing and Frontline Publishing

For a complete list of Pen & Sword titles please contact

PEN & SWORD BOOKS LIMITED
47 Church Street, Barnsley, South Yorkshire, S70 2AS, England
E-mail: enquiries@pen-and-sword.co.uk
Website: www.pen-and-sword.co.uk

Heinkel-Bomber
schiesst Spitfire ab
Heinkel bomber brings down a Spitfire

Eine Rotte Heinkel-Kampfflugzeuge hat über der Insel einen Sonderauftrag geflogen und ist nun im Morgengrauen auf dem Rückflug begriffen. Die letzten Ausläufer der britischen Insel ziehen unter den Flugzeugen vorbei

A two-plane element of Heinkel bombers has carried out a special mission over the island and is now on its way back at early dawn. The last cliffs of the coast are passing beneath the airplanes

Kaum ist die Küste übersprungen, da ruft der Funker eines der beiden deutschen Kampfflugzeuge „Achtung, Jäger von hinten!" Infolge seiner überlegenen Schnelligkeit hat der britische Jäger, der sich beim Näherkommen als eine Spitfire herausstellt, die beiden Bomber bald eingeholt. Aber schon hat ihn der Heckschütze des einen Kampfflugzeugs im Visier und jagt ihm die ersten Feuerstöße entgegen

Hardly have they crossed the coastline when the radio operator of one of the bombers raises the warning cry, "Look out! Pursuit plane behind us!" As the British plane overhauled the two bombers owing to its superior speed, it was seen to be a Spitfire. The rear gunner of one of the bombers has already drawn a bead on him and rips out the first bursts of fire

In den Geschoßgarben des deutschen Schützen dreht sich der Brite in einer weit hergezogenen Kurve ab. Tief unten zieht die Küste vorbei. Es ist nicht anzunehmen, daß der Engländer den beiden Deutschen weit auf See hinausfolgt. Aber mit einem zweiten Angriff ist sicher noch zu rechnen

The British pilot swerves aside from the cones of fire of the German gunner, describing a wide curve. The coast rushes past far below. It is not likely that the British airman will follow the two German planes far out to sea, but a second attack must certainly be reckoned with

Was nun folgt, hat sich blitzschnell ab- gespielt. Unter den Feuerstößen des wackeren Funkers beginnt der Engländer zu „stinken", d. h. er zeigt durch eine weiße Rauchfahne, daß der Benzintank getroffen ist. In der gleichen Richtung weiterfliegend, trägt ihn seine Geschwindig- keit an der von ihm angegriffenen vorderen Maschine vorbei, von der aus diese und die nächste Aufnahme gemacht werden konnten

The sequel took place with lightning rapidity. Under the bursts of fire from the gallant radio operator, the Britisher shows a wisp of white smoke, indicating that the fuel tank has been hit. Continuing his flight in the same direction, his speed carries him on past the front machine that he had attacked, from which it was possible to make this shot and the next one

Aufnahmen: Luftwaffe

Nach kurzem Geradeausflug geht der Engländer, aus dem bereits helle Flam- men schlagen, auf den Kopf und stürzt, gefolgt von einer langen Rauchfahne, in die Tiefe

After flying straight ahead for a little, flames burst out of the British machine and it crashes nose down followed by a long trail of smoke

Und richtig, die Spitfire kurvt erneut ein und setzt sich hinter die vor- ausfliegende He 111, dadurch aber gerät sie in günstigste Schuß- position des Heckschützen der zweiten Maschine

Sure enough, the Spitfire banks again and starts after the He 111 flying in advance, but thereby places himself in the most favorable firing position for the rear gunner of the second machine

3

Das halten Deutiche

German airplanes stand very rough usage

Von Dr. Herbert Müllenbach

In den nun schon der Geschichte angehörenden glorreichen Feldzügen in Polen, in Norwegen und im Westen war es der deutschen Luftwaffe zum ersten Male vergönnt, ihr Können vor aller Welt zu erproben. Damit hat zugleich die deutsche Luftfahrtindustrie, die in ihrer heutigen Form in wenigen Jahren in des Wortes wahrstem Sinne aus dem Boden gestampft worden ist, ihre vom Ausland hin und wieder angezweifelte Leistungsfähigkeit wirkungsvoll beweisen können. Daß sie schöne und auch schnelle Flugzeuge zu bauen versteht, das wußte man schon in Friedenszeiten. Daß diese Flugzeuge aber auch im kriegsmäßigen Einsatz das Vollendetste an neuzeitlicher Flugzeugbaukunst darstellen, haben die Siege der Luftwaffe gelehrt. Zur Überraschung unserer Feinde erwiesen sich die deutschen Flugzeuge in einem bisher für unmöglich gehaltenen Umfang unempfindlich gegen Beschußwirkung. Einige besonders einprägsame Bilder von Flugzeugen, die trotz schwerer Beschädigungen flugfähig blieben, zeigt unser Bericht

Derartige Schußbeschädigungen können deutschen Flugzeugen, hier einem Sturzkampfflugzeug, nichts anhaben

Even a hit like this on a dive bomber cannot harm a German airplane

Zum Bilde links: Durch Unwucht der zerschossenen Luftschraube aus den Trägern gerissener Motor. Der Motor hängt nur noch in den Halteseilen. Das Flugzeug flog mit den beiden anderen Motoren nach Hause

Left: Engine torn from its supports by airscrew out of balance owing to a hit and hanging only from the drag wires. The airplane flew home with the other two engines

Zum Bilde rechts: Beschädigungen einer Ju 52 durch Baumberührung infolge Nebels. Die Maschine ist im Blindflug weitergeflogen und dann sicher gelandet

Right: Junkers Ju 52 badly mauled by coming into contact with trees in a fog. The machine continued its flight, the pilot flying blind, and then landed safely

Flugzeuge aus

The glorious campaigns in Poland, Norway, and in the West, now a matter of history, provided the German Air Force for the first time with an opportunity of demonstrating its skill and prowess to the world at large. The German aircraft industry, which, in its present form, had literally been stamped out of the ground within a very few years, simultaneously had a chance to supply effective proof of its capacity, upon which foreign countries had now and again thought fit to cast aspersion. It had already been well known in peace times that the German aircraft industry knew how to build beautifully designed airplanes that were also remarkable for their speed, but it was left to the victories gained by the Air Force to teach doubters that these planes actually represent modern aircraft design of the most perfect type for service also in warfare. Much to the surprise of our foes, German airplanes have proved to be indifferent to shell fire to an extent hitherto held to be incredible. Our pictorial report shows a few specially impressive photos of airplanes that were able to continue their flight in spite of serious damage

Beschädigte Tragfläche eines deutschen Aufklärers. Das Flugzeug ist mit nur geringer Beeinträchtigung seiner Flugfähigkeit weitergeflogen

Damaged wing of a German reconnaissance airplane. The machine was further flown its flying qualities being only slightly impaired

Die schnellen Kanonen von Abbeville

The Swift Guns of Abbeville

The Experiences of Lieutenant-Colonel Wolf and the Gunners of His Anti-aircraft Defense Battalion

By Hans Wörner

Lieutenant-Colonel Wolf, whose experiences on the western front are here vividly described. He was awarded the Knighthood Cross by the Führer and Supreme Commander of the fighting forces   Foto Scherl

Probably not one in a thousand knows where Süggerath lies, or has ever heard of Prummern, Beggendorf, Freienberg, Übach-Palenberg, Apweiler, Floverich, and Immendorf. When the Creator put Germany together, there was only room left for these dear little hamlets quite at the edge, at the western edge, that is to say, near where Limburg lies, which belongs to the Dutch. And the people in the German district of Geilenkirchen-Heinsberg are of precisely the same cast as those in Dutch Limburg, which means that they are of a solid breed, the mental condition of which might be termed stocky, not easy to get agoing, but of great serenity of spirit. In the early morning the children toddle to the school mass with their wooden clogs; a very decent sort of rye bread is baked there and is spread with thin viscous molasses and thick white cottage cheese, besides the butter. To be born in that district means that one has the benefit of that fact for the whole of one's life.

The gunners of the first battalion of the anti-aircraft Artillery Regiment No. 64 are lying here in December 1939 at the standby. It is worse than cold in that December of 1939, in fact, Siberia has nothing to brag about, compared with Immendorf. A kind of snow that actually consists of hard, dry needles of ice crunches beneath the tires of the motor cycles, motor vehicles, and Krupp tractors. The country is full to bursting with soldiers; so many companies, battalions, detachments, regiments had been crammed into all these little frontier towns, villages, and hamlets, so as to be able to repel any attack at once. But the war, on account of which these soldiers are waiting at the standby, that peculiar war is evidently lying in civilian billets also and sleeping away one week after another.

The new year presents itself. Springtime is well on the way. And then one fine morning the bombshell in Norway bursts.

Will the battalion now be sent to Norway?

The battalion waits and waits, but everything proceeds smoothly in Norway and no one devotes a thought to the antiaircraft battalion.

In a situation like that, one naturally begins to think about his commander and his comrades.

The battalion had long since welded together its officers and gunners and consolidated itself into the form it had assumed on the Dutch frontier at the time of the campaign in Norway. Lieutenant-Colonel Wolf, the commander, who disposed of no lessenergy than experience, had taken care of that. He had made his hand smartly felt, where that seemed to be necessary, and had taken pains to make a formation out of his battalion which should be fit for the greatest achievements. He ticks off nobody, but helps everyone to slough his old self and to assume the form that beseems a soldier. He does not drill-discipline a man, but molds him. Our Lieutenant-Colonel therefore knows, long before the battalion receives its baptism of fire, that it will stand

the acid test. Apart from himself, only a few of his officers have had experience of active service in the Great War, but they are all of the finest metal: very active, ardent, critical, but not to be broken. Lieutenant-Colonel Wolf often thinks that he could wish no one better officers than he has himself.

The men had been recruited in the Rhineland, so that Rhenish blood flows in their veins; it is manœuverable, starts well, and responds readily. Men from Brandenburg or Silesia might perhaps be easier to lead, but Lieutenant-Colonel Wolf trusts his big-hearted men from Düsseldorf to come up to the expectations reposed in them. He does not have a moment's difficulty in thinking their thoughts, and, vice versa, in getting them to enter into his thoughts. His aim is not by any means to be respected simply because he happens to be Lieutenant-Colonel and commander of the battalion, but he wants to prove to himself and to others that his authority is deserved.

Of the career of that man much might be told, but we shall be as laconic as his soldierly way demands. He is of 1899 vintage and his home town is Brunswick. In 1917 he joined up as aspirant officer in the 4th Hanoverian Infantry Regiment in Hameln on the Weser. By the end of the year he had already been in the trenches for weeks in an inferno of spattering clay, shrieking shells, and a welter of appalling bloodshed.

Concerning his experiences of that period, there is little to be got out of the present Lieutenant-Colonel Wolf. He passes through the ordeal, emerges unscathed from the tremendous struggle, and takes his discharge.

Fifteen years roll by before the great change comes for him. He again becomes a soldier in the General Göring Regiment. Captain Wolf leads the 12th company at Neuhammer. In the summer of 1935 there is an inspection by the Führer and General Göring. The regiment is mechanized, everything is mechanized, even down to the regimental band.

That very same summer there is a test of breaking strength. For a fortnight—fourteen days and fourteen nights—manœuvres all through Germany, incredible feats of marching, travelling at full tilt with blacked out vehicles.

The winter brings with it the reorganization of the regiment and it is taken over by the Air Corps in 1936. In 1937 it parades before the Führer and marches to the Reich Party Rally. Wolf is now serving with light anti-aircraft defense guns. At first within the cadre of the General Göring Regiment, but the number of regiments begins to show a notable increase about that time, in some cases by division, in others by detailing cadres, or by forming new staffs. Wolf, now Major, is sent to Lippstadt and shortly thereafter to Düsseldorf.

When war breaks out, he is Major and commander of an anti-aircraft battalion.

On May 9, 1940, meanwhile promoted to Lieutenant-Colonel, but still commander of the same battalion, he is standing at the frontier at Grotenrath over against Limburg.

Alarm!
May 9, 1940.
13.59 hrs.
A beautiful clear day and the sun is shining as if it were alreday June. The air is mild and fragrant, filed with a fine odor of bitter, cool grassland earth. Glorious marching weather. The roads are hard and dry, fit to be trodden by millions of wellingtons. But is it the right weather for dying? Perhaps it is, buddy, but it's still better for victory!
13.59 hrs. Codeword Hindenburg 10,035.
14.28 hrs. Codeword alarm!
At 16.00 hrs. conference of commanders.
Thus Lieutenant-Colonel Wolf sees his battery commanders at 16.00 hrs. for the last time before the advance. Captain K. of the 2nd battery is not present, as he is taking part in a training course somewhere or other for ground targets. Oberleutnant (First Lieutenant) M. is commanding the 2nd battery in his place. Lieutenant-Colonel Wolf hopes that Captain K., whom he very highly esteems, may still turn up.
Commanders in conference.
Frederick the Great is reported to have said on a similar occasion that he would conquer, or "We shall never see one another again, gentlemen!" Lieutenant-Colonel Wolf certainly never said anything of the sort.
The batteries move into their lie-out positions. Their mission is to protect the advance of the division. Oberleutnant E. with his 3rd battery, the self-same Oberleutnant E. who had trained himself for weeks to fire upon receipt of mysterious dot signals at still more mysterious targets that he can only see on the map, has vanished.
The night before May 10.
Everyone understood that it is not a mere matter of exercises this time. The whole frontier area is full of troops. The night is echoing to the dull rolling sound of a huge strategic concentration, and the roads are chock-full of soldiers moving up in dense masses to be as close to the frontier as possible, and still other formations are approaching, either from the neighborhood or from further off in the back areas. They come marching, riding, and driving from every nook and every hamlet, out of every sunken road and over every bridge. It is inconceivable where they all come from. Their numbers are legion, and indescribable what they carry with them in the way of equipment and weapons, accoutrements, and stores, besides special training and confidence. A nation of men arises here, a great legendary nation composed entirely of armed heroes equipped with marvellous weapons.
May 10 begins with a pale, early dawn. At 3 o'clock the hands of a wrist watch can just be made out by holding the wrist quite close to one's eyes.

6

At half past 3 many thousands of men peel themselves out of their greatcoats, at 4 o'clock hundreds of engines are started up to test them. And a few moments later some one here points to the pale sky, over there a group of motor cyclist gunners look up, and further off some one cries out . . .

For at that moment a roll of thunder approaches from the east, a swelling roar of great howling engines. The German Air Corps is steering a western course, an inconceivable thundering of countless aero engines fills the air. Over the heads of the nation of men flies a second nation of men against the foe. Pursuit planes, arrows, bundles of arrows in the sky—a furious whistling and hissing.

Dive-bombers, like hammers flung savagely to the west, come storming up with a snarling roar like a crouching animal and pass on.

There is at thunder of roaring engines, glittering glass turrets flash by, bomb wells are already rattling—gigantic creatures of bombers, forts with wings. The ground troops yell, wave, laugh, shout, and relapse into silence again. Then suddenly slower aircraft rock their way above them from east to west, the trusty angular Ju 52 transport planes.

05.35 hrs.

A loud cry of "Sieg Heil" rises from afar and resounds far off.

The motor cyclist gunners start their engines like racing cyclists, Krupp engines spew furious ignitions rearwards.

The advance begins.

Endless columns of troops are rolling, riding, and marching along every road, every farm track, every woodland path—serpentines of formations and columns, companies, batteries, regiments, artillery, engineers, infantry, anti-aircraft artillery, tanks, and motor cyclist gunners. Who can describe the scene! Far to the front is heard a sputter of rifle-fire, no more than a few rounds, over at the road a burst of fire from a light machine-gun, while a light battery gallops over the fields in great form, as though there were actually something to fire at in the vicinity.

In reality, there were no targets—not even for the anti-aircraft artillery. Its orders were to protect the advance of the division by taking up battery position as far in the van as possible, waiting until part of the division had passed, then limbering up again, and racing to the front once more, in that way continuously protecting the division against air attack.

But no enemy aircraft are to be seen. Nothing but German machines flying in masses in the direction of the enemy, returning, and flying westwards again. The burghers of Limburg are friendly and decidedly obliging. They even wave to us in these neat little hamlets, actually wave and greet us with "Heil Hitler!" The advance proceeds rapidly, although all the bridges have been blown.

The van crosses the Juliana Canal even before midday and the point reaches the Maas before evening. But only a few of the light guns have had a chance of firing, none of the big 8.8 cm. guns at all. Nothing doing! And yet we have a surprise. Captain K. of the 2nd battery suddenly appears, smilingly reports his return from his training course to Lieutenant-Colonel Wolf, and takes over his battery, while Oberleutnant M. returns to brigade headquarters. He had been battery commander for the whole day of the advance and the whole of that splendid day he had not had a chance to fire a single round. He perhaps consoles himself that evening on the Maas with the thought that no one of the whole battalion had fired a single round—with the sole exception of Captain B., who had dealt with a few ground targets with his 2 cm. guns and had even brought in a few astonished and bewildered prisoners, rosy Dutchmen, who did not known what war is.

And yet one of Lieutenant-Colonel Wolf's battery commanders had actually been firing furiously—and how! He had been blazing away like a battle-cruiser since 11.00 hrs. in the forenoon. That was E., Oberleutnant E., with his secretly trained 3rd battery.

E. had silently disappeared very early in the morning. His order tells him that he of all the men behind the Limburg frontier was perhaps the one who had least time to spare. The whole German army is in a hurry, but Oberleutnant E. is in a much bigger hurry. He has orders to take up a position at 11.00 hrs. on a Belgian field that he had naturally never seen and which, for all he knew, might in the meantime have been flooded, or covered with barbed wire, or somehow or other made completely unsuitable for a heavy battery of anti-aircraft artillery to go into line there.

E. accordingly had a hunch that it might be a good idea to reach that Belgian field as far as possible before 11.00 hrs. He is tingling to his fingertips. When he looks aloft and sees one of these big Ju 52 in the sky, he feels like bursting with haste.

So E. tears along, as hard as he can. At 5.35 hrs. he was not half as close to the frontier turnpike, as he would have liked to be. He squeezes forward now, resorts to all sorts of dodges to get his battery along, his drivers honk and shout to be allowed the right of way just for a short while, just for the few minutes needed by E. and his madly driving battery to overtake.

Five times, six times, time and again he had to get off the road into the fields and Krupp engines are going like mad. But E. has no time. And by great good luck he actually squeezes his way forward and cheats the whole van. Finally he overtakes tanks; first heavy tanks, then light tanks. Astonished eyes in very indignant faces watch his proceedings from the loopholes in the roofs. The tank troops know very well that they are the point of the army—what does the crazy battery commander want anyhow? What did you say? Overtake us? Absolutely out of the question.

And yet, somehow, it seems to come into consideration after all. E. waves, honks, yells, laughs. The heavy tractors are slithering halfway in the ditches, but E. overhauls the tanks. Finally he has a free road before him—a trifle rather dangerous, perhaps, but, at any rate, free.

In spite of that, he arrives 20 minutes late at his Belgian meadow. It is dry and firm, and the battery takes up its position.

It is getting on for evening and hundreds of rounds have been fired. That evening there was no day's objective for the 3rd battery; no rest, no food, no repose—nothing, of course, but a cigarette now and again.

A Fieseler stork, one of these funny-looking ungainly machines, slips up and lands near the 3rd battery. An officer of high rank steps out and receives E's report, casts a glance at the sweating gunners hard at work, at the never-ending supply of ammunition, at the piles of empty cartridge cases—nods and says that the advance is going on nicely.

Oberleutnant E. keeps on blazing away the whole of May 10; evening falls, but he keeps on—the night through and the next day until well on in the afternoon. Not until then is he allowed to withdraw.

It is now left entirely to his genius for calculation to work out the whereabouts of Lieutenant-Colonel Wolf and the bulk of his battalion, whom he should now rejoin.

E. packs up and clatters off. He has naturally not a ghost of an idea that he will have to travel for a long while before he finds the battalion again.

During the night preceding the second day of the advance Lieutenant-Colonel Wolf waited with his batteries east of the Maas until the engineers had got their bridges ready. He is in the middle of an incredible crowd from which it was practically impossible to extricate oneself. All the muzzles of the batteries are directed to the west of the summery nocturnal sky, but there is no more sign of enemy aircraft during the first night on enemy soil than there had been on the first day of the advance.

The bridge was ready about 3 in the morning. Lieutenant-Colonel Wolf with a number of B's light guns was one of the first who were allowed to cross. He was soon followed by the 4th battery and Captain K. with his heavy 2nd battery.

The muzzle of the heavy anti-aircraft gun is reared threateningly towards the sky   Foto : PBZ

7

Tag und Nacht, pausenlos, hämmert die Luftwaffe auf Flugplätze und Rüstung und — Nerven der Engländer. Tag und Nacht fliegen die Heinkels, die Dorniers, die Junkers, die Messerschmitts, und wie die deutschen Flugzeuge alle heißen, über die Insel. Unser Bild zeigt eine Heinkel „He 111" beim Überfliegen der Kanalküste

By day and by night the German Air Force keeps uninterruptedly hammering away at the airdromes, armament factories, and nerves of the island, which the various types of airplanes—Heinkels, Dorniers, Junkers, Messerschmitts, or whatever they may be called—visit at all hours of the day and night. The photograph shows a Heinkel He 111 flying over the Channel coast

Hier fallen ihre Sprengbomben. Sie treffen Docks und Hafenanlagen (Mitte) und Eisenbahnen (oben) von Tilbury an der Themsemündung   Aufn. PK Wanderer (2), Luftwaffe (1)

Here they unload their demolition bombs, hitting the docks and harbor works (center) and the railroads (above) of Tilbury Port on the north shore of the Thames

(Rechts) . . . und sie treffen mit Brandbomben die kriegswichtigen Industrieanlagen der Hafenstadt Eastbourne an der Kanalküste, südlich Londons. Dieses Bild ist besonders interessant, da es die im sogenannten Schüttwurf geworfenen kleinen Brandbomben deutlich erkennen läßt. Das Ziel dieser gefährlichen Geschosse ist auf dem Bilde nicht zu sehen. Es liegt über dem Bildrand. Im Kreise eine vor den Brandbomben geworfene Sprengbombe

Right: . . . and here the incendiary bombs land in the important armament plant at Eastbourne on the Channel coast, to the south of London. This photograph is particularly interesting, because it plainly shows the small incendiary bombs being dropped in shoals at a time. The objective of these dangerous projectiles lies above the top edge of the illustration and is therefore invisible. Within the circle can be seen a demolition bomb dropped before the incendiary bomb

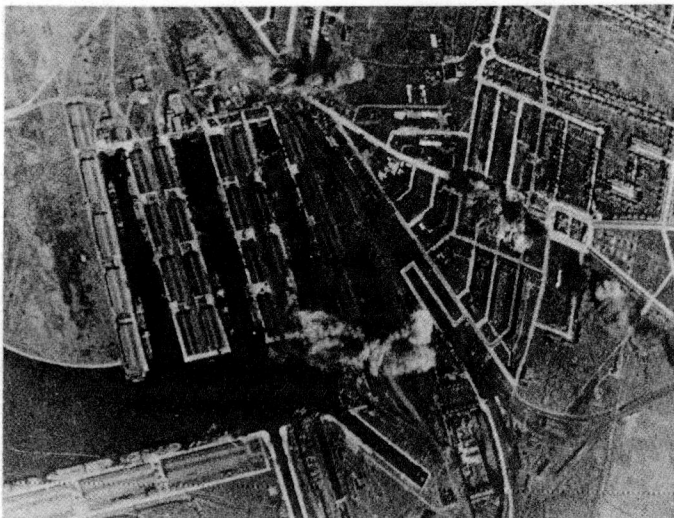

haben es so gewollt!

They did not want it otherwise

FLUGPLÄTZE
vernichtet!
Devastated Airdromes

Das Bild links stellt den britischen Flugplatz Gosport dar. Seine Hallen weisen schon erhebliche Zerstörungen durch deutsche Bombenabwürfe auf. Von besonderem Interesse ist aber an dieser Aufnahme die nicht ungeschickte Tarnung des Rollfeldes. Aus der linken oberen Ecke des Bildes reicht ein Waldzipfel bis zur Straße. Diesen Wald haben die Engländer über den ganzen Flugplatz gezogen, und zwar durch eine Tarnbemalung, die außerdem bebaute Felder und Hecken vorzutäuschen sucht. Die deutschen Kampfflieger lassen sich aber auch durch die geschickteste Tarnung nicht irreführen

Left: The airdrome at Gosport. The hangars have already been seriously damaged by German bombs. A specially interesting feature of this photograph is the rather clever way in which the runway has been camouflaged. The tip of a wood at the top left corner stretches as far as the road, but the wood has been drawn over the whole of the airdrome by camouflage painting that further endeavors to imitate cultivated fields and hedges. German bomber pilots, however, decline to be deceived by even the most skilful camouflage

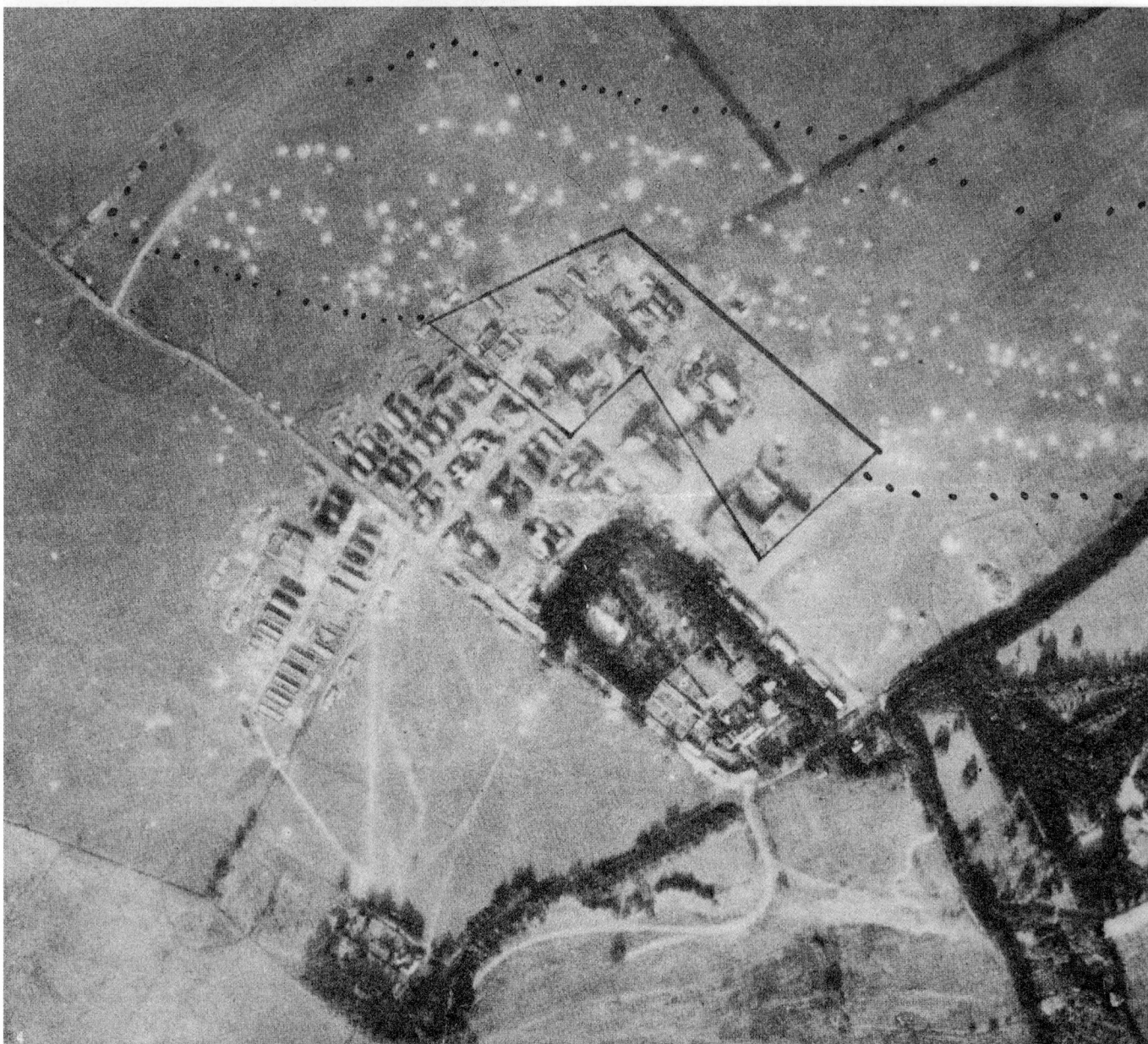

Die Aufnahme rechts zeigt den Flugplatz Warmwell während des deutschen Bombenangriffs. Die Flughafengebäude liegen völlig unter deckenden Bombensalven begraben

Right: The airdrome at Warmwell during a German air raid. The buildings are completely buried beneath salvos of bombs

Das Luftbild links zeigt den britischen Flugplatz Lympne. Die Flugplatzgebäude innerhalb der umrandeten Fläche sind durch deutsche Bombenabwürfe restlos zerstört. Die punktierte Linie deutet eine Unzahl von Treffern im Rollfeld an

Left: The airdrome at Lympne. The buildings within the enclosed area have been completely destroyed. The dotted line indicates numerous hits on the runway

Aufnahmen Luftwaffe (4)

Zum Bilde rechts: Der Flughafen London-Hornchurch im Bombenfeuer. Auch hier liegt die Mehrzahl der Bomben auf dem Flugplatz. Die in Unterkünften und Hallen einschlagenden Bomben sind durch Kreise eingefaßt

Right: The airdrome at Hornchurch near London during an air raid. Most of the bombs have landed in the airdrome itself; those lying on the men's quarters and halls are marked by circles

11

Ein Angriff und feine Wirkung

An Air Raid and Its Effect

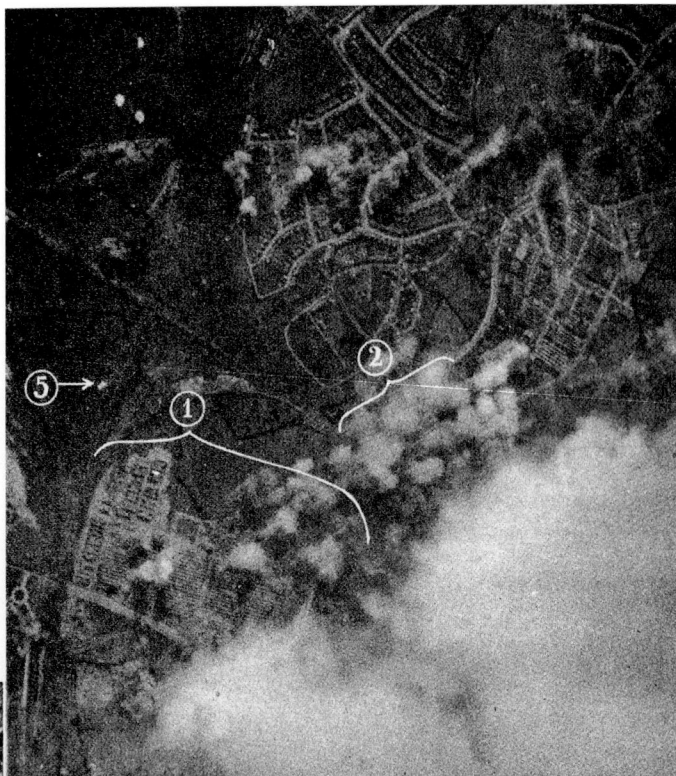

Unsere Aufnahmen haben das große Flugzeug-werk von Filton zum Gegenstand. Das Bild links ist wenige Tage vor dem Angriff auf-genommen, der das Werk nahezu vernichtet hat. Deutlich erkennbar sind neben der Bahnlinie die riesigen Werkhallen, deren Tarnbemalung gegen Fliegersicht schützen soll. Das Luftbild beweist aber, daß der Anstrich der Dächer allein nicht genügt. Die Hallen sind durchaus klar zu erkennen. Das Bild oben ist während des ersten Bombenangriffs aufgenommen. Das Hauptwerk ist in der linken unteren Ecke zu erkennen. Mitten im Werk schlagen Bomben ein. Das etwas kleinere Zweigwerk oberhalb der quer durch das Bild laufenden Bahn ist von Bombensalven vollständig eingedeckt. Die weißen Stellen in der rechten unteren Ecke des oberen Bildes sind Wolken, die sich zwischen die Erde und die Kampfflugzeuge geschoben haben. Das obere Bild läßt mit aller nur wün-schenswerten Deutlichkeit erkennen, daß da unten, im Flugzeugwerk von Filton, die Hölle ist. Einschlag neben Einschlag prasselt in die großen Hallen. Dieses Werk wird nicht mehr viel Flugzeuge herstellen.
Die Zahlen bedeuten (1) das Hauptwerk, (2) das Nebenwerk, (3) sieben aufgestellte Flugzeuge, (4) drei Flugzeuge am Boden, (5) Sperrballone am Boden, (6) die Startbahn, die mitten durch den Flugplatz führt   Aufnahmen Luftwaffe (2

Left: An air photograph of the large aircraft factory at Filton taken a few days before an air raid that practically destroyed it. The huge sheds beside the railroad are plainly to be made out. They have been camouflaged, but the photo shows that it is not sufficient to paint the roofs alone, because the sheds can easily be distin-guished. Above: A photograph taken during the first air raid, showing the chief plant in the left lower corner. Bombs are falling in the center of the factory and the smaller plant just above the railroad running across the photo is com-pletely covered by salvos of bombs. The white patches at the lower right corner are clouds that have interposed themselves between the ground and the bombers. The top photograph shows as plainly as can be desired that hell upon earth has broken out in the aircraft factory at Filton; one bomb after another is landing in the large sheds. This factory will not turn out many more aircraft
The figure (1) indicates the main works, (2) the smaller plant, (3) seven aircraft set up, (4) three airplanes on the ground, (5) barrage balloons on the ground, (6) the runway passing through th airdrome

12

Zeichen-Erklärung

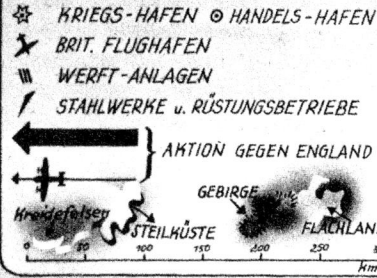

✵ KRIEGS-HAFEN ⊙ HANDELS-HAFEN
✈ BRIT. FLUGHAFEN
⫴ WERFT-ANLAGEN
⚡ STAHLWERKE u. RÜSTUNGSBETRIEBE

← AKTION GEGEN ENGLAND

GEBIRGE

Kreidefelsen STEILKÜSTE FLACHLAND

km

SHETLAND-INS.

Sumburgh

ORKNEY-INS.

Kirkwall
SCAPA FLOW

Thurso
Wick

927 m

MORAY FIRTH

Fraserburgh

1130 m Inverness

1039 m Aberdeen

1343 m 979 m

Perth Dundee
FIRTH OF TAY

Rosyth FIRTH OF FORTH
Leith

Greenock EDINBURGH 528 m
Glasgow

Kilmarnock Selkirk

Dumfries 842 m

HEBRIDEN

NORD-KANAL

NORD-IRLAND
BELFAST

Ramsey

MAN Barrow

Carlisle

Workington
Darlington

Stockton

NORDSEE

ENGLAND

Blyth
Newcastle Tynemouth
Gateshead South Shields
Sunderland
Hartlepool
Middlesbrough Whitby

Scarborough
Bridlington

Lancaster York

Preston Burnley Leeds Goole Hull

Blackb. Bolton

IRISCHE SEE

ANGLESEY LIVERPOOL Manchester
Birkenhead Stockp. Sheffield Grimsby

Holyhead Chester Chesterf. Lincoln

Bangor Mansfield

Dolgelly Stocke Nottingham The Wash

Derby Kings Lynn Norwich Gr. Yarmouth

520 m Shrewsbury Walsall Lovestoft

Wolverhampt. Leicester Peterborough

Birmingham Coventry Cambridge Ipswich

Worcester Northampton Felixstowe

Gloucester Bedford Colchester Harwich

Oxford Luton

Milford Llanelly Rhondda Newport LONDON Southend
Pembroke Swansea Sheerness
Cardiff Bristol Reading Croydon Ramsgate
Bath Aldershot Reigate Hastings Dover
Barnstaple Southampton Brighton Calais
Exeter Bournemouth Cowes Newhaven Boulogne
516 m Portsmouth
Devonport INS. WIGHT
Portland BELGIEN

Penzance Plymouth Dartmouth

Falmouth

SCILLY INS.

DER KANAL

Alderney Cherbourg Le Havre
Guernsey KANAL KÜSTE
KANAL-INS.
Jersey

IRLAND IRISCHER FREISTAAT DUBLIN

SÜD-KANAL

BRISTOL-KANAL

ATLANTISCHER OZEAN

Vernichtungsschläge auf Englands Rüstungszentren

Als im Ausgang des 18. Jahrhunderts in ganz Europa die Industrialisierung begann, war es vor allem Großbritannien, das sich mit aller Macht den ratternden und stampfenden Maschinen verschrieb. In Birmingham, Coventry, Leicester, Burton, Bromwich, Derby, Manchester entstanden große Industriezentren. Diese Zusammenballung der englischen Industrien auf bestimmte Städte und Gebiete rächt sich nun bitter. Die Tatsache, daß es konzentrischen Luftangriffen meist schon während einer Nacht gelang, für die Fortführung des Krieges äußerst wichtige Fabrikorte dem Erdboden gleichzumachen, beweist, daß die wirtschaftliche Kraft Großbritanniens auf Tod und Verderben den deutschen Bomben ausgeliefert ist. Wenn nun in der englischen Presse der Rat gegeben wird, die gesamte Midlandindustrie schleunigst nach dem Norden Schottlands zu verlegen, so spricht man nur aus, was man bisher versäumt hat. Um mit den Worten Chamberlains zu sprechen: „Die Omnibusse wurden auf allen Linien verpaßt . . .!"

Zeichnung Otto W. Hempel

British Armament Centers receive Destructive Blows

England was the pioneer of the industrial revolution in Europe that set in towards the close of the 18th century and was the country that devoted all its energies chiefly to the development of the steam engine and the introduction of the age of machinery with all its unlovely features. The new industries were concentrated in certain towns and areas in England, such as Birmingham, Coventry, Leicester, Burton, Bromwich, Derby, and Manchester, in a way that is now bitterly revenging itself. The fact that concentric air raids have succeeded, mostly in the course of a single night, in razing to the ground certain manufacturing centers of vital importance for the conduct of the war, proves that the economic power of Great Britain has been handed over to destruction and ruin by German bombs. When the British press now advises the bodily removal of the whole of the industry in the Midlands as speedily as possible to the north of Scotland, that is merely belated recognition of a point that has hitherto been neglected. To use Chamberlain's expression, "The bus on every line has been missed"

STUKAS am Feind

Dive Bombers in Action

A Descriptive Report from Three Fronts

By Josef Grabler, War Correspondent

Right after the first "storks" had taken off, the crews of the Peltz squadron had an opportunity of seeing the stuff these infantrymen were made of. The General was the first to take off, with an infantryman behind him, and then the whole group of the slow-flight aircraft took off, each carrying besides the pilot a few infantrymen with weapons and ammunition. Suddenly one of the "storks" seems to be in difficulties, it rises from the ground, but immediately flops back and the machine takes fire, while the crew jump out. An infantryman from Silesia, burdened with a heavy machine gun, had been seated in that plane. Upon clambering out with his heavy machine gun on his back, he goes up to the next machine just about to take off, as placidly as if nothing hat happened, opens the door and lugs out a young fellow, one of his comrades, by the scruff of the neck, takes his place inside with his machine gun, and off he goes.

Is this supposed to be war?

The Peltz squadron had to escort the "storks" and protect them with bombs and machine guns, their chief mission being to get rid of any air defense and heavy machine guns by attack from the air. Not long after taking off, Oberleutnant Peltz saw that the "storks" had landed and were standing about on a meadow near a farm, while others, which had meanwhile been overtaken by the speedier dive bombers, were just landing. Peltz circled round the farm at about 150 ft. and saw the infantrymen beneath him climbing out of the machines and bringing a table out of the farm. Peltz could hardly believe the evidence of his own eyes when a white tablecloth followed and immediately thereafter infantry came out of the farm with a succulent breakfast. That could all be seen quite plainly from the low height as which Peltz was flying. And that is supposed to be the war in the west with all its terrors? Indignant cries were heard in his headphones, confirming that his crews had precisely the same notions about that curious conduct of war that he had himself.

The squadron leader flew higher to have a better look about. But far and wide no military objective was to be seen that would have been worth a single round. Only a lone short-distance scout plane, a Henschel Hs 126, greeted the stuka crews by wobbling in a friendly way. Now Oberleutnant Peltz knew from his experience in the campaign in Poland that these short-range scouts had more than once pointed out worthwhile objectives to the dive-bombers. Conversation was impossible, because the scout had a different frequency. Peltz accordingly nosed up to the scout, who slowly described a curve, while the observer waved. That can only mean one thing: there must be an objective round about after all and sure enough the friendly scout leads them to an airdrome. There is a hangar, which is closed, but no aircraft are to be seen, so that a few rounds are fired into the hangar, which may perhaps bring something out. But nothing does come out and the squadron flies home. Pilot and wireless operator are disconcerted. It had never before happened that they had brought back their bombs from a raid and it is a poor comfort that the other squadrons of the wing had fared no better.

In the afternoon, the squadron started for a like action and once more there was nothing doing. Not a single military objective was to be seen. On their way back, they saw the first German vehicles crossing the Luxembourg-Belgian frontier. A gigantic snake of an army rolled over the roads to the west and south-west. Here and there four columns were marching abreast. The Stuka crews broke into a cold sweat at the thought of an attack by hostile aircraft on the comrades of the army down below. But nothing at all happened, as far as they could see. The fact is hardly credible, but it cannot be disputed that the squadron returned from that mission also with their bombs and ammunition intact. The ground sergeant asked indignantly whether he should lay out bombs in readiness at all. The ground personnel were so disappointed that they were no longer on speaking terms with the crews. That was the second mission of May 10, 1940, the day on which the German army moved out of their winter quarters on the Siegfried line to fight the great battles in Flanders and France. But the poor fellows of the dive-bomber formations, as they laid themselves to rest in the straw, were as disappointed as the disgruntled ground personnel, who had run out on them.

The ground personnel disappointed

According to the reports of the situation, the head of the army had already penetrated far into Belgium. Finally, during the forenoon came the order for their new mission, giving as objective a village where the advanced guard hat met with resistance, which the dive bombers were asked to break down. They flew at 6,600 ft., just as in peace time, and looked for the foe. But nothing was to be seen. They dropped lower to 30 ft. and flew over the village, but there was literally nothing to be seen; it had evidently been evacuated. Not a soul was to be seen on the streets and only a few animals were wandering about the fields. On his own responsibility, Oberleutnant Peltz flew 30 miles further west. Again there was nothing to be seen. They returned at a low altitude. Finally the head of the army appeared on the fine asphalt road, along which they were flying. Armored reconnaissance cars and other vehicles had halted at the side of the road; the crews were sitting in the ditch and breakfasted. Here also everything was as in times of peace. Only the ground panels, which showed that the vehicles were German, led to the conclusion that a war was in progress after all.

For the third time the squadrons brought back their bombs with them. The crews climbed indignantly out of their machines, while the ground personnel hardly condescended to look at them. And these guys are supposed to be dive-bomber pilots, their scowls seemed to say. Oberleutnant Peltz examined everyone of his men. No one had seen even one single enemy.

Then came an order to attack the fortifications of Neufchatel. These were the first blockhouses since Modlin upon which heavy Stuka bombs were dropped. The squadron was surprised to find no air defense. Here also no enemy was to be seen outside the blockhouses.

The next mission was to attack columns on the roads leading to the fortress of Givet. One road was allotted to each squadron. That seemed to be a worth-while target at least; for no one could really have imagined these columns; they simply must be there. Actually, however, there was not a thing to be seen, the roads were bare. The squadron flew further without the

escort of fighter planes until near Givet Oberleutnant Peltz thundered along the road at the head of the crowd, until he finally had enough of it. Flying in a wide arc, he recrossed a wood that the had just flown over and dropped a little bomb into the trees. Then things began to hum! The smoke of the explosion of the bomb had hardly reached the tops of the trees before stampeding horses plunged out of the wood, followed by soldiers and more and more soldiers. Well, well, who'd have thought it, said Peltz aloud into his laryngophone. And then there was a bit of bustle. The squadron hammered as hard as they could into the wood and into the men and animals down below. Dusting out that wood with the little bomb had well repaid the trouble.

After the German tanks had advanced beyond Bouillon into open country, they encountered vigorous opposition on the part of the French at a point where a detour was impossible, and the squadron of Oberleutnant Peltz was ordered to clear the way for them. The day was still young and visibility was impeded by ground fog through which only the hill-tops emerged. Gradually, however, the mist lifted and Oberleutnant Peltz, while flying over a wood, observed the presence of large numbers of motor vehicles, but he was unable, is spite of flying low, to make out whether these were hostile tanks ot our own, and was therefore unable to order an attack. Upon landing on his return, however, he was met by a report from our tanks that the French were attacking in large force, from which it was evident that the tanks seen had actually been French after all. The squadron accordingly thundered back, after having received instructions to attack the blockhouses at X, should no more tanks be observed on the road between Bouillon and Sedan. Flying at an altitude of about 10,000 ft., the squadron arrived at the point of their presumptive activity. It had meanwhile developed into a brilliant summer's day. The road stretched into the distance far below the wings of the dive-bombers and Oberleutnant Peltz dropped to 6,500 ft. and then to 5,000 ft., in order to search the road and its immediate vicinity. Suddenly the cry was raised,

"Look out, pursuit planes behind us!"

The warning cry, heard for the first time in the campaign in France, acted like a trumpet call; for the Stuka crews had not hitherto met with hostile planes in the west. But there was not much time for meditation, because the phosphorus filaments were already hissing through the squadron. The air-gunners kept blazing away for all they were worth. The squadron had meanwhile nearly reached Sedan and the fortifications for which the bombs were intended lay far below. In spite of continuous attacks by pursuit planes, who could only be kept at bay by the air gunners, the squadron managed to drop their bombs, but then there was only one thing to be done in face of the superior numbers of the French pursuit planes, and that was to step on the gas and beat it for home. The French followed the squadron for a little while until a French plane was shot down, at which howls of delight were heard in the headphones. It is impossible to say whether their fuel was becoming exhausted, at all events, the joyful fact remained that they thereupon showed the large cockades on the lower surfaces of the wings and sheered off.

Mit dem Kriegsverdienstkreuz
1. Klasse mit Schwertern
ausgezeichnet

General der Flakartillerie Rüdel

General der Flakartillerie v. Schröder

General der Flieger v. Witzendorf

Generalleutnant Kastner-Kirdorf

Generalleutnant Bodenschatz

Generalleutnant Goßrau

Generalleutnant Doerstling

Ministerialdirektor i. RLM Fisch

Fliegerbummel durch Wien

Airmen Take a Stroll through Vienna

Die deutschen Kulturschätze in den Museen finden ebenso großes Interesse wie die Baudenkmäler der Stadt. Unten der Brunnen am Michaelerplatz

The great treasures of German culture in the museums arouse as much interest as the architectural monuments of the town. Below: The fountain at the Michaeler-Platz

Immer wieder wird die von Geschichte und Romantik umwobene Donaustadt unseren Soldaten zum Erlebnis. Natürlich ist das Wahrzeichen Wiens, der „Steffel", eines der Hauptziele ihres Stadtrundganges

A visit to the town on the Danube famous in history and romance is always an unforgettable experience for our soldiers. St. Stephan's Cathedral, one of the landmarks of Vienna, popularly known as the "Steffy", is naturally one of the chief sights to be seen on their walk round the town

Wenn man sich an den vielen Kunstschätzen müde gesehen hat, dann geht's in den Prater, wo die Schießbuden besondere Anziehungskraft ausüben.   Aufn. PK Sturm (4)

When art treasures begin to pall, a visit to the Prater is indicated, where the shooting galleries form a great attraction for the present visitors

16

Dive Bombers in Action

Oberleutnant Peltz at last found time to inspect his squadron and found that two machines were missing. That was unfortunately only a bitter confirmation of what he had already seen; during the air fight a Ju 87 had withdrawn with a trail of smoke behind it. Oberleutnant Peltz throttled down to let the squadron pass and was able to ascertain by the marks of the various machines that it must have been Leutnant Haller. At that moment, the squadron was just flying over the German front lines, Peltz saw a tall pillar of smoke rising from the ground. That would not of itself have attracted any special attention, because all sorts of things were burning in the neighborhood, but Oberleutnant Peltz happened to have sighted precisely that smoke, being animated by an indefinite suspicion. He accordingly flew lower and, sure enough, a Ju 87 — Haller's machine — was ablaze there. In spite of the severe damage to the plane, he had after all succeeded in reaching his own side of the lines. Peltz dropped to a low height above the ground and saw Haller, his face as black as that of a nigger, frantically waving.

The infantry help

Haller appears to be uninjured, but his gunner is lying motionless beside a tree. Help is evidently urgently needed. But how is that to be managed? A bright idea strikes Peltz as he discovers infantry on the march on a small road not far from where the emergency landing had taken place. He climbs a little and writes a note, with his left hand on the control column: "Wounded airman 300 metres west of the road beside burning plane. Needs help." Placing the note in a message-bag, he dives down again over the infantry, who were dislocating their necks watching the pilot doing funny stunts just overhead. A few feet above the head of the battalion, Peltz lets the message-bag with its long colored streamer flatter down and sees a number of infantrymen running to pick it up. If the wounded man can still be helped at all, his safety is now assured; for a surgeon always accompanies an infantry battalion.
While flying after his squadron, now disappearing over the northern horizon, Oberleutnant Peltz reflects that flight leader Oberleutnant Unbehauen is still missing, as far as he had been able to observe. He is unable quite to grasp the fact that something should have happened precisely to that Sunbird, nicknamed Zaratza. Peltz is rather depressed, as he finally lands, at the thought that the very first air combat in the west should have cost him two losses. Two machines are gone. One was that piloted by Leutnant Haller, which he had sighted ablaze on the ground, and the other was that of Oberleutnant Unbehauen, about whose whereabouts he still knows nothing. It is no comfort to hear that the other squadrons of the wing have also suffered losses during the attack by the French pursuit planes.
Peltz is called to the telephone. And who should report himself, but Zaratza the Sunbird, radiant as ever!
"Quite right, chief", he reports, „Landed smoothly on German territory, although with 65 hits. Can you send a "Stork" round at once? Petrick has two gunshot wounds in the abdomen. Landed at such and such a place. If I was able to land with the Ju 87, you can certainly pull it off with the "Stork"."
"I'll come along myself right away", replies Oberleutnant Peltz. "In fifteen minutes at the outside you may expect me."
And then everything must go at top speed.

Man in distress

The "Stork" is already waiting with its engine running, started up by speedy hands; for the personnel had at once understood from fragments of the telephone conversation what had to be done. Oberleutnant Peltz runs to the "Stork", just as he is, and climbs in. The door is flung to behind him and off he goes. The emergency landing ground, the second that he had had occasion to view from the air that day, is soon located. A Ju 87 standing in an open field is hardly an object that can easily be overlooked, when the approximate location is known. The picture that presents itself closely resembles that shown by the machine of Leutnant Haller. The radio operator is lying on the grass beside the plane and Zaratza is waving. The resemblance with the situation of Haller and his crew, seen just a few minutes previously, is so strong that the observation subconsciously strikes Oberleutnant Peltz, as he lands, that Zaratza is not black in the face, as Haller had been.
Peltz brings the "Stork" to a stop a few feet away from the Ju 87 and jumps out. Non-commissioned officer Petrick is lying quiet and pale on his back. He appears to be unconscious, his combination suit is saturated with blood.
"We'll set him on the middle seat. You take the rear seat, Zaratza, and hold him tight. Take a hold."
The wounded man is cautiously carried the few steps to the "Stork". Oberleutnant Unbehauen climbs in first, grasps the non-commissioned officer under the arms and helps him into the plane, while Oberleutnant Peltz lifts his feet. Petrick groans. Finally they manage to lift him on the seat, where he collapses. Zaratza embraces him with his arms from behind and holds him tight.
Within 65 minutes after receiving the two bullets, the air gunner Petrick is lying on the operating table. It may be added here that he has meanwhile fully recovered, but the doctors left no doubt on the point that it would have been impossible to save him but for rapid transport to hospital.
At last Oberleutnant Unbehauen finds time to report his experiences in the air combat to his squadron leader.
"Petrick must have been wounded at the very beginning of the attack by the enemy planes. I see the tracer filaments constantly flitting about the cockpit and hear a cracking and clicking in the engine, but Petrick is not shooting. I yell to him, "Shoot, boy, shoot", and the poor devil actually pulls himself together and shoots off, as I have seen, five drums of ammunition, with which he brought down the French pilot. Then he collapsed. Isn't it too bad to think that precisely Petrick, who was given the nickname of "stop-butt" on account of his waistline, must actually serve to stop a couple of bullets!"

To the front in a taxi-cab

That afternoon Leutnant Migeot arrived in a French taxicab after a more than adventurous journey. He had had to make an emergency landing with numerous hits in the engine after the fight with the attack planes. His radio operator was

17

badly wounded and unfortunately died soon after landing. Migeot had no idea where he had come down and did not know whether the territory had already been occupied by our troops, or whether it was still in French hands. But he said to himself, as he told us, that only bluff could help him. Armed with his two guns and that of the dead gunner, he wandered to the nearest farmhouse and first of all asked for something to eat, because he was very hungry. Then he demanded a car at once, putting on his most martial air. Supported by his two guns, he uttered frightful threats in case of treachery. He did not himself believe that he would pull it off, but the incredible happened: a car actually came round in half an hour! The chauffeur first had the articles of war read to him, the two guns lending emphasis to Migeot's remarks, and then off they went. Migeot told the chauffeur to drive him as quickly as possible to the German lines. And once more the unlikely happened; Leutnant Migeot reached the head of the German infantry without having a brush with French troops. It was then no great distance to the field airdrome.

Shortly afterwards Leutnant Haller also arrived with his hand already in a plaster of Paris dressing; he had sprained it at the emergency landing.

Attack on Chémery

The breakthrough at Sedan had succeeded. The German tank divisions wheeled to the right and accomplished their historic drive to the sea at Abbeville. The French made furious exertions to take the tanks in the flank and from the rear, so that the stuka crews had often to carry out attacks for the relief of the tanks. Once there was an attack on Chémery, the order expressly stating that French tanks in and around Chémery were not to be attacked after 12 o'clock, the German staff having calculated that the German tanks would have reached the place by that time. That limitation of the attack in point of time was intended to prevent the dive-bombers from bombing their own tanks. Peltz saw large numbers of tanks on the battlefield near Chémery, but neither crosses nor cockades were to be made out, owing to the dust they raised. Peltz made his squadron form a defensive circle round him and dived in order to see whether he had to do with friend or foe. Suddenly the cry was raised, "Pursuit planes coming from the sun!" Peltz zoomed up to his squadron at once and already saw the white phosphorus filaments buzzing through the air. A Ju 87 had plainly been hit and Peltz recognized to his dismay that it was the commander's plane. He gave orders by radio for the squadron to collect in the air space above Sedan. The commander's machine was already smoking and Peltz with his squadron placed himself over and above him as cover. A French Morane zoomed up steeply in front of the wing and thereby got in the way of the concentrated fire of the fixed weapons of the pilots. That French plane simply burst asunder and its parts flew in all directions — the engine-cover, metal sheeting, fairings, and finally the wings. In the meantime, as the stuka crews noticed to their joy, German pursuit planes had arrived and a Morane was shot to pieces by a German pilot before their eyes in a really wonderful way, that plane also breaking up into its component parts. The squadron collected over its own ground at Sedan, while the commander flew home. It was afterwards found that his gunner, Oberfeldwebel (First Sergeant) Herzog, had been killed by two cannon shots. Major Sigel himself had been lightly grazed on the neck, but the burn fortunately merely caused a painful blister. He reached home safely, although his machine had been riddled like a sieve.

"Hold on! Our own tanks!"

The squadron once more advanced on Chémery from Sedan, but had hardly reached the battefield, before the troublesome Moranes once more made their appearance. An air combat took place, this time without incident, and the squadron flew back to collect over Sedan, after which they started a third time for Chémery.

The little town lies straight ahead on the course. Huge conflagrations are raging and enormous clouds of smoke are ascending into the sky. Numerous tanks can be seen moving out of the town in the direction of the German ines. That can only be the French. Peltz orders an attack and the squadron dives behind him. He has a group of these tanks exactly sighted in the reflecting sight, and will be pressing the bomb release knob in a few seconds; his bombs will be dropping and his crews behind him will be getting rid of their bombs too! At that very moment he recognizes the svastika flag on a tank and immediately gives the order by wireless, "Don't drop a bomb! Our own tanks!" The order is given and received in a split second during the actual nose dive — and not a man of the Peltz squadron drops a bomb! After having gone through three air combats, the crews were still so keenly alert that they received and understood the command of thei squadron leader even during the terrific pace of a nose dive. By a hairsbreadth death did not drop out of the sky on their brothers-in-arms below.

There was a mite of breakage when the dive-bombers finally landed, because several machines had been knocked about quite a bit by the repeated air combats. A Ju 87 performed the craziest exploit of all, a cannon having registered a hit on the oxygen bottle, which had promptly exploded. Simply everything on that machine wobbled while in the air; everything had been torn apart, and the tail unit was hanging practically by the operating rods of the controls alone. The machine dissolved into its component parts as it landed, but not a man was injured.

The warfare that had played such a great rôle in Poland began anew. Hostile columns were attacked by bombs and machine-gun fire and the dive-bombers inflicted frightful losses on the enemy. Defence by the enemy attack planes had meanwhile become very feeble, so that our dive-bombers were once more able to fly alone

"Excuse my rudeness in venturing to drop past you!"

"Hot stuff, Bill! Where did you pick up that keen nose dive?"
"From the last burst of fire from the Messerschmitt!"

without being escorted by their own fighters and to carry out strafing on their own account. It was sometimes pure target practice. Peltz often caught himself wondering even during a dive whether he should drop a 250 kilo bomb, or whether a 50 kilo bomb would do the trick. Every bomb dropped was observed by one's comrades and was the object of sharp criticism by wireless. Anyone missing his target had to hear himself abused as "Uhrmacher" (watchmaker), which of course is not intended to convey any aspersion on that worthy gild; it is merely a technical expression used by the dive-bomber crews. After having got rid of their bombs, pilots and gunners would rake the crowd on the ground with their machine guns.

"Spitfire behind Anna!"

The left wing of the German army had meanwhile rolled up the French front in the direction of Calais and the military defences of that town were assigned to the Peltz squadron as new objectives. Even at the very first approach a picture presented itself to his crews which none of them will ever forget. The British island lay bathed in sunshine, as if within touching distance, separated from the Continent merely by a strip of water that looked from that great altitude as if it were no more than a stonethrow across. So that was the island that had started the present war! The island to whose debit all the consequences of the war will be booked. The crews knew that the British were still in Calais and were prepared to drop their bombs on them with specially friendly greetings.

Horizontal bombers had already been at work on Calais before the stukas and the town was ablaze at several points. Many ships lay in the harbor and in the roads; the enemy was evidently bolting. Clouds of smoke were being driven by the wind towards the south-east, so that the squadron was unable to approach from the land side, but had to go out to sea, whereby they got within range of British pursuit planes who came over the water in a few minutes from Dover and Folkestone to lie in wait for their prey. Oberleutnant Peltz was aware of that and had previously informed his pilots and wireless operators of the possibility of attack from that quarter. While flying over the coast north-east of Calais at an altitude of some 11,500 ft., in order to proceed out to sea, he first looked around for hostile planes. It is a mistake to talk of the devil! Like a shot from a gun, evidently swooping down from a great height, a Spitfire whizzes past Peltz and makes an elegant curve to get behind him. The British pilot does that so neatly that he is practically directly beneath and behind the tail unit of the squadron leader's machine after having flown out the curve. It is unnecessary for half the squadron to yell out "Spitfire behind Anna!" (as the machine of the leader is called); Peltz has already observed that fact with all desirable clarity. Peltz depesses the nose of his ship and thunders earthwards in the expectation that the British pilot will immediately follow suit. After having dived for a short distance, Peltz runs out the nose-dive brakes, to slacken the speed of the dive, and the British pilot, unable to brake his descent, promptly whizzes past him at one side. "See you again, buddy", cries Peltz, "Some other time perhaps." But that Britisher will never find another chance of meeting German dive-bombers again. Peltz has hardly called his friendly parting greeting after him, when another airplane shoots past him like a shadow in the same direction after the British plane. Peltz has just time to recognize the beam crosses in a hazy way. Now there is no need for anxiety. Peltz pulls out his machine and looks down, where the German Messerschmitt is just shooting down the British plane. The whole occurrence from the appearance of the Spitfire until he was shot down was over in a few seconds, and now the bombs of the Ju 87 are hailing on the ships down below in the harbor. It was impossible to observe details of the hits, everything being wreathed in dense clouds of smoke.

England im Bomb

England under a Hail of Bombs

Von panischem Schrecken erfüllt muß die Bevölkerung die Angriffe der deutschen Luftwaffe in den Luftschutzkellern über sich ergehen lassen, und die Hauptschlagadern des englischen Verkehrswesens wurden so empfindlich getroffen, daß überall im Lande Zufuhr- und Versorgungsschwierigkeiten auftreten, die England unabwendbar dem Chaos entgegentreiben

The panic-stricken population must submit to the attacks of the German Air Force in the air-raid shelters, while the main traffic arteries in England have been so severely damaged as to cause serious difficulties by dislocating transport and supplies all over the country. All of which helps to drive England towards the inevitable chaos

So ziehen tagtäglich Deutschlands Kampfflieger in geschlossenen Verbänden gegen das Inselreich · Aufn. Luftwaffe (1)

Day by day closed formations of German bombers raid the island kingdom

Links: Einer der deutschen Messerschmitt-Zerstörer über der britischen Ortschaft Bexhill an der Südküste Englands

Left: A German Messerschmitt destroyer over Bexhill on the south coast of England

Rechts und rechts oben: Die Aufnahme A zeigt den englischen Fliegerhorst Lympne in der Grafschaft Kent zu Beginn des Krieges, als die deutlich erkennbaren Hallen noch nicht getarnt waren. Das Luftbild B gibt den Platz wieder, wie er sich den Blicken unserer Aufklärer nach dem deutschen Luftangriff darbot

Right and right above: Photo A shows the English airdrome Lympne in the county of Kent at the beginning of the war before the hangars, which can be plainly seen, had been camouflaged. Air Photo B shows the airdrome as seen by our reconnaissance planes after the air raid

enhagel

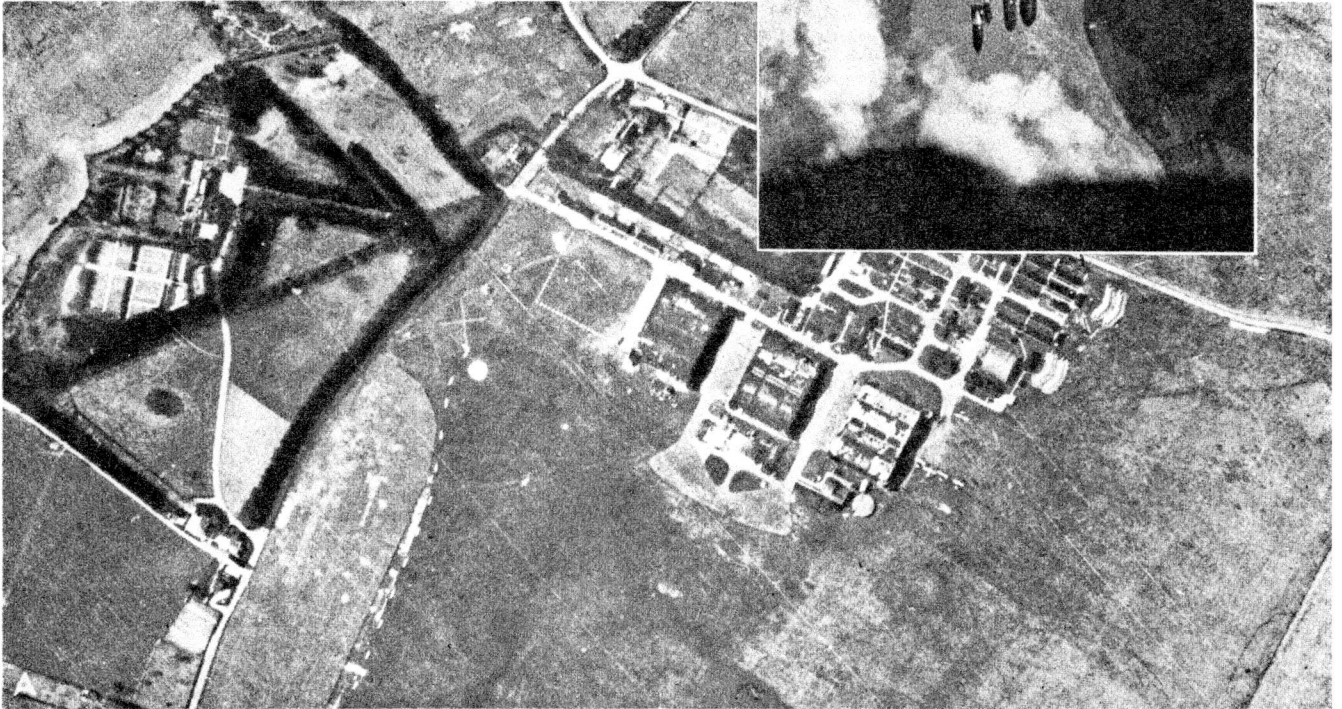

Jetzt auch Liktorenbündel über England

The Lictor's Fasces now over England also

Wie aus dem Bericht des Oberkommandos der Wehrmacht vom 25. Oktober hervorging, hat der Duce einige Verbände seiner Kampfflieger an den Kanal geschickt, von wo aus sie an den Flügen der deutschen Luftwaffe gegen London und die britische Insel teilnehmen

The bulletin of the German Chief Command of October 25th announced that the Duce had sent several formations of his bombers to the English Channel to take part in the raids of the German Air Force on London and the British Islands

Als Erkennungszeichen tragen die italienischen Flugzeuge neben dem weißen Kreuz auf dem Seitenleitwerk das dreifache Liktorenbündel

The Italian aircraft bear the triple lictor's fasces as emblem beside the white cross on the vertical tail surfaces unit

Aufnahmen von Kriegsberichter
Josef Grabler

Evviva il Führer! Es lebe der Duce!" Das Bodenpersonal eines italienischen Kampfverbandes freut sich mit den Männern vom Reichsarbeitsdienst, die ihm den Flugplatz hergerichtet haben, damit nun auch sie in den Kampf gegen die Insel eingreifen können. Die Männer vom RAD sind mit Kreuzen gekennzeichnet, sonst könnte der Beschauer sie nicht unter den Italienern herausfinden

"Evviva il Führer! Es lebe der Führer! (Long live the Führer! Long live the Duce!) The ground personnel of an Italian bomber formation express their joy with the men of the Reich Labor Corps, who have laid out their landing ground, that they can now also engage in the struggle with England. The men of the Labor Corps in the photo have been marked by a cross; for they would otherwise be hard to pick out among the Italians

Die zweimotorigen Kampfflugzeuge der Italiener sind auf den Flugplätzen an der Kanalküste eingetroffen. Neben ihrer Schnelligkeit zeichnen sie sich durch eine kampfkräftige Bewaffnung aus

The twin-engined bombers of the Italians have arrived at the airdrome on the Channel coast. Apart from their speed, they are noteworthy for the fighting power of their armament

Noch steht dieses italienische Kampfflugzeug nach der Landung ungetarnt auf dem Rollfeld. Bald wird es auf seinem Liegeplatz unter der Tarnung verschwinden, die es der Feindsicht entzieht

This Italian bomber is still standing open to view after landing, but will soon be hidden from enemy view under its camouflage

Während die Italiener zur Feldküche abgerückt sind, halten die Männer vom deutschen Reichsarbeitsdienst die Wacht bei ihren Flugzeugen. Dieser Bomber sieht durch das Augenpaar, das auf die Bugkanzel gemalt ist, wie ein gefährliches Untier aus und wird es in den Augen der Engländer auch sein

The Italians have left for the army kitchen, while the men of the Labor Corps keep watch over their machines. The pair of eyes painted on the bow turret makes the bomber look like a dangerous monster—as it doubtless will be in the eyes of the enemy

Der halbierte Britendampfer

A British Steamer Cut in Two

Nothing Escapes German Scout Pilots

Noch vor den letzten großen Angriffen der deutschen Luftwaffe auf Swansea hatte einen großen britischen Frachtdampfer im Bristolkanal sein Schicksal erreicht. Schwer angeschlagen konnte das Schiff sich gerade noch ins flache Wasser der Küstennähe retten, wo es unter der Einwirkung von Wind und Wellen gänzlich auseinanderbrach. Die Briten können sich nicht leisten, so viele Tonnen wertvollen Eisens, wie sie ein moderner Dampfer darstellt, brach liegen zu lassen. Wenn der Dampfer nicht mehr als solcher zu verwenden ist, dann muß wenigstens das Eisen als Schrott geborgen werden. Ihre Versuche, den Dampfer zu bergen, gelangen nur zum Teil. Während das Achterschiff allen Bemühungen widerstand, konnte die vordere Hälfte des Schiffes abgeschleppt werden. Sie wurde in Swansea, einem Hafen am nördlichen Ufer des Bristolkanals, ins Trockendock gebracht. Auf dem unteren Bild ist das Vorderschiff, durch einen Pfeil gekennzeichnet, deutlich im trockengepumpten Dock zu sehen. Die beiden Aufnahmen, eine Meisterleistung deutscher Fernaufklärung, beweisen wieder einmal, unter welch genauer Beobachtung alle Vorgänge auf der britischen Insel liegen

Aufnahmen: Luftwaffe (2)

A large British freighter met its fate in the Bristol Channel some time before the last big raids on Swansea by the German Air Corps. It was badly knocked about and just managed to reach shallow water near the coast, where it was beached and broke up under the action of wind and waves. The British cannot afford to leave the tonnage of valuable steel represented by a modern steamer to lie about uselessly, and at least the scrap metal had to be salved although the vessel itself could no longer be used. Efforts to salve the steamer were only partly successful. The stern resisted all attempts at salvage, but the forepart of the ship was towed to Swansea, a port on the north shore of the Bristol Channel, where it was drydocked. The lower photo clearly shows the forepart of the ship (marked by an arrow) lying in the dock, which has been pumped dry. These two photographs are a masterly piece of German long-distance reconnaissance work and prove once again that everything that goes on in the British Isles is kept under close observation

STUKAS am Feind

Dive Bombers in Action

A Descriptive Report from Three Fronts

By Josef Grabler, War Correspondent

The Inferno of Dunkirk

After the fall of Calais, the last strong point left to the British forces was Dunkirk, which became the culmination of the greatest outflanking battle hitherto fought in the present war. The British were pushed further and further back, and found no other way out than to board their ships and clear off. It may be noted in passing that they thereby betrayed their allies, the French, to an extent that would never have been credited. The French fought desperately with their backs to the town of Dunkirk against the onslaught of the German troops. The British, on the contrary, withdrew a company here, a battalion there, one after the other, from the fighting line, marched them to the harbor and the beach, and there embarked them. It is not so well known that the British adopted a measure to save at least part of their Expeditionary Force, which at any rate has the merit of originality. As soon as it appeared certain that they would not be able to hold their position on the Continent, they mobilized everything on the south-east and south coasts of England that was capable of floating at all; besides steamers and tugs of every description, they sent off even the tiniest power-boats, that could hold only a few men. The whole of that gigantic armada was sent to Dunkirk to save whatever it was still possible to save. It will readily be understood that the mobilization of these craft enabled the British to transport part of their Expeditionary Force back to their island home, because the German troops were unable to reach the town in time to prevent that operation, the British having blown up the sluices and thereby inundated the whole area round about Dunkirk. Under these circumstances, it was only natural that the German Air Corps made a merciless clearance of the British transporter fleet.

In the experience of the dive-bomber crews, Dunkirk represented one of the dramatic climaxes of the whole war up to that time. All hell seemed to have broken loose there. Horizontal and dive-bomber formations uninterruptedly dropped their deadly loads into the doomed town. It was hardly necessary to take accurate aim over Dunkirk and it was anyhow practically impossible to do so, owing to the dense pall of smoke in which the town was continually enveloped. Every bomb scored a hit, because the allied forces were compelled to collect enormous masses of troops in the town itself, since the free space at disposal was steadily growing less. They simply did not know where to dispose their troops; for in the town of Dunkirk was penned up a whole army that had originally been in occupation of all Flanders and part of northern France. These troops were now all crowded together in the narrow space of Dunkirk and every house in the town was crammed full of soldiers, as was later revealed. They had erected tents on all the open spaces, and the whole neighborhood of the town, as far as it was still occupied by the French, was congested with troops and vehicles. The dive-bomber crews made a less agreeable observation over Dunkirk of the same nature as they had already made over Warsaw. The concentration of so many troops naturally led to the massing of anti-aircraft artillery in a very confined area and countless anti-aircraft guns were firing in and round about Dunkirk.

Third-class ticket for Dunkirk

The blazing oil tanks in the harbor were the chief source of the enormous clouds of dense smoke lying over Dunkirk. When Peltz and his squadron dived, everything was at first black with smoke; nothing was to be seen at all, visibility simply did not exist, and targets could only be dimly made out after having

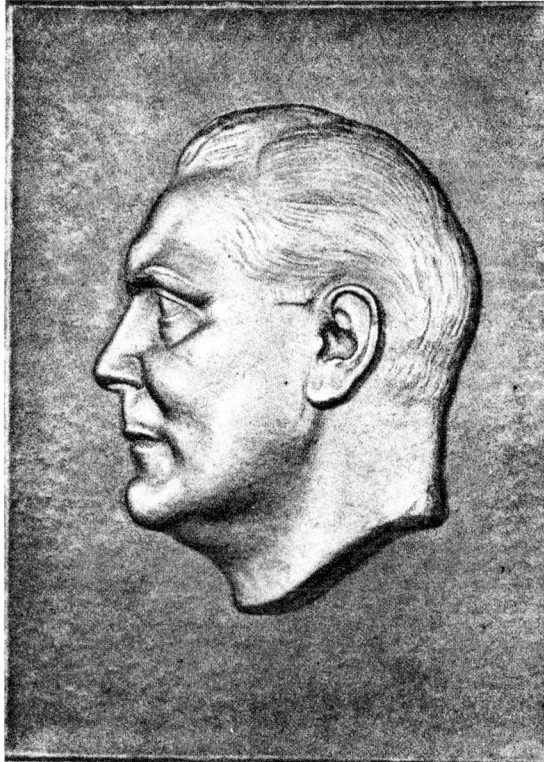

REICH MARSHAL HERMANN GÖRING
Obergefreiter (Air Force Corporal) Hans Böhler of Neu-Ulm, the romantic town on the Danube which produced one of the pioneers of aviation, the often unjustly derided "flying taylor", created this extremely successful plaque of our Reich Marshal. His performance must be rated all the more highly, as the young sculptor is self-taught and had to seek his way to plastic art without any assistance from others. Hans Böhler, who is now wearing the blue-gray uniform of the air soldier, justifies the highest expectations and the Reichs Marshal has taken occasion personally to express to him recognition of that fact

pierced the layer of smoke. The bombardment of Dunkirk from the air was so concentrated that a pilot had literally to watch out that he did not get a bomb in the neck from his comrades flying above him. The approach to that last bulwark had long since ceased to be a problem. Even hidden by banks of cloud, Dunkirk was not to be missed, because countless numbers of anti-aircraft shell-bursts were to be seen, even above the clouds, at the point where the town ought to lie. Hostile air-craft were hardly ever to be observed over the town and only German planes were to be seen. Oberleutnant Peltz and his squadron attacked Dunkirk eight times altogether. When the squadron took off during those days, the ground personnel merely remarked, "Third-class ticket for Dunkirk, without changing!" It frequently happened during an approach that whole groups of Heinkel horizontal bombers of the He 111 type passed through the dive bombers and the pilots and gunners of the latter could then watch with satisfaction the bombs dropping from all the bomb-wells of these formations.

The British forces at first carried out their evacuation operations practically only under the cover of night. But the ring of the German troops steadily closing in on the town made the situation so acute that they were no longer able to confine themselves to night operations. It was only a matter of a few days until Dunkirk would have to fall, so that the British were compelled to continue their flight by day also. The heavy shipping traffic between Dunkirk and England caused thereby was naturally meat and drink to the dive-bomber crews; for the small point targets, such as presented even by large vessels, were their own exclusive domain. They had hitherto bombed land objectives only were now to attack floating targets for the first time. The squadron experienced their greatest day when they flew out to sea, a few days before the fall of Dunkirk, to seek their prey. The squadron flew over the coast at a medium height, left it behind, and the British ships were already to be made out ahead, looking like toys from that altitude.

It must be a big freighter

Oberleutnant Peltz gazes round about. The large numbers of small fry swimming down below are not worth while, they can be raked with machine-gun fire. A big freighter must provide a target for the heavy bombs. Peltz flies further out over the Channel and soon sees something better afloat out there. As he reaches the ship with his crews, he can make out that it is a vessel of at least 5,000 tons, steering at full speed for the English shores. That one must be polished off and with it many a warrior of old England will be sent to Davy Jones's locker! Peltz orders his squadron to attack the ship with all bombs. It is very heavily armed with anti-aircraft guns and knows what is awaiting it. The deck is reddened by the flashes from the muzzles of the guns, smaller vessels in the vicinity are firing with light anti-aircraft guns. The transporter starts to zig-zag, before Peltz begins his nose-dive, and the foam in its wake wriggles like a twisted tail. Peltz dives, the steamer comes closer at a terrific rate, growing in size to meet him. Suddenly he sees a gun of larger caliber standing amidships and, while diving, gives the machine just a slight correction by means of the joy-stick, so that the reflecting sight can seize that gun. Another moment and it will be time to drop the bomb. Now for it! The sight is directed with the utmost accuracy on the big gun. According to all human calculation, the bomb must hit it. Peltz pulls out and once more centrifugal force with its giant fist thrusts him back on his seat. But only for a split second and then he lightly banks the machine to such an extent that he can observe his hit. The explosion has already taken place, he never

A Thrust at England's Flank

The German Air Corps in Norway

April 9th is the first anniversary of the day on which the Führer and supreme commander-in-chief of the national defense services by his inspired strategy brought about a decision of far-reaching importance. The military occupation of Denmark and Norway anticipated by a few days the invasion of Norway by the British navy, which had actually already set out, and thereby undid the thrust at the flank of Germany planned by England. Every difficulty, however great, was overcome by lightning rapidity of action and masterly cooperation on the part of all arms of the service, so that the intended threat to Germany was reversed and England, which had once more missed a chance, in spite of its superiority at sea, suddenly found its own flank threatened.

The German Air Corps took a decisive part in that operation, which is unparalleled in the annals of war. In spite of most unfavorable weather and uncertain landing conditions, it occupied the most important bases and airdromes over a stretch of some 900 miles, transported parachute troops and air-borne troops in the speediest way possible to the points where they were to be brought into action as far off as Narvik; besides being simultaneously ready to repel raids by the British Air Force, they escorted the extensive troop transports by the German navy, destroyed many units of the British navy, and successfully took part in the ground fighting, wherever required. It must be left to later historians to recognize and assess the value of that gigantic performance. The timely appearance of the new volume of the Adler series bearing the significant title "Stoss in Englands Flanke" (A Thrust at England's Flank) just before the anniversary is therefore the more to be welcomed. It unfolds the course of the operations before our eyes both by means of dramatic narratives of the experiences of those who took part in the fighting, as well as by a profusion of particularly telling illustrations.

An introductory chapter plainly brings out the great tasks and difficulties that confronted the military leaders on April 9, 1940. The mountainous country of Norway was upon the whole easy to defend and difficult to attack. Only those directly concerned can really appreciate what it meant at that time to occupy such a country with its innumerable fjords and small islands, between which the enemy might be lying in wait anywhere, its paucity of communications, and its almost insuperable mountain barriers. The book introduces us vividly to these realities and then describes the strategic advantages that the German forces, more particularly the air service, won for themselves by the new lie-out position for the further course of the struggle with England, advantages upon which it is impossible to place too high an estimate. The enemy have meanwhile had occasion over and over again to feel in their own person that German bombers are no longer obliged to confine themselves to starting from the German Bight, but have much shorter approach flights to all the important armaments centers of the island and not only consume less fuel, but can also carry a much greater weight of bombs.

But the campaign in Norway would never have been so rapidly and so victoriously concluded had it not been for the brilliantly organized supply of men, military materials, munitions, and stores. A special chapter of the book is therefore devoted to the air transport formations, which, as the order of the day issued by the commander-in-chief of the Air Corps expresses it, "created in selfless unobtrusiveness and the most untiring exertions the provisos for the success of the undertaking". What the air transport formations succeeded in doing, borders on the miraculous. They flew by day and by night, they pushed forward with lightning rapidity to the most distant posts and everywhere supplied the fighting troops with all necessities. Many a heroic deed that merits special mention is described in this book.

The air transport formations are above all most closely connected with the name of Narvik. The heroic struggle of German parachute troops and air-borne troops against an almost overwhelming superiority of numbers has long since passed into history as a brilliant example of unconquerable German soldiership. That glorious defense is the real center of the campaign in Norway and forms the climax of the book. One who

took part in the fighting there describes no less dramatically than comprehensively the heroic life and struggles of the defenders of Narvik and the self-sacrificing devotion of the Air Corps. In this narrative too, as in many of the other contributions, the successful action of our horizontal and dive-bomber formations against the "invincible British navy" takes life again before our eyes. Bombs of the heaviest type received the British landing fleet and equally destructive bombs hit the same fleet of transporters a few weeks later on their flight from Narvik to the home harbors. Battleships, cruisers, and large troopships then experienced one disastrous day after another and the British Admiralty was willy-nilly forced to recognize that no navy, however strong it may be, can operate for any length of time within the range of action of a superior air service.

One point in particular is brought out with satisfactory clarity by this publication: the unique success achieved was only made possible by far-sighted cooperation of all units of the Air Corps. In spite of wind and weather, the reconnaissance formations carried out intensive observation work, followed up the movements of the British fleet, and gave the bomber formations and pursuit squadrons the possibility of immediately attacking. Pursuit pilots and anti-aircraft artillery night and day protected the air space over Norway. The ground personnel, hardly disembarked on the Norwegian airdromes, did their duty with sangfroid and marvellous discipline. The air force signals corps were tirelessly ready for duty and maintained connection between the formations, strung far apart as they were, but also with headquarters at home.

It is practically impossible to do more than hint at the contents of the book within the scope of this article, but the headings of a few chapters may be quoted here: "Dive bombers versus British Fleet", "Airmen Escort a Convoy", "British Troopship Reported", "Big Bomber Flies over the North Cape", "German

After the Raid

Butler: "Did anyone knock?"   (Marc Aurelio)

Pursuit Pilots on the Northern Polar Circle", "Bombs on the Arctic Ocean". They simultaneously bring out individual phases of the tremendous struggle of the German Air Corps in Scandinavia. It may be remarked in passing that one who knows Norway particularly well gives the reader an interesting insight into the thought and feeling of the Norwegians.

Taken as a whole, the new Adler volume gives us a vivid impression by word and picture of the boldest undertaking in the German annals of war, as the Führer and supreme commander-in-chief of the national defense services has termed the campaign in Norway. Those who were there will find in these narratives "their" fight and "their" experiences related over again. But the home front, more especially, the youth of Germany, should take the book into their hands with a feeling of pride and gratitude, and with the unfaltering determination to emulate these deeds and to carry out whatever they undertake. For the virtues of the highest soldiership, death-defying courage, self-sacrifice, and stubborn tenacity were realized in fact during the campaign in Norway.

Dive Bombers in Action

observed the flash. But an enormous black mushroom is shooting up precisely at the point where the gun had just been standing. The heavy bomb had landed amidships. Flashes appear at a number of points on the ship. Several bombs also fall beside and behind it. The work of his comrades. Their machines are diving on the ship from all sides. A hail of bombs takes place. Peltz can see the splinters hissing through the water, the crests of the waves spraying over them. As he zooms up, he sees once more a heavy bomb landing in the middle of the deck, shortly followed by another on the quarterdeck. A jet of flame shoots up amidships. Peltz is now far away from the ship attacked, which he can only see is still smoking, but there can be no doubt that it has had enough.

And now the small fry are for it! Motor boats, yachts, and fishing cutters. Craft of every description are swimming about, some with the bow towards England, others towards Dunkirk. These provide targets for machine-gun fire, not very different from the way the squadron has had sufficient practice of in Poland and France in low-flying attacks on marching columns. These small craft also try to escape by zig zagging, but it doesn't help much. Hardly one of the crowded boats but smarts under the bursts of fire from the machine-guns of pilot and gunner.

During the next attack in the afternoon the crews of the Peltz squadron see that "their" ship has been beached and is still smoking. It must have turned with the last strength at command and dragged itself back to the French coast, where it was run aground. That day brought a proud bag: the wing had sunk four transporters and a destroyer.

The battle in France

After the fall of Dunkirk there was a brief interval of rest until June 5, 1940, when the great offensive over the Somme was opened. Once more the dive-bomber crews had the experience of a discussion of their mission of historical importance as they stood round their commander in a tent by candle-light. They all consulted their maps and noted the objective, a village to the south-east of Amiens, where a high French staff had their headquarters. After discussing the mission, Major Sigel spoke a few words, pointing out to his officers that they would be flying in a few minutes in advance of the greatest offensive of all time.

The hurricane bombardement of the artillery at the front was still thundering over the airdrome as the squadron took off in the dark, in order to be over their objective in the early dawn. Shortly after taking off a sight presented itself to their eyes, such as only their fathers before them had seen during the Great War at the time of the battles of machinery. From one end of the horizon to the other stretched the glare of the flashes from the heavy artillery engaged in pulverizing the French positions. It was a solemn impression to experience from that altitude, much as an unconcerned spectator, that tremendous push by the German army. The whole line of the Somme scintillated as if huge electrical discharges were taking place. Further to the south, the impacts could be seen lying close together. Flames were shooting up, wherever one looked. The explosions of the discharges and impacts swallowed up the noise of the engine. The impression made by the magic of fire on the Somme was thus all the more spectral. Oberleutnant Peltz has his squadron well together, although it is still dark, and it has not become much brighter by the time they are a short way off their objective. Peltz looks at the clock. The raid has been timed for 5.05 a.m. There are still a few minutes to go. He banks in a wide curve, so as not to be above the objective earlier than the time set. Peltz once more looks back to where the artillery duel is proceeding below. It has risen to a hurricane of fury, as can be recognized from the much more increased concentration of fire. Under the overwhelming impression of the scene, the squadron leader almost forgot to approach his objective in time. It is a small place, rather larger than a village, but still not a town. Numerous vehicles are to be seen on the streets and at the outskirts of the place. It seems to be just the right kind of place for a raid, being evidently well occupied and just of the right size that the bombs of his squadron can completely cover it in. The raid goes off smoothly. Every bomb scores a hit and the objective is soon enveloped in clouds of smoke. While on his way back, Peltz sees a machine of another squadron crash in flames. It probably chanced to get in the trajectory of an artillery projectile and received a direct hit. After the capitulation of Paris, the French front began to give way everywhere. When the French troops did offer resistance, the dive-bombers lammed in and made the sparks fly. During the further advance the French mostly arranged rallying positions to the rear, usually by strengthening up villages by throwing up field fortifications. After the German infantry had taken a bulldog hold, rarely more than half an hour elapsed before a dive-bomber formation appeared and completely pulverized the islet of resistance.

French defense by pursuit planes had practically ceased to exist, so that dive-bomber crews were able to take liberties that would have been self-prohibitive, had enemy interceptor planes been abou. Conditions were once again as in Poland, where everything that had a propeller had been smashed within a few days. During an attack near Troyes the Peltz squadron pulled off a great coup. The sun had just risen and was breaking through the nocturnal veil of haze that still hung over the ground. Oberleutnant Peltz was flying in the direction of Troyes at an altitude of 1600 ft. when he discovered an endless column of enemy motor lorries. He broke up the squadron to crack that nut. Once again there was merry hell down below on that road, as the vehicles crashed into trees, bucked into the ditch, or exploded under mechine-gun fire and a hail of bombs. Oberleutnant Peltz was just climbing a little higher, in order to get a better view of the effect, when he suddenly saw a gigantic spurt of flame from a group of lorries that stood for a few seconds over the column and finally reached a height of over 3,000 ft. That had been ammunition—that had!

General von Richthofen was at that time commanding officer of the air corps to which the Pletz squadron belonged. The General was constantly hustling about with a Fieseler "Stork" to keep an eye on weather conditions and even to find objectives. He was rather astonished at first to find machine-gun hits in his machine. The go-ahead action on the part of the commanding officer had its reward not only from a tactical point of view, but the General solved the problem of improving the mechanization of his formations in a way that left nothing to be desired. One fine day, that is to say, he spots during a reconnaissance flight an enormous park of automotive vehicles belonging to the French army, the German advance

having proceeded so rapidly that the French had had no time remove them. After landing, the General promptly tips off his formations by telephone that large numbers of lorries are standing at the place he had reconnoitred and hints that there might be a chance to provide themselves with any vehicles they needed. The Peltz squadron, which could long since have done with a replenishing of their park, does not need to be told twice, but packs off a lorry with a number of drivers to the front, where the party is one of the first to arrive. First come, first served. It was a real driver's paradise and the men from the Peltz squadron could afford to be finical. They helped themselves only to lorries

of eight cylinders and upwards, and of these only the very best makes.

The First Attacks on England

Soon there was fresh work. Floating objectives were now assigned to the squadron after it had stood the test so remarkably well in attacks on transporters. The next raids were on British convoys attempting to run the blockade of the Channel. These flights over long stretches of sea were a trifle uncomfortable at first, because a dive-bomber pilot has of course only one engine; when that cuts out, there is nothing for it but a dip in the "drink" with all its disagreeable consequences. Although the crews were provided with life jackets, they had no yearning for a cold footbath. The anxiety felt about the single engine often led subconsciously to a certain feeling of uneasiness. Did it not just conk? Not a bit of it! The engine is roaring quietly in its sonorous way, as it has always roared. Merely imagination playing tricks! After the first few raids, they had familiarized themselves with flying

over the sea, thanks to no inconsiderable extent to the unbounded confidence that the pilots were able to place in the work of their mechanics.

At first there was occasionally a hitch with the convoys and many a bomb missed its target. The British skippers tried a new trick of dodging aimed bombs. When an attack was reported, they did not rush off at full speed in zigzag, as hitherto, but in circles. That was very awkward for the dive-bomber crews, until they had found out the arc, and more than once fervent, but unholy Bavarian expressions were to be heard in the headphones. In a short time, however, the squadron had got in its hand and many a proud British steamer was sent to the fishes.

Peltz flew with a large formation in the first attack on England, a raid on London. Unfortunately the raid had to be broken off owing to the very bad weather conditions, which made a flight in formation very difficult. During the return flight there was a little misadventure, which in reality was not one. Peltz had been flying back blind and dived through the clouds, when he knew that the French coast lay beneath him, in order to catch a glimpse of the earth. He had barely reached the open and recognized the coastline below, when "Archie" opened a furious fire. Fortunately, the machine was not hit, but the crew were hopping mad. That cursed anti-aircraft defense! We'll show them this time! Arrived home, Peltz at once got on the phone and rang up everyone he could reach to work off his wrath. But he speedily calmed down when he finally got hold of the officer commanding the anti-aircraft defense, who spoke a few soothing words. "My dear man", he said, "there's no great call to get your dander up. We recognized you all right as a German machine, but what you evidently failed to recognize was the Bristol Blenheim interceptor behind you, which was evidently out for your scalp. My gunners shot it down not very far behind you." Peltz vowed never again to bawl out "Archie"—at least until the next time.

The cold season made the raids on England more difficult. Although the machine is almost perfectly equipped against the risk of ice-formation, by means that need not be discussed here, still there was one troublesome feature. Blind flying often seemed to take no end when zooming up to find the open, the clouds appeared to go up all the way to heaven, and the result was that the windows of the cockpit became covered with ice, thereby eliminating free vision, one of the most vitally essential elements of flying.

Whale Hunting

Although the cry of "Interceptor!" is not exactly music in the ears of a bomber pilot, Peltz had perforce developed a method that enabled him always to shake off enemy pursuit planes. When on his way to his objective above the clouds in brilliant sunshine, Spitfires or Hurricanes were almost always sure to turn up. Fortunately these troublesome insects revealed their presence at a great altitude in good time by the white condensation streaks. Then the first thing to be done according to a well-tried recipe was to get into the clouds. Peltz had barely disappeared from view when he changed his course; he flew for a time on the wrong course and then cautiously poked his nose out into the open. The pursuit planes had mostly gone off by then, looking for the enemy on the old course and waiting till he came to the surface again. His crew gave that method of shaking off the British pilots the name of

In rasendem Flug ist der Stuka in die Tiefe gestoßen, soeben ist die Bombe ausgelöst worden und wird nach wenigen Sekunden treffsicher im Ziel liegen
Aufnahme IFM

Rapidly flying, the Stuka has rushed downward; the bomb has just been released and will hit the mark in a few seconds

"whale-hunting", because whalers, like the British pilots, are after a big fish that also doubles under water. There is no fear that British pilots will reap any benefit from the publication of that dodge, because they will already have noticed for themselves that the German bomber pilot, who again and again destroys precisely their most valuable military objectives, is not to be diverted from his objective. When the faithful Ju 88 was homeward bound and flying blind, leaving nameless destruction behind it, the gallant crew were accustomed to chant their battle-cry to the well-known tune "Wir haben den Kanal, wir haben den Kanal — noch lange nicht voll" (which might be freely endered "We have not filled the Channel, we have not filled the Channel—by a very long way"). And now the reader is invited to make the acquaintance of that crew, whom there will often be occasion to mention. Besides the pilot and commander, Oberleutnant (Flying Officer) Peltz, there was the bomb-aimer Oberfeldwebel (Sergeant-Major) Rauscher, meanwhile promoted to the rank of Leutnant (Pilot Officer) for bravery in the presence of the enemy. The radio operator was Oberfeldwebel (Sergeant-Major) Schönchen, while Feldwebel (Sergeant) Klaar acted as rear gunner. All three of the same hard timber as their commander. Men who would be prepared to fetch the devil's grandmother out of hell, as all in the day's work.

German bomber muscles in on a British airdrome

Once more Peltz and his crew are off for England. Over the Channel, the weather was all that could be desired, but the low clouds steadily tail off as they approach their objective. Peltz is still 4,600 ft. up as the last veil of cloud flits by and then the machine is in the open; there is no further protecting mass of cloud in front, which is not quite healthy for a lone plane that aims at worrying the Britishers a mite.

Peltz flies a little further at the risk of running up against enemy pursuit planes in that wide open expanse of sky. He must decide quickly. His objective is still far off and is not to be reached under the present circumstances, so that he must seek a substitute target, because there can be no question of carrying that nice little load of bombs back home with him. At the worst, there is always London, but that would be merely a makeshift target that appears to Peltz and his crew to be hardly a fair deal. They are accustomed to better objectives.

The pilot has now left the protecting cloud cover quite a distance behind him, but can detect no worth-while objective for his precious bombs, however, much he looks about him in every direction. Suddenly he spots an airplane several miles away over to the left that is travelling away from him and seems to be intending to land. At all events it is plainly descending. But if the pilot is going to land, he will most likely do so on a landing ground. Peltz nudges Oberfeldwebel Rauscher beside him, who has also noticed the plane and is of the same opinion as his commander, without many words passing between them. Airdromes are always worth-while objectives.

Peltz has long since started the slight deviation from his course that brings him on the track of the landing Britisher and in a very short time they have the landing ground before them. That was some landing ground! That was much more than an ordinary kind of landing ground, it was the real thing in airdromes. There was a steady coming and going of aircraft and a number of machines stood in a bunch together, evidently alongside the gas pits, and there were extensive hangers close by. "O boy!" says Peltz, "Me for that".

Now a raid on a British airdrome in bright sunshine out of a blue sky is not quite as simple a matter, as it looks, because the British are accustomed to protect their airdromes by plentiful use of anti-aircraft defense artillery, more especially light weapons, that are rather awkward for any low-flying machine. Oberleutnant Peltz knows all about that and his crew naturally know that too, but they hope to pull it off by acting on their well-tried maxim that much can be done by bluff, where bashfulness would not have a look-in. Peltz has long since laid his plan, as he descends in a wide turn and manœuvres himself towards the airdrome. A training course seems to be in progress down below, because aircraft are constantly flying round the airdrome, and Peltz intends to muscle himself into that traffic as if he belonged to the gang. Peltz has completed his turn and is flying straight for the airdrome; he can even recognize the landing cross ahead. Rauscher says, "Pursuit planes are taking off", but Peltz only shrugs his shoulders; it is scarcely to be supposed that they are after him, because he does not seem to have been noticed yet. Several machines are landing simultaneously and others are whirring in from the left. There are all sorts of types among them, but Peltz has no time to bother about them. His attention is concentrated on the crowd of machines ahead at the gas pits. Suddenly a red streak flits past the front turret. Then again; more and more of them. "They've spotted us now!" But the firing stops at once and Peltz sees the reason why; there are too many British machines in the air, so that the anti-aircraft defense cannot shoot properly. Rauscher has his hand on the bomb release gear, but Peltz stops him and banks sharply to make an about turn. The approach has failed. It passed very close to the objective, so that the bombs would not have exerted their full effect.

"Down with the bombs!"

The numerous British planes in the air appear not to have noticed as yet what is going on. Some land, but others take off, while others are flying round the airdrome, as if nothing had occurred. "That is very nice of these guys", says Peltz, "because in that way they are preventing their own artillery from firing." At a very low altitude Peltz approaches the target again in a sharp curve and once more the tracer munition of the light anti-aircraft guns whistles past. But not a single hit is scored.

Birmingham

Das Bild zeigt die durch eine punktierte Linie eingerahmten Singer-Werke in Birmingham, ein für die britische Rüstung lebenswichtiges Werk, das Panzer und Kraftwagen herstellte. Die Aufnahme zeigt das Werk vor dem Angriff. Die Hallen scheinen gegenüber dem unteren Bilde dunkel, da sie noch nicht mit Tarnanstrich versehen sind

This illustration, taken before the air raid, shows the Singer Works in Birmingham framed by a dotted line. This factory was of essential importance for British armaments and manufactured armored and motor cars. The sheds appear dark compared with the photograph below, because they have not yet had their camouflage coat of paint

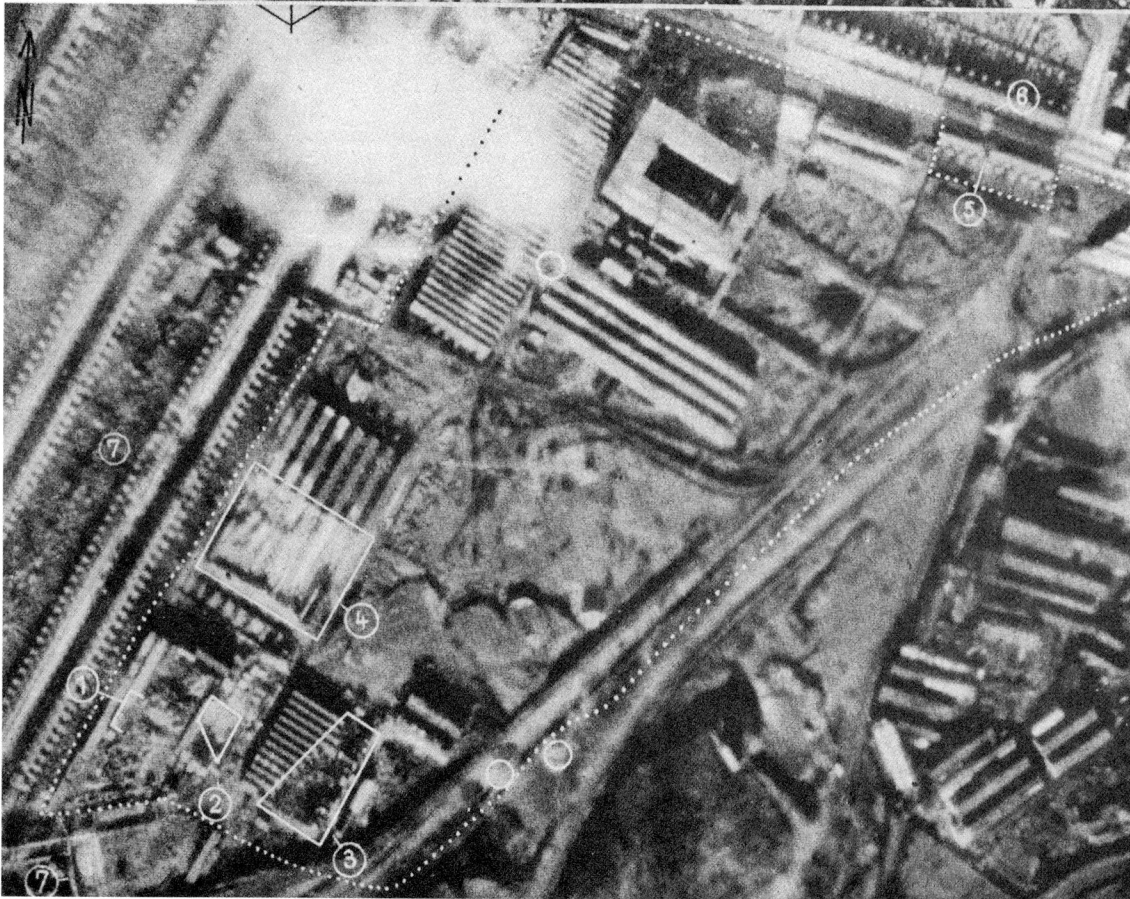

Inzwischen ist ein Angriff deutscher Kampfflugzeuge über das Werk hinweggebraust. Die schweren Zerstörungen sind deutlich sichtbar. Sie sind durch weiße Umrahmungen kenntlich gemacht. Einzelne Bombeneinschläge sind durch einen Kreis eingefaßt. Die Zahlen bedeuten im einzelnen: (1), (2), (3) und (4) zerstörte oder beschädigte Hallen. Bei (5) hat eine Bombe einen Häuserblock getroffen und teilweise auseinandergerissen. Dies ist an der Schattenlücke auf der Straße, durch (6) gekennzeichnet, besonders deutlich zu sehen. Mit (7) sind Zerstörungen außerhalb des Werkgeländes bezeichnet

Aufn. Luftwaffe (2

Meanwhile a raid by German bombers has whirled over the plant. The damage inflicted is framed by white lines and is obviously serious. Bomb hits are marked by a circle. The figures (1), (2), (3), and (4) indicate destroyed or damaged shops. At (5) a bomb has struck a block of houses and partly demolished it, as is particularly evident from the gap in the shadow on the ground (6). Damage outside the factory grounds is to be seen at (7)

Luftwaffe blockiert die britische Insel

Einen überzeugenden Beweis, mit welcher Genauigkeit die deutsche Luftwaffe die für die Briten lebenswichtigen Anlagen zu treffen weiß, bietet diese Bildmeldung eines Aufklärers. Das an der Südspitze der Dockhalbinsel von Southampton gelegene große Kühlhaus (3), in dem riesige Mengen von Gefrierfleisch eingelagert waren, ist durch Bomben vernichtet worden. Der Ausfall sowohl dieser Anlage wie der hier gelagerten Vorräte ist ein schwerer Schlag gegen die britische Ernährungswirtschaft. John Bull muß längst das tun, was er uns zugedacht hat: den Riemen enger schnallen. Bei (1) liegt ein Überseedampfer im Trockendock, mit (2) sind Schiffe gekennzeichnet, die an den Piers entladen werden, und bei (4) sind wieder Sperrballone zu sehen, die auf Schiffen verankert sind und sich durch ihre Schatten auf dem Wasser verraten

Aufnahme Luftwaffe (Scherl)

The Air Force Blockades the British Island

This photograph brought back by a reconnaissance plane proves convincingly the accuracy with which the German Air Force is able to hit vitally important plants. The large cold storage warehouse (3) situated at the southern extremity of the docks peninsula of Southampton, containing enormous quantities of frozen meat, was destroyed by bombs. The loss of this plant and its contents is a heavy blow for the British foodstuff industry. John Bull has long since had to tighten his own belt—as he intended us to do. An ocean liner is lying in the dry dock at (1), while (2) marks ships discharging at the quays. At (4) other balloons are also to be seen; they are anchored to ships and betray their presence by their shadows

30

31

So jagten wir sie

Die Besatzung des deutschen Kampfflugzeuges nimmt auf dem Fluge gegen den Feind noch eine Stärkung zu sich. „Bitte Platz nehmen zum ersten Mittagessen", hatte der Funker eben gerufen, als er die Bordverpflegung verteilte. Der Beobachter läßt den Flugzeugführer wählen: „Lieber Vollmilch- oder bittere Schokolade?"

The crew of a German bomber enjoys a snack on the way to their objective. The wireless operator in his function as steward has just called out "Please take seats for the first lunch", and is distributing the board rations. The observer gives the pilot his choice. "Milk chocolate or bitter?"

Aufn. PK Grosse (2), PK Schaller (1)

Jetzt wird es Ernst! Nach längerem Fluge über der Nordsee ist das erste feindliche Schiff in Sicht gekommen (Bild rechts). Der Beobachter übernimmt jetzt die Bedienung des Bug-MG's. Das Kampfflugzeug setzt zum Angriff an

Matters are now becoming serious. The first enemy ship has just come into view after a long flight over the North Sea. The observer is now attending to the bow machine-gun and the pilot manœuvers for attack

in den Grund

How we sent them to the Bottom of the Sea

Die Bilder dieser Seite stellen eine Episode aus den Kämpfen der Luftwaffe während des Frankreich-Feldzuges dar. Nach Ablauf des Jahres 1940, das in den Sommermonaten den glorreichen Feldzug gegen Frankreich in sich schloß, ist es gut, einen Blick zurückzuwerfen auf die Taten der Luftwaffe, die entscheidend zur schnellen Beendigung dieses Feldzuges beigetragen haben

Weiter geht der Flug ins Feindesland hinein. Rechts und links die Flugzeuge der Kameraden, steuert der Kampfflieger dem nächsten Ziel entgegen

Bombers penetrate further and further into enemy territory towards their next objective with their comrades on all sides

Ran

In starken Verbänden flogen die deutschen Kampfflieger gegen den Feind. Mehrere Einsätze an einem Tage waren, begünstigt durch das durchweg schöne Wetter, keine Seltenheit

Powerful formations of German bombers raided the enemy and several raids on a single day, favored by good weather all through, were nothing uncommon

Aufnahmen: PK-Grosse (PBZ), PK-Folkerts [(Scherl) Atlantik], PK-Sprotte (Atlantik), PK-Sprieth (Atlantik), PK-Schödel [(PBZ) Scherl]

Das Ziel ist erreicht, ein Eisenbahnknotenpunkt bei Rethel. Wenige Bomben genügten, um diese wichtige Einmündung zweier Gleise nachhaltig zu zerstören. Alle sitzen haargenau

The objective, an important railroad junction near Rethel, has been reached, and a few bombs sufficed to cause serious damage, destroying the two lines of rails. Every bomb hit the target with great precision

Feindlicher Widerstand hat die Stadt Sedan zum Schlachtfeld gemacht. Stukas und Kampfflieger mußten eingreifen, um den Feind niederzukämpfen. Das Bild rechts zeigt Sedan während des Kampffliegerangriffs

Enemy resistance turned the town of Sedan into a battle-field. Stukas (dive-bombers) and horizontal bombers had to be employed to outfight the enemy. Right: Sedan during an attack by bombers

an den Feind

Up and at Them!

Diesmal gilt der Angriff feindlichen Truppenansammlungen. Bombe auf Bombe verläßt die Schächte, um in der Tiefe Tod und Vernichtung zu säen. Die feindliche Jagdabwehr war nicht untätig. Dieses nach der Landung aufgenommene Bild zeigt die Bombenwanne mit der mehrfach durchschossenen Glasverkleidung und die leeren Hülsen der Patronen, die der MG-Schütze verfeuert hat

Concentrations of troops form the target this time. Bomb after bomb leaves the wells, dealing out death and destruction below. The enemy fighter planes were not idle. This photo was taken after landing and shows the bomb well with numerous holes in the glass fairing and empty shells fired by the gunner

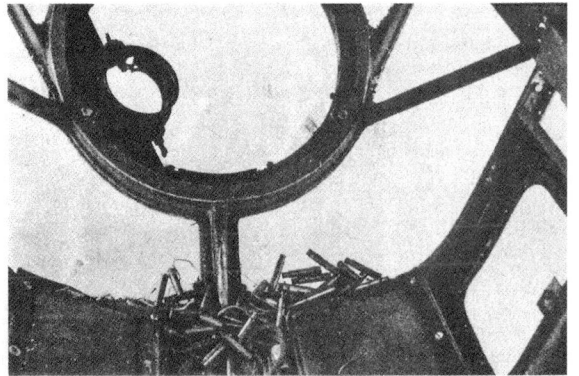

Nach der Landung stellt sich heraus, daß der feindliche Jagdflieger-Angriff doch nicht „so ohne" war. Die Maschine hat zahlreiche Treffer bekommen

It was found on landing that the attack by enemy fighters had not been exactly harmless, as evidenced by traces of numerous hits

Bomben Albions

Auch hier liegen wieder zwei unwiderlegbare Bilddokumente vor uns, die deutsche Aufklärer aufgenommen haben. Sie zeigen ein britisches Rüstungswerk in Southampton-Woolston vor und nach dem deutschen Bombenangriff. Links ist die ganze Anlage unversehrt, wobei (1) eine Montagehalle zeigt, (2) eine Werkhalle. Bei den Hallen sind große Materialvorräte aufgestapelt. Links führt eine Eisenbahnlinie vorbei. Eine gewisse topographische Verschiedenartigkeit der beiden Aufnahmen ist darin begründet, daß das linke Bild, bei Ebbe aufgenommen, mehr Land zeigt als das rechte, das bei Flut gemacht wurde.

Das Bild rechts läßt die verheerende Wirkung des deutschen Bombenangriffs klar zutage treten. Die Werkhalle (1) ist getroffen und durch Feuer vollständig zerstört. Im Dach der Montagehalle (2) klafft das Einschlagloch einer schweren Bombe. Sie wird im Innern das Ihre getan haben. Die Hallen (5) und (6) sind gleichfalls schwer getroffen und teilweise ausgebrannt. Auch in diesem Falle wurden die Wohnhäuser links neben den Hallen (5) und (6) nicht angetastet. Interessant ist ferner, daß das große Schiff und die vielen kleinen Fahrzeuge, die auf dem linken Bilde das Wasser beleben, auf der rechten Aufnahme bis auf ein einziges Schiff verschwunden sind.

Über dem unteren Bildrand ist eine Werft zu sehen. Die Schiffe, die hier teils im Wasser, teils auf den Gleitbahnen liegen, sollen hier ausgebessert werden. Ihre große Zahl läßt eindeutige Rückschlüsse auf den Reparaturbedarf der meerbeherrschenden Flotte zu. Und damit die Ironie nicht fehle, ist auch dieses Rüstungswerk durch eine Ballonsperre „geschützt". Auf dem rechten Bilde steht rechts unten über dem Wasser eine solche Gummiblase. Die Sperre hat weder unsere Kampfflieger daran gehindert, den befohlenen Zerstörungsauftrag durchzuführen, noch unsere Aufklärer, am hellen Tage diese Aufnahme zu machen. Wie hier, so sieht es in zahlreichen anderen kriegswichtigen Anlagen Großbritanniens aus. Nach britischen Eingeständnissen ist allein die Flugzeugproduktion durch den Ausfall vieler Werke so gestört worden, daß ein Ersatz der abgeschossenen Flugzeuge längst nicht mehr möglich ist. Wie unsere Jäger übereinstimmend berichten, versuchen die britischen Jagdflieger, jedem Kampf mit deutschen Jägern auszuweichen. Sie haben, Befehl, nur noch Bomber anzugreifen. Es kommt hinzu, daß die von unseren Jägern oder von der Flak als abgeschossen gemeldeten Flugzeuge bei weitem nicht die volle Zahl der britischen Verluste darstellen. Ein erheblicher Prozentsatz ihrer Maschinen kommt aus den Luftkämpfen so beschädigt zurück, daß sie aus Mangel an Reparaturwerken für längere Zeit ausfallen.

So läßt die deutsche Luftwaffe ihre vernichtenden Schläge weiter auf die britische Rüstung niedersausen bis zu dem Ende, dem Churchill in seinem Amoklauf unentrinnbar zustrebt.

Aufnahmen Luftwaffe PBZ

36

auf Rüstung

Bombs

on Britain's Armaments

Here again we present irrefutable testimony of the effect of G. bombs in the shape of two photographs taken by German reconnaissance planes, showing a British armament factory at Southampton-Woolston before and after an air-raid. The photo at the left shows the whole plant untouched, with assembly shed (1) and machine shop (2), while large stocks of materials are piled up near by. A railroad line will be seen at the left. The two photographs show certain topographical differences, because that at the left was taken during low tide and shows more dry ground than the other at the right, which was taken during high tide.

The photograph at the right plainly shows the devastation and havoc wrought by the German bomb raid. The shop (1) has been hit and completely destroyed by fire. A hole in the roof of the assembly shed (2) indicates the point of entry of a heavy bomb that doubtless did its duty in the interior. Sheds (5) and (6) have also been badly hit and are partly burnt out, but the dwelling houses close by remained undamaged. A further interesting point is that the large ship and the numerous small vessels that animate the water in the illustration at the left have disappeared in that at the right, but for a single ship.

A wharf will be seen just above the bottom edge of the picture. The ships, lying partly in the water, partly on the slipways, are here for repairs. The large number of these vessels permits of drawing unequivocal conclusions on the repair requirements of the fleet that rules the waves. And there is a spice of irony in the fact that this armament factory also is "protected" by a balloon barrage; one of them is visible above the water in the right lower corner of the photo at the right. The barrage neither prevented our bomber pilots from carrying out their mission of destruction, nor hindered our reconnaissance pilot from taking his photographs in broad daylight.

Numerous other plants of military importance in Great Britain present much the same appearance. It is conceded by the British authorities themselves that the output of aircraft alone has been disorganized to such an extent by so many factories having been put out of operation that it has for long been impossible to replace the machines shot down. Our fighters unanimously report that the British pursuit planes try to avoid a fight with German fighter planes and have been ordered, in fact, to attack only bombers. It is further a fact that the aircraft reported as having been shot down by our fighters or our anti-aircraft defense by no means represent the total British losses, because a large proportion returns from air combats in such a damaged condition as to be unfit for action for a long time owing to the scarcity of repair shops.

Thus the German Air Force further hammers away at the destruction of British armaments up to the bitter end towards which Churchill is irretrievably straining.

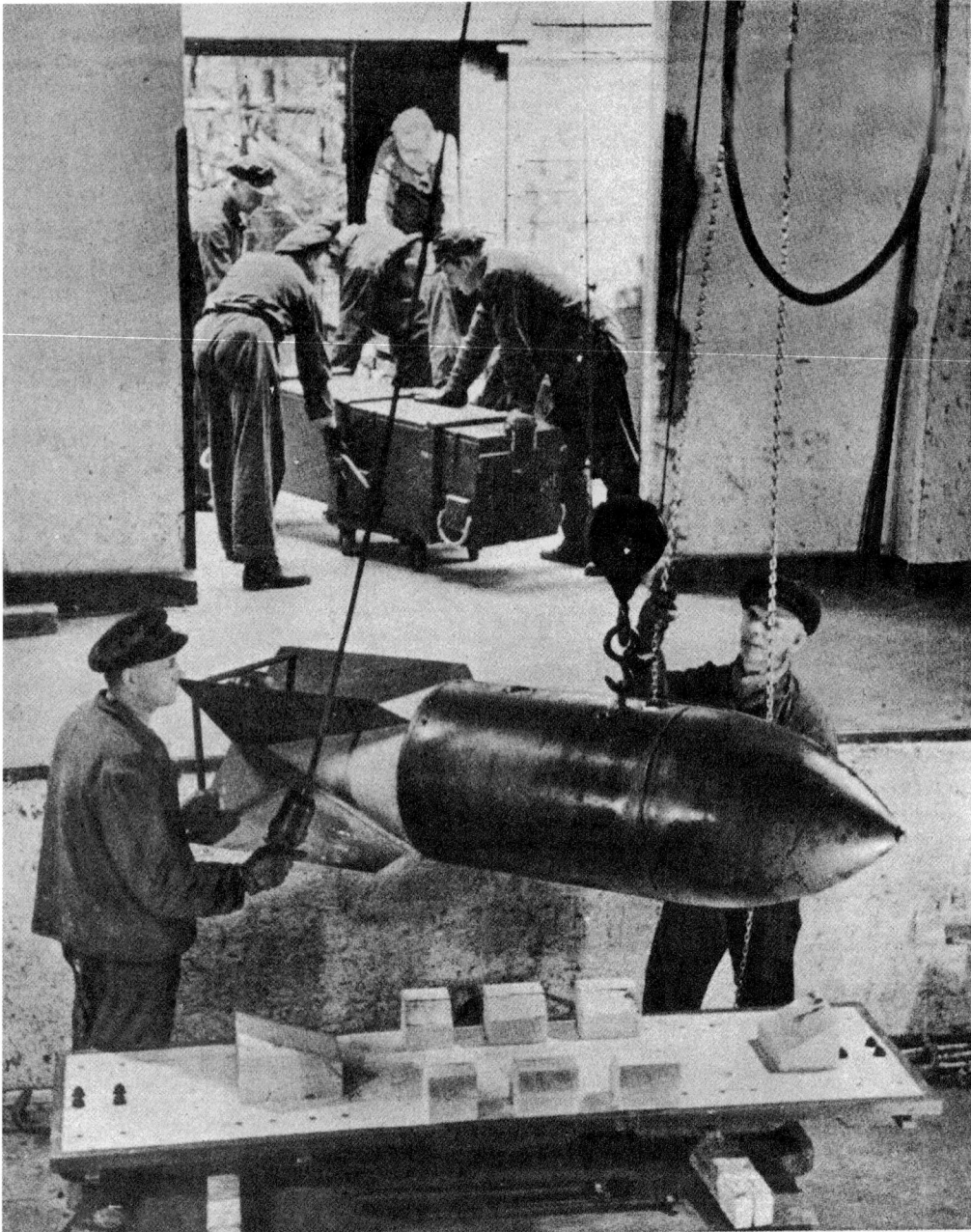

Der uns von Englands Plutokraten auf-
gezwungene Krieg hat sich anders
entwickelt, als Churchill und seine
Helfershelfer es sich erträumt hatten.
Pausenlos rollen die deutschen Vergel-
tungsflüge über das Inselreich dahin.
So wird es bleiben, bis deutsche Bomben
Europa den Weg zu friedlicher Neu-
ordnung bereitet haben

The war thrust upon us by the British
plutocracy has taken rather a different
course from what Churchill and his
associates dreamt of. The German re-
prisal raids are rolling ceaselessly over
the island kingdom and will continue to
do so, until German bombs have prepared the way for a peaceful new order
of things in Europe

Die Bombe ist fertig und wird
nun (Bild oben) in eine feste
Kiste verpackt, um an die Front
transportiert zu werden

The bomb is ready and is now
(illustration above) stowed in a
strong packing case for transport
to the front

Unsere Flieger können sich auf
das Material verlassen, das
ihnen die Heimat liefert. Bild
links zeigt das Abdrehen der
Rümpfe und Spitzen schwerer
Bomben   Aufn. Senckpiehl (s

Our pilots can depend on the material that the home country
supplies them with. Left: Turning
the body and tip of heavy bombs

In diesem Wald, den unser Bild
rechts zeigt, sind unvorstell-
bare Mengen von Bomben aufgestapelt. Tag und Nacht gehen
die Züge zur Front

Right: Incredible quantities of
bombs are piled in the wood
shown. Trains leave day and
night for the front

Sie werden Churchill „besuchen"

Hier stellt man riesige Bomben für England her

Going to pay a visit to Churchill

The gigantic bombs for England are prepared here

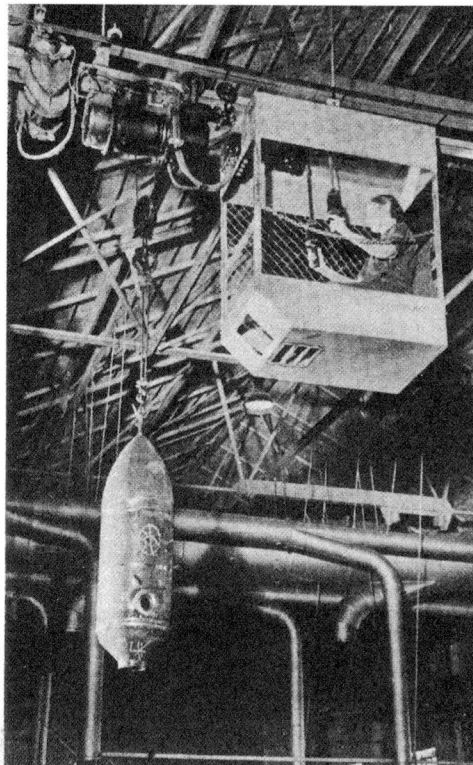

Bombe auf Bombe schwebt durch die Luft, vorerst allerdings nur in der Montagehalle . (Bild rechts)

Bomb after bomb floats through the air, at present, it is true, only in the assembly shed, shown at the right

Schwere Brocken in Reih' und Glied. Am laufenden Band (Bild links) rollen sie zum Verladeplatz

Rows of heavy bombs. The bombs roll to the loading place on the belt conveyor (left)

Durch Flakbeschuß zertrümmerte Kielflosse eines Sturzkampfflugzeugs. Die Maschine ist damit noch über 100 km
geflogen und im Heimathafen glatt gelandet   Aufn. JFM (8)

Vertical fin of dive bomber shattered by anti-aircraft shell. The machine flew more than 100 km. in this condition and landed at the base airdrome without any trouble

Auch dieser Volltreffer einer Flakgranate in der Tragfläche
einer Ju 52 konnte die Sicherheit des Flugzeugs nicht gefährden

Not even this direct hit in the wing of a Ju 52 could endanger the reliability of the airplane

Bei einem Angriff auf Küstenbefestigungen kam eines der eingesetzten Sturzkampf-
flugzeuge beim Abfangen dem Wasser zu nahe. Dabei verlor es das gesamte
Fahrwerk; außerdem wurde die Luftschraube leicht verbogen. Das Flugzeug flog
damit im Verband zu dem noch über 120 km entfernten Heimathafen zurück und
landete glatt auf der Rumpfunterseite

One of the dive bombers came too close to the water when pulling out during an attack on coastal fortifications whereby it lost the whole undercarriage and the airscrew was slightly bent. In that condition the machine returned in formation to the base airdrome more than 120 km. off and landed smoothly on the underside of the fuselage

Zerschossener Rumpf eines Sturzkampfflugzeugs. Die Flug- und
Steuersicherheit wurde dadurch fast gar nicht beeinträchtigt

Riddled fuselage of a dive bomber. The flying qualities and control of machine were practically unimpaired

Diese Heinkel He 111 wurde über dem Kanal von englischen Zerstörern gejagt. Trotz zahl-
reicher Treffer landete sie glatt auf einem Fliegerhorst in Deutschland   Aufn. PK Grabler

This Heinkel He 111 was chased by British destroyer machines while over the Channel, but it landed smoothly at an airdrome in Germany in spite of numerous hits

Die He 111 ist startbereit für den Nachtflug, die Besatzung an Bord. Ein Motor läuft bereits, der zweite wird sofort anspringen

The He 111 ready for its nocturnal trip and the crew are aboard. One engine is already running, the other will start in a moment

Nachtflug gegen England

Night Raid on England

Ist schon bei Tage jeder Feindflug eine Leistung, die an die Besatzungen hohe Anforderungen stellt, so häufen sich die Schwierigkeiten beim Fliegen in der Nacht. Daß unsere Kampfflieger ihr Handwerk verstehen, beweisen die großen Erfolge ihrer nächtlichen Angriffe gegen militärische Ziele in England. Sie haben es nicht nötig, wie die Engländer aus riesigen Höhen Bomben ziellos abzuwerfen

Heavy as are the demands made on an airplane crew during a daytime raid, all difficulties are vastly increased on a night raid. The outstanding successes achieved by our pilots on their night raids on military objectives in England prove that they thoroughly understand their job. They do not need to drop their bombs at random from a tremendous altitude, as British airmen are accustomed to do

Besonders schwierig und verantwortungsvoll ist die Arbeit des Beobachters beim Nachtflug. Mit Kursrechengerät und Karte, die er von Zeit zu Zeit mit der Taschenlampe beleuchtet, findet der deutsche Beobachter seinen Weg   Aufn. PK Grosse Weltbild (2)

The observer has a particularly onerous task of great responsibility during a night raid. He finds his way by the aid of a course calculator and a map, now and again using a torch to illuminate it

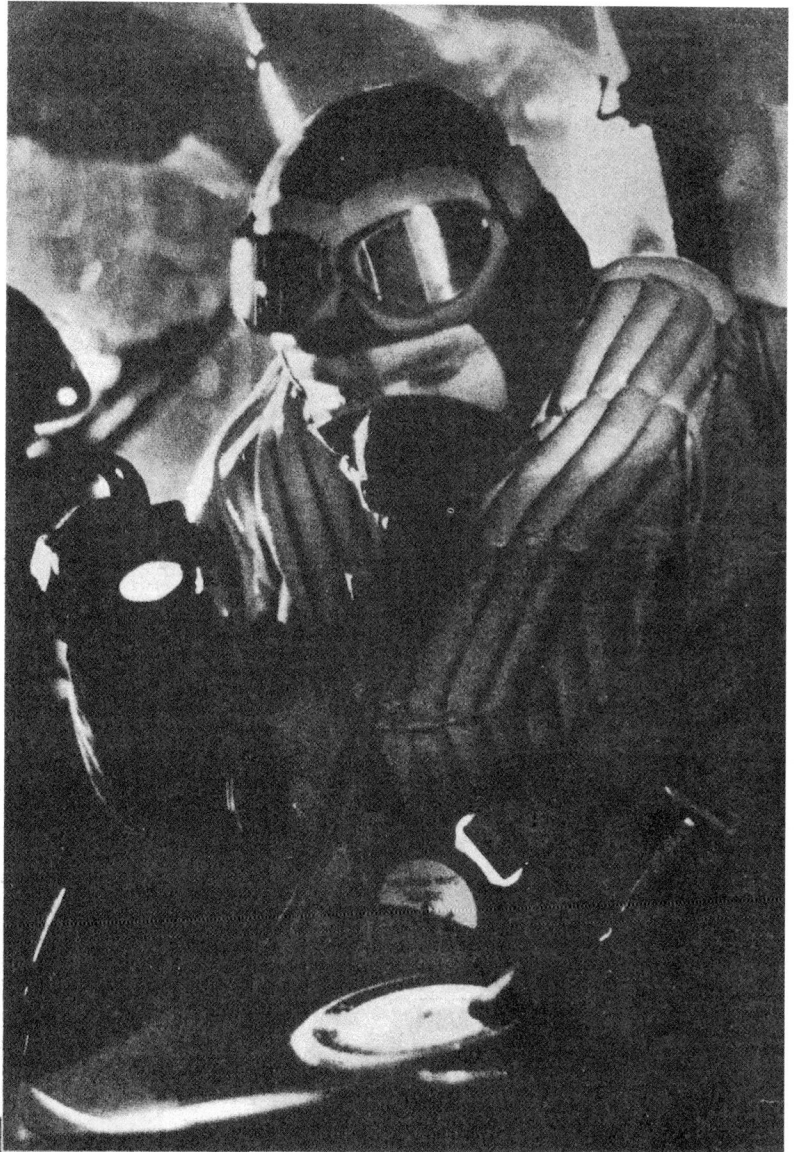

Auch der Bordwart hat ein verantwortungsvolles Amt. Während des Fluges überprüft er eingehend die Einstellungsvorrichtungen an den Bombenschächten   Aufn. PK Grosse-Presse-Hoffmann

The flight mechanic has also a responsible task and takes the opportunity during flight of carefully inspecting the adjusting devices on the bomb wells

Am nächsten Abend bietet der Liegeplatz der Kampffliegerstaffel das gleiche Bild. Wiederum sind die Besatzungen um den Staffelkapitän versammelt und starten zum neuen Nachtflug gegen England   Aufn. PK Grosse-Atlantik

The same scene presents itself next evening at the airdrome of the bomber squadron. Once more the crews assemble round their squadron leaders before starting again on another night raid on England

41

LN in Paris und am Kanal

LN — die Abkürzung für die Luftnachrichtentruppe — ist jedem Soldaten der Luftwaffe und des Heeres ein festumrissener Begriff. Die Männer mit dem braunen Kragenspiegel sind im wahrsten Sinne des Wortes die Führungstruppe der Luftwaffe. Sie ermöglichen der Führung, in jedem Stadium des Kampfes ihre Verbände fest in der Hand zu behalten und einzugreifen, wo es not tut

Every soldier serving in the German Air Force and the army is thoroughly familiar with the letters "LN", the abbreviation for "Luftnachrichtentruppe" (Air Intelligence Service Troops). The men with the brown tab on the collar of their uniforms form the leading unit of the Air Force in the most literal sense of the word. They enable the command to keep a firm hand on all formations at every stage of the battle and to engage whenever necessary

Bild rechts: In Paris mußte selbst eine Siegesgöttin sich dazu bequemen, das Feldkabel in ihre erhobene Rechte zu nehmen

Right: Even a goddess of victory in Paris had to put up with holding the field cable aloft in her right hand

Die vielfach verschnörkelten Laternenträger in Paris eignen sich vorzüglich zur Aufnahme von Kabelleitungen

The often very ornate lamp-posts in Paris are splendidly adapted for carrying cable lines

Neugierig schauen die Pariser zu, wie deutsche Luftnachrichtenmänner an einer Seine-Brücke entlang ihre Kabelleitungen legen

The Parisians curiously watch the men of the LN as they lay their cables along a bridge over the Seine

Es hat viel Arbeit gekostet, in Paris all die Fernsprechleitungen zu legen, die die Luftwaffe in diesem Zentrum benötigte. Die Luftnachrichtentruppe hat hier alle Anforderungen erfüllt

A great deal of work was needed to lay all the telephone cables in Paris that the Air Force needs in this center. The LN met all requirements here in a few days

Air Intelligence Service Troops in Paris and at the Channel

Wo die Anlegung von Fernsprechleitungen sich verbietet, sei es, daß eine Sprechverbindung nur vorübergehend benötigt wird, sei es, daß die Lage der Anschlußstelle zu ungünstig wäre, da tritt, wie hier auf dem Dach eines Pariser Hochhauses, das tragbare Funkgerät in Tätigkeit

When it is not feasible to lay a telephone cable, for example, when a connection is only temporarily required, or when the location of the junction would be too unsuitable, the portable radio apparatus comes into action, as shown here on the roof of a Parisian skyscraper

Bild links: Man muß selbst gesehen haben, mit welcher Findigkeit die Luftnachrichtenmänner jede Möglichkeit ausnutzten, um ihre Leitungen zu verlegen. Selbst in zerstörten Ortschaften bleibt die Errichtung von Masten auf Ausnahmen beschränkt

Left: The ingenuity with which the men of the LN utilize every possibility of laying their cables must be seen to be believed. The erection of poles remains an exception even in destroyed villages

Fw 190 jagt

Der siegreiche Abwehrkampf am Kanal

Selbst die äußere Form des Rumpfes der Fw 190 wirkt wie ein Sinnbild der ungeheuren gedrängten Kraft, die der Doppelsternmotor BMW 801 zu entfalten vermag — fast winzig nimmt sich dagegen der Jagdflieger aus, der doch die Seele dieses Kampfinstruments ist und Motor und Waffen überhaupt erst zur Wirkung bringt

Der Start eines Jagdfliegers zum Angriff ist der Kampf um Sekunden. Wenn die Lautsprecher ihr „Gefechtsalarm!" über den Platz beulen, beginnt ein Wettrennen der Flieger und der Warte zu ihren Flugzeugen. Jeder weiß „wie im Schlaf", was er zu tun hat, und nach erstaunlich kurzer Zeit rollt die Maschine zum Start

Alle Versuche der Briten, ebenso wie im vergangenen Jahr mit stärkeren Kräften den Einflug in die besetzten Westgebiete zu erzwingen, scheitern an der deutschen Abwehr. Meist werden die feindlichen Verbände schon vor Erreichen der Festlandküste von den deutschen Jägern zum Kampf gestellt. Die dabei erzielten Erfolge aber sind nicht nur dem überlegenen fliegerischen Können und der größeren Kampferfahrung der deutschen Jagdflieger zu danken, sondern ebenso auch der hervorragenden Waffe, die ihnen mit dem neuen deutschen Jagdflugzeug, der Focke-Wulf Fw 190, in die Hand gegeben wurde

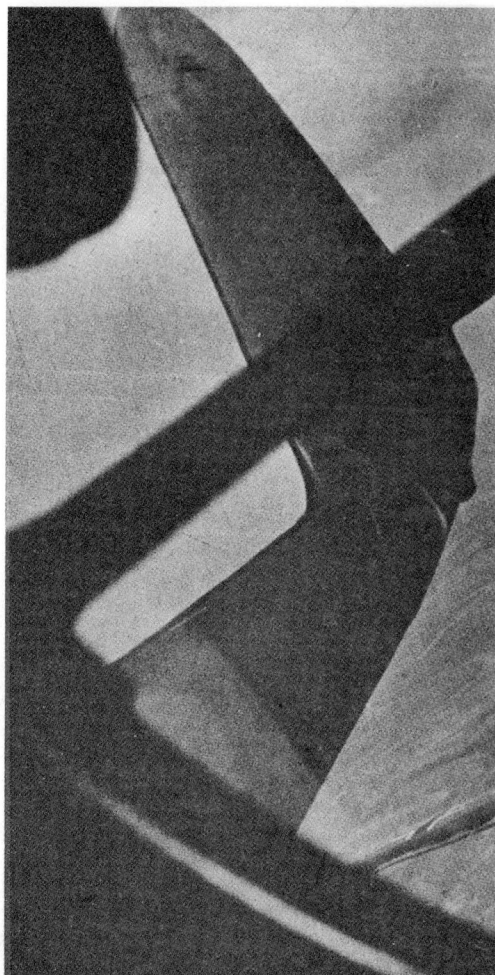

Über dem Kanal, der nun schon seit den Tagen von Dünkirchen der Schauplatz immer neuer Jagdkämpfe geworden ist ... An vielen Punkten vor der Küste sieht man hier noch Wracks liegen, die entweder aus der Zeit des britischen Rückzugs stammen oder von späteren Angriffen auf Schiffe Zeugnis ablegen

Spitfire

Eine Spitfire in gefährlicher Lage: Dicht hinter ihr hängt die Fw 190. Auch die Wendigkeit seines Flugzeugs wird den britischen Piloten kaum mehr retten, denn die Focke-Wulf ist nicht nur ebenso wendig, sondern obendrein schneller

Ein glücklicher Schnappschuß auf dem Filmstreifen, der das Ende einer Spitfire und im Vordergrund die siegreiche Focke-Wulf zeigt. Aus einer Höhe von Tausenden von Metern sind die Flugzeuge in ständiger Kurbelei bis dicht über den Boden hinabgedrückt worden, ehe es dem deutschen Jagdflieger gelang, den vernichtenden Feuerstoß anzubringen

Aufnahmen PK-Luftwaffe

Links: Heimflug nach dem Kampf. Über das wohlbekannte Land geht es zurück zum Fliegerhorst, wo die Kameraden gespannt auf den Ausgang des Kampfes warten

STUKAS

Oberleutnant Hans Wilde, Staffelkapitän der 7. Staffel. Sein „Steckbrief" im Drehbuch lautet: Großer Flieger. Freude am Kampf. Rauher Spötter. Haßt Sentimentalität. Liebt „schräge" Musik. Raucht Pfeife. Inhaber des Spanienkreuzes. Sein Name im Zivilleben: Hannes Stelzer

Oberleutnant (Flying Officer) Hans Wilde, Squadron Leader of the 7th Squadron. His characteristics according to the scenario: A great pilot. Delights in a scrap. Tone of rough mockery detests sentimentality. Has a liking for music of sorts. Smokes a short pipe. Decorated with the Spanish Cross. His name in civilian life is Hannes Stelzer

Unten: Stabsfeldwebel Niederegger, die wahre „Staffelmutter". Er ist streng und energisch, aber stets gerecht und hilfsbereit. Er kennt die Gewohnheiten eines jeden und ist immer besorgt, daß es „seinen" Offizieren und Leuten gut geht. — Darsteller: Lutz Götz

Below: Staff Sergeant Niederegger, heart and soul for the Squadron. Strict and energetic, but always just and ready to help. He knows everyone's habits and always makes a point of seeing that "his" officers and men want for nothing. Played by Lutz Götz

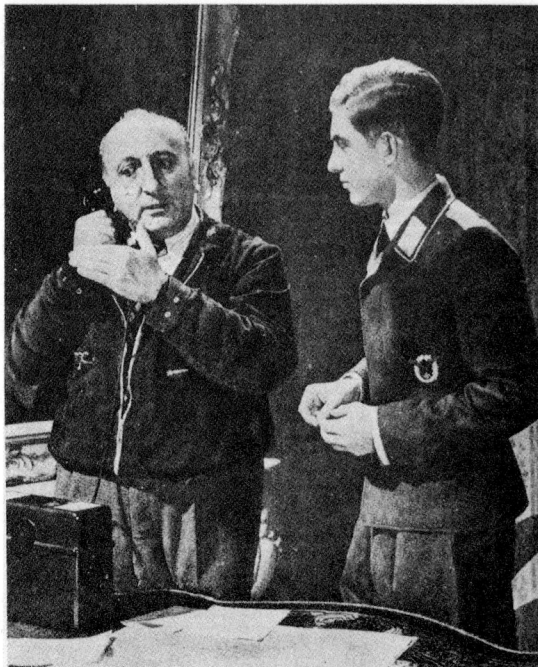

A field airdrome somewhere in France. A couple of Stukas (dive bombers) ready to take off. Airmen in full outfit with weatherbeaten countenances. Cries and commands on all sides. In reality we are standing on the Ufa lot in Babelsberg, where a new film is struggling into being. A film that is to be a heroic epic of our Air Corps and a monument to inviolable comradeship. It is intended to be a vivid presentation of the struggle and victory of our airmen in France based on the plain and unadulterated truth.

At the present time there is one film director in Germany who possesses not only the artistic power, but also the full inner justification for the production of such a film, and that is Professor Karl Ritter, the pilot of the Great War. He grew up, as few others have done, with the beginnings of aviation in Germany, he experienced its smashing after the Great War and its reconstruction under Reich Marshal Hermann Göring, and now he is once more in the fighting line. To be able to fly and to be allowed to fly, that is the secret pivot of a life unusually prolific in excitement and tense situations. He began his reminiscences in unadulterated at Würzburg dialect by saying, "I am really quite an old eagle. Even as a boy, I was intended for the army and so found myself in barracks, became Fahnenjunker (Aspirant Officer), and lieutenant of engineers. In 1909 I married and became airman, although that was not such a simple matter as it is today. Whoever wanted to fly,

Der Spielleiter des Stuka-Films, Prof. Karl Ritter, zeigt seinem jüngsten Darsteller Johannes Schütz, wie er eine Szene spielen soll

Professor Karl Ritter, director of the Stuka film, shows his youngest actor, Johannes Schütz, how a scene should be played

Ein neuer Film
von
Prof. Karl Ritter

Prof. Karl Ritter's New Film

Der Kommandeur der Stuka-Gruppe, Hauptmann Bork, am Bombenzielgerät. Er verkörpert den Typ des deutschen Fliegeroffiziers, einfach, unpathetisch, ein vorbildlicher Führer seiner Mannschaft. Stets ist er der erste am Feind. In der Rolle: Carl Raddatz

Captain Bork, Commander of the Stuka wing, at the bomb sight. A typical German Air Corps officer, unaffected, without pathos, an exemplary leader of men. Always the first at the foe. Played by Carl Raddatz

had to provide his own machine. I began to build one for myself and, in order to make more rapid progress, applied to my superior officer to have a fitter, a carpenter, and a coachhouse placed at my disposal. His reply was terse and to the point, "The man's crazy!" But in the end I got my way and the contraction actually flew. I do not know whether young men of today can appreciate what that meant to me. But I must confess that I did not always land in the orthodox way: something always broke, but I cheerfully repaired the damage and started again, until I was finally officially seconded in due form for instruction in aviation. And then, as throughout my whole life, the aim was to learn and to keep on learning. In 1911, I passed my tests as certified pilot on a monoplane of my own construction and received my membership card No. 121 of the Fédération Aéronautique Internationale."

From that day on, Lieutenant Ritter of the Third Royal Bavarian Battalion of Engineers knew no peace. He devoted all his energy to promoting military aviation in the Bavarian Army and had firmly resolved to be transferred to the Air Corps, when the Great War broke out. He left for the front as officer of engineers, but was soon seconded to the Air Corps, took part in numerous undertakings and

Deutsche Infanterie wird von feindlichen Tanks bedrängt. Stukas greifen ein und vernichten den Gegner

German infantry hard pressed by enemy tanks. Dive-bombers take a hand and destroy the enemy forces

Zum Bilde unten: Am Schluß kehren Kameraden, die vermißt waren, zur Staffel zurück Und alle sind wieder beisammen zum Kampf gegen England

Below: Comrades who had been missing finally return to the squadron. They are now all united again for the struggle with England

Mit dem Kriegsverdienstkreuz I. Klasse ausgezeichnet

Dr. h. c. Heinrich Koppenberg

Dr.-Ing. e. h. Claudius Dornier

Prof. Dr.-Ing. e. h. Ernst Heinkel

Professor Willi Messerschmitt

Anläßlich des Jahrestages der Machtübernahme hat der Führer eine Reihe besonders verdienter Männer ausgezeichnet. Das Kriegsverdienstkreuz I. Klasse mit Schwertern wurde u. a. verliehen an:

General der Flakartillerie Rüdel,
General der Flakartillerie v. Schröder,

General der Flieger v. Witzendorff,
Generalleutnant Bodenschatz,
Generalleutnant Goßrau,
Generalleutnant Doerstling,
Ministerialdirektor im Reichsministerium für Luftfahrt Fisch.

In Anerkennung ihrer besonderen Verdienste bei der Durchführung von Kriegsaufgaben verlieh der Führer ferner das Kriegsverdienstkreuz I. Klasse den Betriebsführern Dr. h. c. Heinrich Koppenberg, Professor Willi Messerschmitt, Professor Ernst Heinkel, Dr. Claudius Dornier. Aufn. Scherl-Bildarchiv (4)

STUKAS

gained the Iron Cross, Class I. Aviation did not lose its attraction for him, even after the War. He worked out plans for the organization of sporting aviation and finally became the creator of German aviation films of the heroic stamp. "Pour le Mérite" was the first of these, in which he gave final form to the pride and bitterness of his own experience in the Great War. It was followed by the "Legion Condor", a film of the German volunteers in the Civil War in Spain. Karl Ritter himself, supported by his son, photographed the decisive phases of that war, being often on the move for hours on end from morning to night. He sat for twelve hours in a plane, while hostile anti-aircraft guns banged away at him. Thus arose a faithful picture of the war on foreign soil, of the spirit that animates our airmen, and of the planes that proved to be superior in every respect to the enemy machines. And now a new film is being shot, in which men and dive bombers occupy the center of interest.

Two unusually bright and vivacious eyes in sharply cut features impress themselves on the listener, as Professor Ritter vividly and tersely describes his new commission. "It is the aim of this film," he said, "to present the German airman as he really is for the benefit of our own people and also of countries abroad. They are simply young lads, hearty and straightforward, who do their duty unostentatiously as a matter of course without talking about it; human beings with a healthy sense of humor and unquenchable joy in life. Just as they often presented themselves to me on an airdrome in France. Some would be reading, others having a game of cards, others playing music, or otherwise diverting themselves in their own fashion. Then came the order for action and a few seconds later they would be climbing with the same quiet assurance into their machines, and taking off on a raid. Only those who have actually been present can really have any conception of the stuff that these men are made of, and the psychical and intellectual forces that enable them to hold out even in the most trying situations. That is the reason why a film that purports to deal with these men can only be made by one who is himself an airman, just as everyone who knows war only from hearsay must call a halt before portrayal of war itself. Personal experience is essential." Karl Ritter was once again at the front during the campaign in the West. He points to two Ju 87 dive-

bombers standing before us and proceeds with his description. "These planes belong to the wing to which I was attached in the West. I intended at first to travel about and to visit several field airdromes, but then I decided to remain from start to finish with the same wing. That proved to be the right course. For I had full experience of everything in that way: everyday routine, work, fighting, and victory. That reality has entered into the film, which contains no invented incidents. I was able to document even the most trifling episodes of the scenario by bringing only events that actually occurred. And the characters too are exactly such as are to be met with on every field airdrome. Beside the commander, the paragon leader of his wing, there is the comrade with artistic temperament who cannot do without his piano, even in war, to play Beethoven and Wagner. The dashing Flying Officer, a favorite of fortune in every situation in life, is paralleled by the definitely unlucky fellow who fails at everything. All of them, officers and men, differ altogether in temperament, but all are of one mind when the time for action comes."

The action of the film covers six weeks of the campaign in France. Stukas thunder over the battlefields in the West and swoop on the enemy, forts are shattered, moles burst asunder, and ships blow up. In spite of that, however, Professor Ritter would prefer not to call the film a "war film", but rather a "soldier's film"; for the most important factor of the war is the man and comradeship. It is not a matter of chance that a dive-bomber wing occupies the foreground of interest. That branch of the service to a great extent determined the course of the campaign in France; it has impressed itself most forcibly on the mind of the German people and throughout the world, and it gives the clearest possible expression to the absolute will to victory.

It is a particular pleasure to watch Professor Ritter at work. The old soldier, as he is, has fused his co-workers into a genuine team—artistes, camera-man, scenic artist, the writer of the scenario, and musicians, they are all members of the "Old Guard" with whom he has shot many successful films. His closest collaborator is his son Heinz, who also made the open-air shots for the Stuka film. "The most difficult problem," he tells us, "was to get diving Stukas before the camera and I have to thank the comradely spirit of the dive-bomber wing that I succeeded at all. Day by day the boys flew as if it were the most natural thing in the world, until the shots were perfect."

So much at least is certain. This film will meet the ideas of the front-line fighter. It will be a document of soldierly spirit and genuine comradeship, such as only the common struggle can bring forth

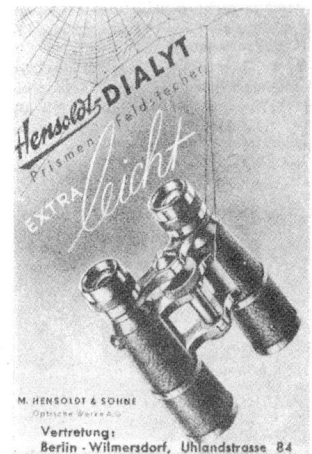

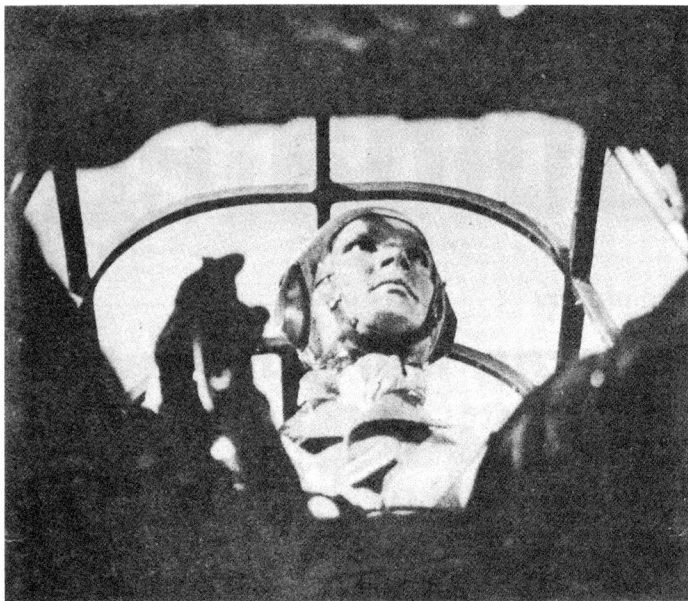

Staffelkapitän Wilde auf der Suche nach dem Feind. Eben noch hatte er sich auf dem Feldflugplatz mit seinen Kameraden vergnügt unterhalten, Sekunden später, nachdem der Einsatzbefehl gegeben ist, besteigt er ruhig und sicher seine Maschine und startet gegen den Feind

Squadron Leader Wilde on the look-out for the enemy. He has just been having a chat
with his comrades on the flying-ground; then comes the order for action, and a few seconds
later he is climbing quietly and determinedly into his plane to start on his commission

„Wir konnten uns gerade noch so durchschlagen." Mit diesen Worten meldet sich
Staffelkapitän Oberleutnant von Bomberg, der mitten im feindlichen Gebiet zur
Notlandung gezwungen war, bei seinem Kommandeur zurück

"We were just able to scrape through." Squadron Leader, Flying Officer von Bomberg,
who has had to make a forced landing in enemy territory, reports his return to his
commander

Unermüdlich sind die Männer
vom Bodenpersonal an der
Arbeit. Sie schaffen Munition und
alle sonstigen Ausrüstungsgegenstände heran und erweisen sich
stets als die besten Kameraden
der fliegenden Besatzungen

The ground personnel are untiringly at work, bringing up
ammunition and all the other
equipment required. They always
prove themselves to be the finest
comrades of the flying crews

Aufnahmen
Ufa-Krahnert (10), Schaller (1)

Stukas sind den Kameraden der
Infanterie in Frankreich zu
Hilfe gekommen und haben den
Weg frei gemacht. Die Infan-
teristen jubeln und winken hinauf

Stukas have come to the relief
of their comrades of the infantry
in France and have cleared the
way for them. The infantry are
cheerfully waving up to them

49

Flieger und Soldaten

Airmen and Soldiers

Gedanken zum 6. Jahrestag der Luftwaffe am 1. März 1941

Thoughts about the Sixth Anniversary of the German Air Corps on March 1, 1941

By Fieldmarshal-General Milch

The Air Corps forms the point of the German sword. In that branch of the service will be found united the highest qualities of the German aviator spirit and German soldiership. Further than that, the German Air Corps is not only in the main a creation of National Socialism, but, as it presents itself to us, would be inconceivable did not the conditions of National Socialism exist. For that reason its development, its mission, and its victories are inseparably connected with our leader Adolf Hitler and with the man who created it at his command, Reich Marshal Hermann Göring.

From the day on which the Captain and last commander of Richthofen's pursuit squadron vowed to his comrades in the very midst of the disaster of 1918 that he would resuscitate that squadron, a straight undeviating path, the various stages of which testify to an indomitable will and a unique creative force, leads to the marvellous victories in Poland, and from the North Cape to the Bay of Biscay, and now also to the Mediterranean.

After Compiègne and Versailles had utterly shattered military aviation in Germany and had practically throttled what remained of aeronautics to that country, aviators and soldiers had each to go their own several ways and they did so in the full confidence that the day would yet come when their paths would once more converge. It would have been impossible for either to account for that feeling of confidence under the existing political conditions and the tenets of life that then prevailed. They bore that confidence in their breasts and set to work as men of action, silently, stubbornly, and doggedly. The aviators cooperated with men of science and created gliding, a field in which they accomplished not only the whole of the first decisive achievements, but continuously created also world records. They stood uninterruptedly and without reference to the sacrifices thereby involved at the head of international aviation.

Air traffic in Germany took its origin in the most humble circumstances. In spite of the onerous conditions due to the throttling of German aeronautics by the enemy, German commercial airplanes performed exploits the historical importance of which will one day come to be fully recognized. The unity of German air traffic was created, often as the result of wearing struggles, and protected against any possibility of its exploitation by private speculation. By that means the foundations of the Deutsche Lufthansa were well and truly laid, the finest air traffic organization in the world, which serves all other undertakings of similar nature as a model and the air transport of which was and still is not only the most dependable, but at the same time also the safest service existing.

Some few pilots of the Great War remained as soldiers in the little Reichswehr or in the ranks of the police forces, where they devoted themselves wholly to the preservation and further development of those soldierly virtues that have made the German soldier the best in the world, and further spent their creative energies on the everlasting deeds of German soldiership. When fate chose the creator and leader of the National Socialist movement to be the leader of the whole German people and of the German Empire, not only his airmen, but also his soldiers stood at his disposal and Hermann Göring, the living embodiment of both, was entrusted with the task of creating of Germany an Air Corps that should be superior to every other air force. He now forged the aviator spirit and soldiership into a single unit, attaining thereby a pitch of perfection such as could hardly ever have been divined before. Airmen became soldiers once more, and soldiers were again airmen. They aligned themselves by the example of the creator of the German Air Corps and thus created the type of the soldier of the Air Corps who emulates to the inmost depths of his thoughts and feelings the man to whom he owes his development and his being.

The three branches of the German Air Corps—the flying corps, air defense, and air force signals corps—are not three branches of a service that merely coexist and are only combined in respect of organization, but form a compact unit mentally and materially, in their training, and in their employment. And more than that: The German Air Corps as a whole is not a unit by itself, but is in turn part of that perfect unity, as which the German forces with their three services were able to hasten from victory to victory. The master-motto of National Socialism "Gemeinnutz geht vor Eigennutz" (Common weal before private interests) finds its most wonderful fulfilment in deed among the well-known and no less among the countless unknown soldiers of the Air Corps.

No air force has greater flying achievements to show than the German Air Corps. In no service can soldierly austerity be greater than among these men. But nowhere, more particularly, can there be greater readiness for action and a more powerful will to victory. And the most of the men of that branch of the forces are not young in years only, but always and under all circumstances retain youth in their hearts. Everyone who gazes into the eyes of our airplane crews knows the meaning of the eternal value of the figure of Siegfried, the victor with a smile on his face.

The soldier of the Air Corps feels himself one with the worker of the German aircraft industry not only for the reason that his life and victory depend upon his skill; the worker of the aircraft industry did not labor merely to give the fighting soldier the best possible instrument of war. If no relations but these existed

Luftwaffe auf Wacht

Von Norwegen bis Sizilien steht die deutsche Luftwaffe einsatzbereit, um das Großdeutsche Reich und Europa gegen England zu schützen. Von links nach rechts: Kampfflugzeuge Heinkel He 111 über der Schneelandschaft von Narvik. — Flakartillerie auf der Wacht an der Kanalküste. — Seite an Seite mit den italienischen Waffenbrüdern kämpft die deutsche Luftwaffe gegen den gemeinsamen Feind im Mittelmeer

The German Air Corps stands prepared for action from Norway to Sicily to protect the German Reich and Europe against England. Left to right: Heinkel He 111 bombers over the snow-covered landscape of Norway. — The air defense corps on guard on the coast of Flanders. — The German Air Corps is fighting side by side with their Italian brothers-in-arms on the Mediterranean against the common foe

these men was the identical spirit that enabled our glider pilots to set up records that cannot be beaten and drove them to devote their whole energy to new and coming things. At the same time they proved themselves to be bearers and consummators of the spirit that has its quite definite expression in the conception of the "Stosstrupp" (shock troops). It is already a matter of history how the air force of France was in a short space of time utterly shattered after a hard struggle. The struggle with England is still going on. Each single man has again and again proved himself to be chosen by his Supreme Commander to be the executor of the will of Baron von Richthofen "Und dann muss der Gegner fallen!" (And then the foe must fall!). The confidence reposed by the leaders in the troops cannot be greater than the confidence of the troops in their leaders. The public occasionally learns of great missions by which England's defense was again bound to suffer a particularly severe blow, and now and again hears of individual enterprises carried out by specially selected crews, whose flying achievements and military deeds would be unique, were they not matters of course in the eyes of those who accomplished them, as they are for their leaders. The downfall of a world hostile to us is proceeding in an uninterrupted, hard, and stubborn struggle, by which the once so powerful opponent is being steadily ground down and by which the German Air Corps is day by day, and victory by victory becoming stronger and acquiring greater superiority; a world with which, by its own desire, there can be no discussion other than a life and death struggle to the bitter end and to destruction. We know that the victory will thereby be ours. The saying of the Reich Marshal "The German nation must become a nation of airmen", has since been treasured in the hearts of German boys. By the deeds of our Air Corps our boys recognize the spirit which they also will one day have to bear when it is their lot to range themselves among the soldiers of the nation. But the further future will show that there dwells in that spirit not only the greatest power of destruction, but also an enormous creative force of construction. For the aviator spirit and soldiership are not only very high moral ideas, but also values of the utmost extent for the creation of civilization. The desire of airmen and soldiers is rather to be than to seem, and they demand from themselves more than others ask of them. That is their faith, their pride, their happiness, and their silent matter-of-course expression of gratitude to the man to whom they owe all. For that reason also Air-Corps day is a day of the whole German nation.

between the two, neither military achievement, nor engineering skill and performance would be as great as they are. The fundamental and decisive point is the feeling of community existing between soldier and worker which reveals itself as the common will to victory. Each not only knows, but also appreciates the worth of the other, but they feel that they are also standing side by side as comrades in the same fighting line and know to what extent that is so. Without finding it necessary to be aware of the fact, they thus demonstrate daily and hourly the unity of soldier and worker that has grown out of the National Socialism of Adolf Hitler. Comradeship, to be sure, is a matter about which not much is said; its existence is demonstrated in a practical way by deeds.

And these proofs of mutual confidence, of the same will, and of the same discipline find confirmation in the superiority of Germany in the air, as struggled for, attained, and yet steadily growing. Our foes considered all that to be impossible and would not believe it even after they had had to submit to the heaviest blows. They ought to have recognized already by the cam-

paign in Poland that the German Air Corps as incorporation of the aviator spirit and soldiership always bears victory in itself under all circumstances whatsoever. The achiements of airmen and soldiers during the campaign in Norway were no less eloquent. The enemy had nothing of even approximate value to oppose to the cooperation of the three branches of the Air Corps and the three services, but considered the achievements of the German crews in the air as being simply impossible. Our experienced commercial pilots here enjoyed the pleasure of having proved their worth as flying instructors of the young crews. They were themselves engaged on active service and accomplished deeds as far north as Narwik by which they expanded beyond their own stature. After the victory in Norway the Führer and Supreme Commander took occasion to express clearly and plainly the extent to which the Air Corps had contributed to the success of the enterprise and thereby particularly emphasized the combative performance, for example, of the transport groups. Parachute troops and air-borne troops then appeared for the first time. The driving force behind

Aufn. Presse-Hoffmann, PK Klapproth, PK Altvater-Presse-Hoffmann, PK Kranz

Tausende von Gewächshäusern geben der englischen Insel Guernsey, über der seit dem 1. Juli 1940 die deutsche Flagge weht, ihr besonderes Gepräge. Ein Zehntel der bebauten Fläche der Insel liegt unter Glas, so daß schon zu Beginn des Frühjahrs das zarte Treibhausgemüse auf dem Küchenzettel der deutschen Besatzungstruppen erscheint. Große Mengen von Frühgemüse, insbesondere Tomaten, Gurken und Frühkartoffeln, aber treten in Frachten die Reise in das Reich an

Unten: Übervoll hängen die Stauden der in den Treibhäusern unter günstigsten Bedingungen gezogenen Tomaten. Da sie über See versandt werden müssen, werden sie noch in grünem Zustand geerntet

Tomaten aus Guernsey

Eine englische Kanalinsel
liefert Gemüse nach Deutschland

Hier werden die Tomaten, nach Größe und Qualität sortiert, sorgfältig verpackt. Bei dem langen Transportweg ist eine gute Verpackung für die Haltbarkeit der Früchte besonders wichtig

PK-Bildbericht
Kriegsberichter
Mützel (PBZ)

Im Hafen stauen sich die Lieferwagen der einheimischen Produzenten. Tausende von Kisten wandern in den Laderaum des Transporters, um ihre Reise nach dem Festland anzutreten

Der **Adler**

HEFT 21 / BERLIN, 15. OKTOBER 1940

Denmark	35 Öre	Finland	3.50 Fmk.
Holland	15 cents	Norway	35 Öre
Sweden	45 Öre	U.S.A.	8 Cents

HERAUSGEGEBEN UNTER
MITWIRKUNG DES REICHS-
LUFTFAHRTMINISTERIUMS

Major Werner Mölders

Kommodore eines Jagdgeschwaders, dem der Führer
als erstem der erfolgreichen Jagdflieger nach dem 40.
Luftsieg das Eichenlaub zum Ritterkreuz des Eisernen
Kreuzes verlieh

Major (Squadron Leader) Werner Mölders, Commodore
of a fighter wing, the first of the German aces to be
decorated by the Führer with the Oak Leaves to the
Knight's Cross of the Iron Cross

Ehre den Siegern

"Wenn ohne die Tapferkeit des Heeres niemals die errungenen Erfolge hätten erreicht werden können, dann wäre ohne den heroischen Einsatz der Luftwaffe alle Tapferkeit des Heeres doch nur eine vergebliche gewesen." Höheres und uneingeschränkteres Lob konnte der Führer und Oberste Befehlshaber der deutschen Wehrmacht in seiner weltbewegenden Reichstagsrede vom 19. Juli 1940 seiner von Hermann Göring geschaffenen Luftwaffe nicht zollen. Mit unbändigem Stolz und höchster Genugtuung nahm das ganze deutsche Volk an den Lautsprechern die Ehrung seiner jungen, ruhmreichen Luftwaffe auf, die ihr „in Ansehung der einmaligen Leistung" durch die Beförderung ihrer siegreichen Führer zuteil wurde. Und mit dankbarer Zuversicht vernahm das Volk weiter die Erklärung des Führers: „Heer und Luftwaffe sind in diesem Augenblick — da ich zu Ihnen spreche — auch in ihrer Ausrüstung vollkommener und stärker, als sie es vor dem Antritt im Westen waren." Die ganze Welt muß, ob sie will oder nicht, die gewaltige Größe der Gesamtleistung unserer Flieger anerkennen. Das ganze deutsche Volk aber dankt es ihnen durch die felsenfeste Zuversicht: Was auch noch kommen mag, wir halten durch mit euch in zähem Willen zum Endsieg!

Im nächsten Heft des „Adler" bringen wir weitere Bilder von Offizieren der Luftwaffe, die vom Führer und Obersten Befehlshaber der Wehrmacht befördert wurden

Generalfeldmarschall Milch,
Generalinspekteur der Luftwaffe
und Staatssekretär der Luftfahrt

Generalfeldmarschall Milch, Inspector-General of the Air Force and State Secretary in the Reich Air Ministry

*

Zum Bilde rechts: Generalfeldmarschall Kesselring, Chef der Luftflotte 2 und Befehlshaber Nordwest

Right: Generalfeldmarschall Kesselring, Chief of Air Fleet 2 and Commanding Officer of the Northwest District

*

Zum Bilde ganz rechts: Generalfeldmarschall Sperrle, Chef der Luftflotte 3 und Befehlshaber West

Extreme right: Generalfeldmarschall Sperrle, Chief of Air Fleet 3 and Commanding Officer of the West District

Aufn' Scherl-Bilderdienst (9), Presse-Hoffmann (1) Binder (1)

Generaloberst Udet
Generalluftzeugmeister

Generaloberst Keller
Befehlshaber des IV. Fliegerkorps

Generaloberst Grauert
Befehlshaber des I. Fliegerkorps

Generaloberst Stumpff
Chef der Luftflotte 5
und Befehlshaber Nord

Generaloberst Weise
Befehlshaber des I. Flakkorps

Honour to the Victors

Reichsmarschall
des
Großdeutschen Reiches

Marshal of the Reich

Der Jagdflieger des Weltkrieges

The fighter pilot of the Great War

Zum Bilde rechts: Der treue Gefolgsmann des Führers im Kampf um die Macht

Right: The trusty adherent of the Führer during the struggle for power

Zum Bilde rechts außen: Der Schöpfer der jungen, ruhmreichen deutschen Luftwaffe

Extreme right: The creator of the glorious young German Air Force

Reichsmarschall Göring begrüßte bei einem Empfang, den er zu Ehren des italienischen Außenministers Graf Ciano in Karinhall gab, Generaloberst Udet und beglückwünschte ihn zu seiner Beförderung   *Aufn. Robert Kropp*

At a recent reception held at Karinhall in honour of Graf Ciano, the Italian Minister for Foreign Affairs, Reichsmarschall Göring greeted Generaloberst Udet and congratulated him on his promotion

„Seine Verdienste sind einmalige!"

So sagte der Führer in der historischen Reichstagssitzung am 19. Juli. „Ich ernenne ihn daher zum Reichsmarschall des Großdeutschen Reiches und verleihe ihm das Großkreuz des Eisernen Kreuzes." Wer im deutschen Volke hätte nicht dieser Feststellung des Führers aus vollstem Herzen zugestimmt und ihm auch freudig beigepflichtet, als er ausführte: „Ich muß nun an die Spitze jenen Mann stellen, bei dem es mir schwer fällt, den genügenden Dank für die Verdienste zu finden, die seinen Namen mit der Bewegung, dem Staat und vor allem der deutschen Luftwaffe verbinden"

"His merits are unique,"

the Führer said before the Reichstag on July 19th, 1940: "I therefore nominate him Marshal of the Reich and award him the Grand Cross of the Iron Cross." Is there a man among the whole German nation who would not wholeheartedly subscribe to that statement or who would not joyfully assent to his further words, "At the head of all others I must place that man to whom I find it difficult to express my thanks in adequate terms for the signal services that connect his name with the National Socialist movement, the State, and, more particularly, the German Air Force"

55

Der

Neben der unvergleichlichen Tapferkeit des deutschen Soldaten und Fliegers beruht die Schlagkraft der Luftwaffe in ihrer zielsicheren Führung durch den Schöpfer unserer Luftmacht Hermann Göring. Der Reichsmarschall gibt in den Generalstabsbesprechungen persönlich die Befehle zum Einsatz der Luftwaffe. Unser Bildbericht schildert eine Generalstabsbesprechung, die in einem französischen Schloß stattgefunden hat

The striking force of the German Air Corps is based not only on the incomparable bravery of German soldiers and airmen, but also on the purposeful leadership of the creator of our air power, Hermann Göring. The Reich Marshal himself gives the orders for the operations of the Air Corps at the meetings of the General Staff. Our illustrated report describes such a meeting that took place in a French chateau

Reichsmarschall Hermann Göring läßt sich vor Beginn der Generalstabsbesprechung von Generaloberst Udet, dem Generalluftzeugmeister der deutschen Luftwaffe, berichten

Before the meeting of the General Staff begins, the Reich Marshal listens to a report by Generaloberst Udet, the Generalluftzeugmeister

Die Generalstabsbesprechung. Der Reichsmarschall nimmt die Berichte der Luftflottenchefs und Geschwaderkommodore entgegen und erteilt seine Befehle

The meeting of the General Staff. The Reich Marshal receives the reports of the chiefs of the air fleets and wing commodores and gives his orders

Aufnahmen: Eitel Lange (7)

Generalfeldmarschall Sperrle (rechts) und Generalleutnant Kastner-Kirdorf, der Chef des Luftwaffen-Personalamtes

Field-Marshal General Sperrle (right) and Lieutenant-General Kastner-Kirdorf, chief of the personnel section of the Air Corps

56

Reichsmarschall
bei einer seiner
Generalstabsbesprechungen

The Reich Marshal Attends
a Meeting of His General Staff

Generalfeldmarschall Kesselring verläßt nach Beendigung der Generalstabsbesprechung mit General der Flieger Jeschonnek das Schloß

Field-Marshal General Kesselring and General der Flieger (Air Chief Marshal) Jeschonnek leave the chateau at the conclusion of the meeting of the General Staff

Der Reichsmarschall mit dem Chef des Generalstabes der Luftwaffe, General der Flieger Jeschonnek

The Reich Marshal and General der Flieger Jeschonnek, Chief of the General Staff of the Air Corps

Rechts: Nach der Generalstabsbesprechung erteilt der Reichsmarschall dem Generalluftzeugmeister, Generaloberst Udet, noch Anweisungen über technische Fragen

Right: After the meeting of the General Staff, the Reich Marshal gives Generaloberst Udet, the Generalluftzeugmeister, further instructions in technical matters

Es ist so schön Soldat zu sein...

Isn't it great to be a Soldier!

Air Corps Recruits Learn the Essentials of Military Training

Links: Erst heißt es „Gewehr über!" Um die militärische Grundausbildung kommt keiner herum. Bevor einer Flieger, Funker oder Flakartillerist wird, muß er sich schon als Soldat die Stiefelsohlen abgelaufen haben

Left: First, "Slope arms!" No one can dodge learning the essentials of a military training, but must have worn out the soles of a pair of ammunition boots, before he can hope to become airman, radio operator, or anti-aircraft gunner

Oben: Da stehen die Luftwaffenrekruten auf dem Kasernenhof, wo ihnen der Unteroffizier die Anfangsgründe des Soldatendaseins beibringt. Jetzt werden gerade „Griffe gekloppt". Das muß wie am Schnürchen gehen

Above: The Air Corps recruits are standing in the barrack yard learning the first rudiments of military life from a non-com. Manual drill is just in progress and must go like clockwork

Aufnahmen:
Seeger-Mauritius (8)

Auch mit dem Maschinengewehr muß der Luftwaffenrekrut umgehen können. Er hat zum erstenmal Geländedienst, und der Ausbilder belehrt ihn, wie er sich mit dem MG im Gelände vorzuarbeiten hat

The recruit must also know how to handle a machine gun. He has field duty for the first time and the instructor is showing him how to work his way forward with the machine gun

Zur Abwechslung einmal Unterricht im Freien. Da heißt es, den Kopf anzustrengen. Aber der richtige Luftwaffenrekrut weiß auch hier seine Aufgaben zu bezwingen

Instruction in the open for a change. It is a bit puzzling, but a real Air Corps recruit knows how to complete his task here too

Thousands of novel impressions crowd upon the young Air Corps recruit at his entry into barracks. He must learn and keep on learning from the very first day. He is speedily freed from his civilian dress and in four weeks is a new man. When doing manual drill during his infantry training, his thoughts often dwell impatiently on his later calling as airman, radio operator, or anti-aircraft gunner, but he must first have proved his worth as soldier, before he is allowed to turn to the special arm of his choice. There is no difficulty in that, because he is surrounded by comrades imbued by the same spirit and with the same goal in view. They all feel strong through the spirit of community. That is the reason why laughter is nowhere to be heard more often and more heartily than among soldiers, in spite of duty and the heavy strain. Their calling is certainly not a free one, but filled with the most powerful obligation, and yet makes men free and fits them to face life

Stiefelputzen ist die letzte Beschäftigung des Tages, und sie wird mit dem nötigen Eifer betrieben, damit am nächsten Morgen die Kommißstiefel blitzblank sind. Das Lied von der Annemarie gibt der Burste erst den richtigen Schwung

Boot polishing is the last occupation of the day and is carried out with the requisite energy, so that the ammunition boots shine next day. The brush is given the right swing to the tune of Annemarie

Links oben gibt ein Bordfunker an der Morsetaste einen Bericht durch, den die jungen Luftwaffensoldaten abhören und niederschreiben

Left above: A radio operator is morsing a message which the young Air Corps soldiers listen to and write down

Weiße Linien und Kurven auf dem Globus ... Die angehenden Flieger sind gespannt bei der Sache; sie werden mit den Anfangsgründen der Navigationslehre vertraut gemacht

White lines and curves on the terrestrial globe. The budding airmen are receiving instruction in the elements of navigation and are all attention

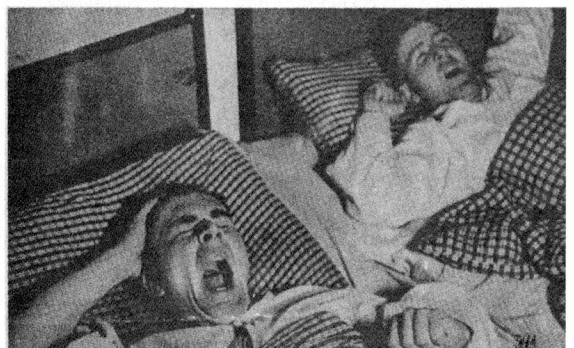

Und dann wird noch einmal herzhaft gegähnt. Nur eine Frage gibt es hier: Wer von den beiden schläft zuerst? Junge Rekruten pflegen nach dem harten Dienst nicht an Schlaflosigkeit zu leiden

And then for a hearty yawn! There is just one point in doubt here: which of the two will be asleep first? Young recruits do not usually suffer from insomnia after a hard day

Wolken, Wellen, Weiten —
das Reich der Seeflieger

Clouds, waves, and far-flung wide open spaces —
there the seaplane pilots hold away

Aufnahme Dr. Wolf Strache

Der Jäger und seine Waffe

The Fighter Pilot and His Weapon

Immer wieder melden die Berichte des Oberkommandos der Wehrmacht große Erfolge der deutschen Jäger. Unter ihnen setzen Männer wie Major Mölders und Major Galland die Reihe der berühmten Weltkriegsflieger fort. Das deutsche Jagdflugzeug hat sich als eine Waffe erwiesen, die dem Gegner bereits schwerste Verluste zugefügt hat. Wo deutsche Jäger auftauchen, da muß der Engländer auf der Hut sein; mit pfeilschneller Gewalt stürzen sie sich auf ihn und lassen nicht ab, bis der Feind zur Strecke gebracht ist

The bulletins of the German High Command again and again report the successful doings of the fighter pilots. Men among them like Squadron Leader Mölders and Squadron Leader Galland perpetuate the line of famous aces of the Great War. The German pursuit plane has proved to be a formidable weapon that has already inflicted very severe losses on the enemy. British pilots must be very wid_awake whenever German fighter planes suddenly swoop upon them like an arrow from the bow, never to let go until the enemy plane has been shot down

Start folgt auf Start, Einsatz auf Einsatz. Der Jäger ist stets bereit, sich auf den Gegner zu stürzen, wo er ihn auch treffen mag

Take-off follows take-off, raid upon raid. The fighter pilot is ever ready to hurl himself upon the foe whenever encountered

Aufmerksam verfolgt der Jagdflieger (Bild rechts) auf dem Frontflugplatz die Rückkehr seiner Kameraden, die eben dem Tommy einen ihrer zahlreichen Besuche auf der Insel abgestattet haben

Right: The fighter pilot at the front airdrome is attentively following the return of his comrades who have just paid one of their numerous visits to Tommy Atkins in his island home

61

Von seinem Sitz, der unbehinderte Sicht nach allen Seiten bietet, sieht der Flugzeugführer jede Einzelheit im Luftraum

The pilot observes every detail in the sky from his seat, which permits of unimpeded view in every direction

Zum Bilde links: Beim Start darf natürlich „Mufti", der Staffelhund, nicht fehlen. Sein Abschiedsgruß hat den Jägern bisher immer noch Glück gebracht

Left: "Mufti", the squadron dog, must of course be present at the take-off. His farewell greetings have hitherto always brought the pilots luck

Der treue Bordwart hilft seinem Flugzeugführer beim Anlegen des Fallschirms. In wenigen Sekunden wird die Maschine zum Start rollen

The faithful board mechanic helps his pilot to adjust his parachute. In a few seconds the machine will taxy to the take-off

Zum Bilde rechts: Ständig fliegen die pfeilschnellen Messerschmitt Me 109 die Kanalküste entlang. Sie werden jedem Feind zum Verhängnis, der sich sehen läßt

Right: The Messerschmitt Me 109 planes are constantly on the wing along the Channel coo·· Swift as an arrow, they spell disaster for every antagonist who shows hime

Aufn. Scherl-Bilderdienst (3), Stöcker (3), Dr. Strache (2), Presse-Bildzentrale (1)

Das Jagdflugzeug hat einen besonders kurzen Start. Kaum hat es vom Boden abgesetzt, da wird auch schon das Fahrwerk eingezogen

The pursuit plane has a particularly short take-off. It has barely left the ground before the undercarriage is retracted

Rechts: Der gefällige Anblick und die schnittige Form des Jägers lassen kaum erkennen, welch eine gefährliche Waffe wir vor uns haben

Right: The graceful aspect and racy lines of the pursuit plane hardly permit of recognizing what a dangerous weapon we have before us

Was ziehen unsere Flieger an?

Die Tapferkeit unserer Flieger, die Güte der Flugzeuge und — nicht zuletzt — die hervorragende Ausrüstung der Besatzungen verbürgen den vollen Erfolg der deutschen Luftwaffe. Wenn die Flieger zum Feindflug starten, fehlt es ihnen an nichts. Gerade jetzt im Winter ist dafür gesorgt, daß sie gegen Kälte und Nöte gewappnet sind. Die Kleidung ist warm und praktisch, jeder Ausrüstungsgegenstand zweckentsprechend und einfach in der Handhabung. Auf langjähriger Erfahrung beruhend, ist die Fliegerkleidung heute technisch so vervollkommnet, daß sie jeder Anforderung gerecht wird: sie ist ein zuverlässiger Schutz und gestattet blitzschnelles Handeln

The courage of our airmen, the quality of their machines, and, to no less degree, the excellent equipment of the crews ensure a full measure of success for the German Air Force. Our pilots lack nothing, when they take off. Every care is taken to ensure their full protection against cold and distress of any kind, in particular at the present season, during the winter. Their clothing is warm and practical, every article of their equipment is adapted for its purpose and easy to manipulate. Clothing for airmen is based on many years' experience and has now been so successfully perfected as to meet all requirements. It affords reliable protection and permits of lightning-like action, since it places no restrictions on the wearer's movements

Die Begurtung scheint äußerst verzwickt zu sein. Tatsächlich ist die Handhabung ganz einfach. Die Scheibe hält alle vier Gurte zusammen, mit denen der Flieger an seinem Sitz befestigt ist. Nach einer kurzen Drehung in Pfeilrichtung genügt ein leichter Schlag auf die Scheibe, um die Gurte zu lösen

The belting makes a very complicated impression, but, as a matter of fact, is quite easy to handle. The disk holds together all four belts, with which the airman is attached to his seat. The belts are released by turning the disk a little in the direction of the arrow and then striking it smartly

Rechts: Dieser rüsselartige Schlauch, den hier der Jäger vor Nase und Mund trägt, ist das Höhenatmungsgerät, mit dem er zum Schutz gegen Sauerstoffmangel bei Flügen in großer Höhe ausgerüstet ist

Right: This trunk-like pipe which the pilot is wearing over his nose and mouth is the respirator for protection against deficiency of oxygen when flying at great altitudes

Zum Bilde links außen: Wenn der Feindflug viele Stunden dauert, kriecht die Ablösung zum Schutz gegen die Kälte in einen bequemen, gefütterten Schlafsack. So gehen die Besatzungsmitglieder am Ziel frisch in den Kampf

Left outside: When a flight lasts many hours, the relief seeks protection against the cold by creeping into a comfortable, well-lined sleeping bag. The crew are then fighting fit when they arrive at their objective

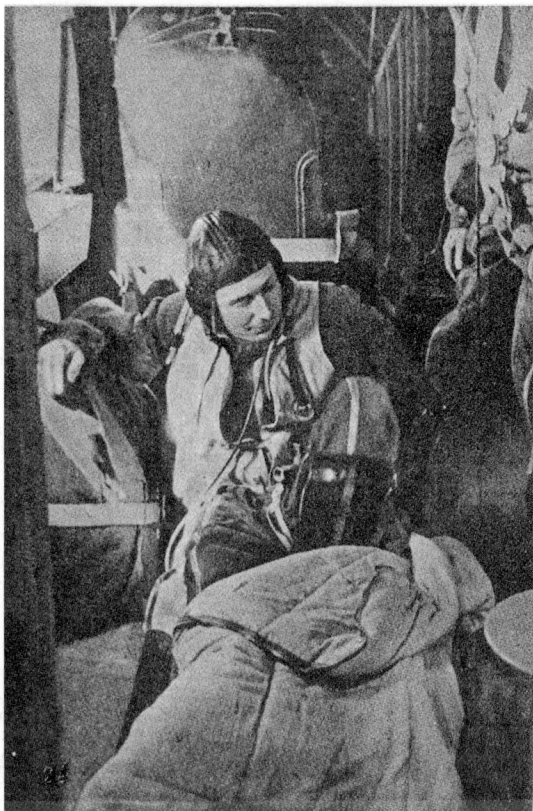

Zum Bilde links: So ist der Flieger gegen größte Kälte gewappnet. Er trägt während der Wintermonate besonders warme, pelzgefütterte Kombinationen und dazu Pelzstiefel, die durch verstellbare Riemen an den Waden eng anschließen

Left: An airman is protected against the bitterest cold during the winter months by wearing a particularly warm, fur-lined combination suit with fur boots, closely fitting the calf of the leg by means of adjustable straps

What do our airmen wear?

Aufn. Scherl-Bilderdienst (3), PK-Platzek (PBZ), PK-Pilz (Atlantic), Dr. Strache, Die Wehrmacht

Neben Pilotenhaube und Brille hat der Flieger ein Kehlkopfmikrophon. Es überträgt die Worte unmittelbar vom Kehlkopf des Sprechers und gestattet trotz Motorenlärm eine einwandfreie Verständigung unter den Besatzungsmitgliedern, was für die geschlossene Kampfkraft von größter Wichtigkeit ist

The airman has a pilot's helmet, goggles, and a laryngaphone, which transmits his words directly from his larynx and permits of intercommunication between the members of the crew, in spite of the noise of the engines. That is of the utmost importance for concentration of fighting force

So sieht die Schwimmweste aus; sie ist mit Kohlensäurepatronen versehen, die bei Berührung mit Wasser Kohlensäure entwickeln. Dadurch wird die Schwimmweste aufgebläht und kann leicht einen Menschen stundenlang an der Wasseroberfläche halten

What a life-jacket looks like. It is fitted with carbonic acid cartridges that develop carbonic acid gas in contact with water, thereby inflating the life-jacket, which can then easily keep a man afloat for several hours

Zum Bilde rechts: Die Fliegerausrüstung wäre unvollständig ohne den Fallschirm, den Rettungsring der Luft, dem schon mancher Flieger sein Leben verdankt

Right: An airman's equipment would be incomplete without a parachute, the life-belt of the air to which many an airman owes his life

15 Jahre

Fifteen Years Deutsche Lufthansa

Vergangenheit und Zukunft begegnen sich: Das war (Bild oben) der Flughafen Tempelhof vor 15 Jahren, gewiß weiträumig und imponierend ... aber so (Bild rechts) wird in dem Deutschland der Zukunft der Weltflughafen Tempelhof aussehen, dessen Bau fast fertiggestellt ist

Past and future meet. Above: Fifteen years ago the Tempelhof airport was certainly spacious and imposing, but the international Tempelhof airport will look differently (right) in the Germany of the future. A beginning has already been made with its construction

Unten: Die Kabine war damals etwas eng, und der Fluggast mußte sich mit Rohrstühlen begnügen. Heute ist das Reisen in einem Großverkehrsflugzeug der Lufthansa ein Vergnügen. 23 Fluggäste haben in bequemen Polstern Platz und werden dazu von einer reizenden Flugbegleiterin betreut

Aufn. Deutsche Lufthansa 10 (Atlantic 1, Stöcker 6), Hansa-Luftbild (2)

Below: A cabin was a trifle narrow at that date and passengers had to be contented with cane chairs. A trip nowadays in a large airliner of the Lufthansa is a pleasure. There is accomodation for 23 passengers in comfortable cushioned seats and a charming stewardess ministers to their needs

Die Deutsche Lufthansa wurde am 6. Januar 1926 gegründet. Sie faßte damals den zersplitterten deutschen Luftverkehr einheitlich zusammen. Mit ihr begann eine neue Epoche der Luftfahrt, die — weit über die deutschen Grenzen hinausgehend — ihr Verkehrsnetz über ganz Europa spannte und bald auch die Brücken zu anderen Erdteilen schlug. Wenn die Leistungen der Deutschen Lufthansa bis Kriegsbeginn schon beispiellos gewesen sind, so werden sich ihr nach Beendigung des Krieges noch gewaltigere Aufgabengebiete erschließen

Zu den Bildern rechts — 1926: Die Post wird in einen einmotorigen Fokker-Hochdecker verladen. 1939: Die Südatlantikpost der Lufthansa landet in Buenos Aires

Right: In 1926 the mail was loaded in a single-engined Fokker high-wing monoplane. 1940: The South American mail plane of the Lufthansa alights in Buenos Aires

Untere Bilder. — Links: Rückkehr der Flieger (von links nach rechts) Kirchhoff, v. Gablenz und Untucht nach dem erfolgreichen Flug über das „Dach der Welt". Kirchhoff und Untucht haben inzwischen bei Erkundungsflügen als Pioniere der deutschen Luftfahrt ihr Leben gelassen. — Rechts: Abschuß des Schwimmflugzeuges Ha 139-B „Nordstern" von einem Flugstützpunkt der Deutschen Lufthansa im Nordatlantik

Left below: Return of the aviators Kirchhoff, von Gablenz, and Untucht (reading from left to right) after their successful survey flight over the Pamirs, the Roof of the World. Kirchhoff and Untucht have meanwhile lost their lives as pioneers of German aviation. Right below: The seaplane Ha 139-B "Nordstern" (Pole Star) is catapulted from a floating air base of the Deutsche Lufthansa in the North Atlantic

Deutsche Lufthansa

Leiſtungstafel

Von 1926 bis 1939 wurden über 192000000 km zurückgelegt; es wurden über 2000000 Personen, über 22000 t Post und fast 20000 t Fracht und Gepäck befördert

More than 182 million kilometres (115 million miles) have been flown between 1926 and 1939; over two million passengers, more than 22,000 tons of mail, and nearly 20,000 tons of freight and baggage have been carried

	1926	1939
Reisegeschwindigkeit der Flugzeuge	140 km/st	280 km/st
Höchste Sitzzahl in der Kabine	9	32
PS-Leistung eines Flugzeuges bis zu	900 Ps	3200 PS
Längste planmäßige Strecke .	1100 km	15300 km
Planmäßige Hochgebirgsstrecken	keine	2 Alpenstrecken, 1 Andenstrecke
Längste planmäßige Überseestrecke	200 km (Ostsee)	3050 km (Atlantik)

Von oben nach unten: Start einer Dornier „Merkur" im Gründungsjahr der Deutschen Lufthansa. Dieses Verkehrsflugzeug wirkt fast wie ein Spielzeug — wenn wir es mit der viermotorigen Junkers Ju 90 vergleichen. Machtvoll, sicher und schnell zieht das Riesenflugzeug seine Bahn

Noch ein Rückblick auf das Jahr 1926: Start einer Junkers G 24, die mit ihren drei Motoren immerhin schon 900 PS leistete

Heute: Die 32 Fluggäste haben Platz genommen, die vier Motoren mit 3200 PS sind bereits angelassen, die Luftschrauben dröhnen, der Riesenvogel wird in wenigen Augenblicken starten

From above down: A Dornier "Merkur" takes off in the year in which the Deutsche Lufthansa was founded. The commercial plane almost looks like a toy, when compared with the four-engined Junkers Ju 90. Powerful, safe, and speedy, the giant airliner pursues its way. Another glance back at 1926: A Junkers G 24 takes off. With its three engines it had after all an output of 900 h.p.

Today: Thirty-two passengers have taken their seats, the four engines with their 3,200 h.p. have been started, the propellers are roaring, and the gigantic bird will take-off in a few moments

Das Gesicht des

The Visage

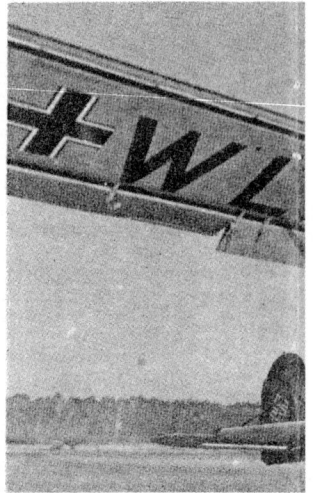

Wie eine Heuschrecke, die in höchster Konzentration im nächsten Augenblick zum Sprung ansetzen wird, so hebt sich der Fieseler „Storch" vom Boden

The Fieseler "Storch" stands on the ground like a grasshopper with tense muscles ready to leap off in a moment

Daß Flugzeuge ein ganz bestimmtes Gesicht haben, wissen unsere Soldaten am besten. So haben sie diesem Zerstörer (Bild unten) das Aussehen eines Haifisches gegeben und damit ein bekanntes Verbandsabzeichen geschaffen

Our soldiers are best aware that aircraft have a well-defined visage and have therefore given this destroyer (below) the appearance of a shark, thereby creating the mark of a well-known formation of the German Air Force

Zum Bilde links: Mit unerhörter Wendigkeit und unwiderstehlicher Kampfkraft stößt der Zerstörer Me 110 vor

Left: The destroyer Me 110 zooms up with incredible manoeuverability and veresistible fighting power

deutschen Flugzeuges

of the German Airplane

Jeder rechte Flieger hat es tausendmal erlebt, daß Flugzeuge mehr sind als Maschinen und tote Gegenstände. Es sind lebende Wesen, mit denen die Besatzungen verwachsen sind wie der Reiter mit dem Pferd. Flugzeuge sind wie gute Kameraden, und ihre Eigenart kommt, genau wie bei den Menschen, am klarsten in ihrem Gesicht zum Ausdruck. Ja — auch Flugzeuge haben ihr ganz bestimmtes Gesicht. Das eine ist angespannt, gewaltig und furchterregend, das andere schmal, ruhig und doch voll vorwärtsstürmender Kraft. Diese Gesichter sind im Augenblick des Kampfes gegen den Feind gerichtet. So sieht sie der Brite, und er erzittert unter den unerbittlichen Schlägen, die unsere Luftwaffe ihm täglich und stündlich erteilt

Every real airman must over and over again have experienced the feeling that aircraft are something more than mere machines and lifeless objects, but rather that they are actually sentient creatures, forming with their crews a single entity, as a rider with his horse. An airplane is like a good comrade and its character, just as with human beings, is most clearly expressed in its face; for even aircraft have a face all their own. One may be tense and gigantic, arousing fear, while another is narrow, quiet, and yet full of driving energy. These faces are directed towards the enemy at the moment of battle and thus it is that Britons see them, as they quiver under the relentless blows dealt out to them daily and hourly by our Air Force

Wie die Facetten eines scharf um sich blickenden, alles erspähenden Insektenauges durch dringt die Vollsichtkanzel des Fernaufklärers den feindlichen Luftraum

As the long-distance reconnaissance plane penetrates the enemy air space, the nose turret which permits of vision in all directions, resembles the facetted eye of an insect with its keen gaze that misses nothing

Der Nahaufklärer (Bild unten) ist sein kleiner Bruder, der auf zierlichen Füßen steht und nicht so hoch und weit hinauswill, aber unseren Soldaten ein unentbehrlicher Kamerad ist

Below: Its little brother is the short-distance scout plane, which stands on graceful feet and does not aim at flying too high or too far, but is an indispensable comrade for our soldiers

Zum Bilde rechts: Massig in seiner geballten Kampfkraft sieht uns das gläserne Gesicht der Heinkel He 111 zwischen den beiden brausenden Motoren an

Right: The glazed visage of the Heinkel He 111 with its concentrated fighting power watches us from between the two roaring engines

Ein gepanzertes zorniges Insekt stößt aus den Wolken nieder — die Henschel Hs 123 während des Sturzfluges. Links: Das Gesicht der Hs 123

An angry armored insect dives from the clouds—a Henschel Hs 123 during a nose dive. Left: The face of the Hs 123

Die Motorhaube der Junkers Ju 87 (Bild rechts) erscheint uns wie der schmale Kopf eines jagenden Windhundes; die Wucht der Tragflächen und des bekleideten Fahrwerks verrät zugleich die vernichtende Gewalt dieses Sturzkampfflugzeuges

Right: The engine cowling of the Junkers Ju 87 looks like the long narrow head of a greyhound. The massive appearance of the wings and the covered undercarriage betray the annihilating power of this dive-bomber

Aufnahmen: Hoffmann, Kücke, Heinricht, PK Ruge, Schaller, Stöcker, Werkaufn.: Dornier, Heinkel, Henschel, Messerschmitt

Zum Bilde links: Als blicke er voll Ungeduld zu seinem Jagdrevier hinauf — so steht der Messerschmitt-Jäger siegeszuversichtlich da

Left: The cocksure Me fighter plane is standing there, as if gazing impatiently at its hunting grounds aloft

Mittelalterliche Helden mit geschlossenem Visier — so stürmen die Kampfflugzeuge Dornier Do 215 gegen den Feind

Dornier Do 215 bombers thunder against the foe, like medieval heroes in armor with their visors down

In 40

Assembled in Forty Minutes

Welch hohen Grad der Vollkommenheit die Serienherstellung von Frontflugzeugen in Deutschland erreicht hat, beweist unsere Bildreihe. Daß ein zweimotoriges Flugzeug in weit weniger als einer Stunde montiert wird und daß vom Beginn der Montage bis zum Probelauf der Motoren nicht mehr als fünf Stunden vergehen, bedeutet eine hervorragende Leistung sowohl der Konstrukteure als auch der Werkmänner. Es ist kein Geheimnis, daß der deutsche Flugzeugbau auf dem Gebiet der Groß-Serienherstellung in der Welt führend ist

Our series of photographs shows the pitch of perfection that the series production of fighting aircraft has reached in Germany. The fact that a twin-engined airplane can be assembled well within one hour and that not more than five hours are needed from starting assembly to the trial run of the engines, is a peak achievement on the part of the designers and the workers alike. It is no secret that German aircraft construction leads the world in point of mass production

8.01 Uhr: Der Rumpf eines Kampfflugzeuges vom Baumuster Dornier „Do 215" wird auf fahrbaren Untersätzen in die Montagehalle gebracht, wo bereits alles zur Aufnahme bereitsteht

8.01 a. m. The fuselage of a Dornier bomber of the Do 215 type is brought into the assembly bay on portable supports. Everything is ready for its reception

8.06 Uhr: Von den Fahrgestellen wird der Rumpf auf Böcke gesetzt. Harte Werkmannsfäuste lassen ihn sanft auf diese neue Unterlage niedersinken

8.06 a. m. The fuselage is removed from the wheel frames and placed on trestles. Worker's rough hands let it settle down gently on the new supports

8.13 Uhr: Während nebenan an einem anderen Flugzeug bereits die Luftschrauben montiert werden, senkt sich das weit ausladende Tragwerk auf den Rumpf

8.13 a. m. The wide-spread wing unit is lowered on the fuselage, while the propellers are already being mounted on another airplane

minuten montiert

8.14 Uhr: Sorgsam geleitet, schweben die Tragflächen an der Laufkatze der Montagehalle auf die Aussparungen im Flugzeugrumpf herunter. Hier ist deutlich eine Motorengondel zu sehen

8.14 a. m. The wings suspended from the trolley hoist of the assembly shed are carefully guided down to the recesses for them in the fuselage. The engine nacelle can here be plainly seen

8.16 Uhr: Während vorn das Tragwerk eingebaut wird (Bild oben rechts), bringt ein zweiter elektrischer Kran das Leitwerk (die Steuerung) an die Montagestelle, wo es von einer zweiten Arbeitergruppe am Schwanzende des Rumpfes aufmontiert wird

8.16 a. m. While the wing unit is being installed in front (illustration at the right above), a second electric crane brings the tail unit (control mechanism) to the point of assembly, where it is mounted by a second group of workers on the tail end of the fuselage

Aufnahmen:
Dr. Wolf Strache

8.25 Uhr: Die Montagearbeit ist zeitlich so organisiert, daß ständig verschiedene Gruppen von Arbeitern an der Maschine angesetzt werden können. Noch während der Montage der Tragflächen und des Leitwerks haben andere Werkmänner die einziehbaren Laufräder angesetzt, andere schaffen gerade das Spornrad herbei

8.25 a. m. Assembly work is organized in such a way in point of time that the various groups of workers can be continuously set to work on the machine. While the wings and tail unit are being installed, other groups of workers have mounted the retractable wheels, while others again are just bringing up the tail wheel

8.28 Uhr: (Bild oben links) Hier setzt ein Arbeiter das Spornrad ein, und in der gleichen Zeit schaffen andere Werkgruppen die Motoren heran

8.28 a. m. Left above: A workman sets in the tail wheel, while other groups of workers bring up the engines

8.35 Uhr: Das Triebwerk (der Motor) ist vom Kran an die Montagestelle gebracht worden. Es ist noch in seiner Aufhängung befestigt, bis die Montage der Motoraufhängung so weit fortgeschritten ist, daß sie den Motor allein trägt

8.35 a. m. The power plant (engine) has been brought up by the crane for installation. It is still in the sling until the assembly of the engine suspension has proceeded so far that it can support the engine alone

8.37 Uhr: Der Motor ist vom Kran gelöst worden. Ein Arbeiter zieht die letzten Verschraubungen fest. Deutlich ist die Motoraufhängung zu erkennen

8.37 a. m. The engine has been released from the crane. A workman is tightening up the last few bolts. The engine suspension can be plainly seen

8.40 Uhr: Kaum ist der Motoreinbau vollendet, sind schon weitere Arbeiter damit beschäftigt, die dreiflügeligen Verstellluftschrauben aufzuziehen. Damit ist die Montage des Kampfflugzeuges im wesentlichen beendet

8.40 a. m. The engine has hardly been installed, when other workers are engaged in mounting the three-bladed variable-pitch propellers. The assembly of the bomber is therewith practically completed

10.45 Uhr: Zwischen der Beendigung der Rohmontage um 8.40 Uhr und jetzt sind alle Anschlüsse hergestellt. Gerade ist ein Spezialarbeiter damit beschäftigt, die Bewaffnung anzubringen

10.45 a. m. All connections have been made between the rough assembly at 8.40 and the present moment. A specialist is just engaged in installing the armament

11.04 Uhr: Ein Fachmann legt die letzte Hand an die Apparaturen im Inneren der Kanzel

11.04 a. m. A skilled workman puts the finishing touches to the equipment in the interior of the turret in the nose of the machine

11.10 Uhr: Jetzt sind bereits fleißige Arbeiterinnen dabei, die Verglasung der Bugkanzel und des Heckstandes blankzuputzen

11.10 a. m. Girls are already busy polishing the windows of the turret and the tail cockpit

13.01 Uhr: Die gesamte Montage ist beendet. Ein neues Kampfflugzeug verläßt die Halle und wird dem Einflieger übergeben

13.01. Assembly is completely finished. A bomber is leaving the shed to be turned over to a pilot to be flown in

75

Heinkel-Jäger

Heinkel Fighters at the Front

an der Front

Unsere Bilder zeigen Aufnahmen von einer Staffel He 113, eines Jagdflugzeuges, dessen Ursprungsmuster vor einem Jahr erstmals den absoluten Geschwindigkeits - Weltrekord mit 747 km/st für Deutschland eroberte. Dieser deutsche Jagdeinsitzer hat inzwischen längst seine Feuertaufe bestanden — in Dänemark und Norwegen ebenso wie über den Schlachtfeldern Belgiens und Frankreichs

Our illustrations show photos of a squadron of He 113 fighters. When this type was brought out a year ago, it won for Germany, for the first time, the absolute world's speed record with a speed of 747 km/hr. (415 m.p.h.). This single-seat fighter has long since undergone its baptism of fire, in Denmark and Norway, and on the battlefields of Belgium and France

Zum Bilde links: Startbefehl! Ein Wart hilft dem Flugzeugführer beim Schließen der Anschnallgurte. Wenige Sekunden noch, und die Motoren beginnen zu dröhnen

Left: The order to start. An aircraftman is assisting a pilot to buckle on his safety-belt. The engines will be roaring in a few seconds

Zum Bilde links: Staffel vor
dem Start nach dem Norden:
Ausgerichtet wie zur Parade
warten die Flugzeuge auf den
Einsatzbefehl

*Left: The squadron before start-
ing for the north. The machines
are drawn up as on parade and
await commands*

Aufnahmen: Stöcker (4)

Kurz ist der Start des Jagdflugzeuges: kaum
hat es den Boden verlassen, da ist auch schon
das Fahrgestell eingefahren

*A fighter needs only a short starting run and has
barely left the ground before the landing gear is
retracted*

Zum Bilde rechts: In steiler Kurve liegend
beweist ein Heinkel - Jäger seine Wendigkeit

*Right: A Heinkel fighter shows its manœuvrability
in a steep turn*

77

The leading unit of the swiftest branch of the forces

Man and Engine in the Wireless Service of the Air Force

"Ihr seid die Träger des raschen und reibungslosen Zusammenwirkens in unserer Waffe. Ihr gebt unserer Waffe die Möglichkeit, den eigenen, alles überrennenden Angriff voranzutragen und den feindlichen Gegenstoß rechtzeitig abzufangen und zum Scheitern zu bringen." Mit diesen Worten kennzeichnete der Oberbefehlshaber der Luftwaffe, Reichsmarschall Göring, das Wesen der Luftnachrichtentruppe, dieses Bindeglied zwischen Angriff und Abwehr, Flieger und Flak, Befehlenden und Gehorchenden jener imposanten Luftwaffe der neuen Wehrmacht, die gleichsam aus dem Nichts entstand und heute schon die Initiative am Himmel Europas an sich gerissen hat. — Was ist das, Luftnachrichtentruppe? Telephonisten? Funker in den Dienststellen der Kommandobehörden? Meldefahrer? Vom Dienst dieser „Führungstruppe", die so wichtig ist für die Verbindungen zwischen Führung und Truppe, und die dafür sorgen muß, daß das Zusammenwirken aller im Gefecht sichergestellt ist, erzählt unser Bildbericht

Die vollmotorisierte Funkkompanie auf dem Marsch. Den Kübelwagen folgen die verschiedenartigen Spezialwagen mit den Nachrichtengeräten. Am Bau der Fahrzeuge erkennt man, welch große Geländegängigkeit von ihnen gefordert wird

Fully motorized wireless company on the march. The open cross-country car is followed by the various special wagons with the wireless equipment. The design of the vehicles shows that they are intended for heavy duty across country

Eine Funkstelle hat auf schmalem, sandigem Wege den befohlenen Standort erreicht. Der Hochwald bietet Gelegenheit für eine natürliche Antenne

Traveling over narrow, sandy tracts, a wireless station has reached its objective. The forest provides a natural antenna

Die Führungsgruppe der schnellsten Waffe

Mann und Motor in Funkdienst der Luftwaffe

"On your shoulders rests the responsibility for speedy and friction-less cooperation in our branch of the service. You provide us with the possibility of pushing forward our own attack, over-coming all resistance, parrying the enemy counterthrust in good time and causing its breakdown." With these words Reichs-marschall Göring, Air Officer Commander-in-Chief, characterized the Air Intelligence Service which acts as connecting link between attack and defense, between airman and air-defense corps, be-tween those giving and those executing orders in the imposing Air Force of the new Defense Forces which arose, as it were, out of nothing and has now secured for itself the initiative in the sky of Europe.—What, it may be asked, is the function of the Air Intelligence Service? Are they telephonists, or wireless oper-ators at headquarters of the commanding authorities, or are they despatch cyclists? Our present pictorial report describes the duties of this leading unit, which is of vital importance for the connections between leader and troops, and has the duty of ensuring the cooperation of all the forces engaged

Eine andere Funkstelle ist in offenem Gelände eingesetzt worden. Hier ist die Errichtung eines Antennenmastes notwendig

Another wireless station has been set up in the open and an antenna mast must be rigged up

Rechts: Nach Aufstellung des Mastes wird die Verbindung mit der Funkstation durch Abrollen eines Kabels hergestellt

Right: After setting up the mast, connection with the wireless station effected by paying out a cable

Zum Bilde links: Hier bilden die Kronen hoher Kiefern eine gute Tarnung gegen Fliegersicht, so daß sofort aufgebaut wird. Der Betrieb kann beginnen

Left: The tops of the tall pines camouflage the site well against air observation, so that the equipment can be set up right away and work can start at once

Ein aufgenommener wichtiger Funkspruch wird schriftlich an die nahegelegene Befehlsstelle weitergeleitet. Hierbei darf kein Wort, keine Zahl verstümmelt werden

An important wireless message just taken down is sent in writing to the nearest command. Not a single word, not a figure must be mutilated

Die in offenem Gelände eingesetzte Funkstelle muß sorgfältig gegen Fliegersicht getarnt werden. Nach wenigen Minuten wird man hier nur noch einen Strauch vermuten

The wireless station set up in the open must be carefully camouflaged against overhead observation. A few minutes later, nothing but a bush would be suspected here

Die Funkstellen liegen oft so dicht am Feind, daß eine Sicherung gegen versprengte oder durchgebrochene Feindteile, Panzerspähwagen oder Baumschützen unbedingt notwendig ist. Ein leichtes MG ist zum Schutze der Funkstelle vorgeschoben worden

The wireless stations often lie so close to the enemy lines as to require protection against isolated enemy units, or a break through, armored reconnaissance cars, or snipers hidden in the trees. A light machine-gun has been brought up for the protection of the wireless station

Größte Beweglichkeit, auch auf versandeten oder vereisten Wegen oder gar quer durch Wiesen und Schonungen, wird vom Funkwagen gefordert. Ist er an der befohlenen Stelle angekommen, beginnt im Innern eine fieberhafte Tätigkeit. Eine Unmenge von Drähten und Schaltern ist zu bedienen, Signale leuchten und summen. Klarer Kopf und schnelle Hand werden vom Funker gefordert

The wireless wagon must be extremely mobile, whether traveling through sand, over ice-covered roads, or across meadows and plantations. As soon as it reaches its objective, the interior presents a scene of great activity: countless wires and switches have to be attended to, signal lamps flash up, buzzers call. The operator must have a cool head and a quick hand

Das Gesicht des

The Face of the Airman

Ein Flugzeugführer des Jagdgeschwaders
Schumacher

A pilot of the Schumacher fighter wing

"Wenn ich das Gesicht eines Hunnen beschreiben sollte, der in 9000 Meter Höhe fliegt und Explosivbomben auf die Erde abwirft in der Hoffnung, daß diese etwas treffen werden, dann würde ich ein halbirres, lüsternes, lasterhaftes, unter den Einwohnern eines Irrenhauses ausgewähltes Gesicht malen, das schallend lacht in dem Augenblick, in dem es seine Sendungen abwirft und mit aufgerissenem Maul danach ausschaut, was geschieht." (Aus einer Predigt des Erzbischofs Partridge von Portsmouth.) Als schlagendste Erwiderung auf diese widerliche Begeiferung deutscher Flieger durch einen hohen Würdenträger der anglikanischen Kirche bringen wir einige Porträte deutscher Flieger des Zeichners Wolf Willrich

"If I were to depict the face of a Hun airman flying at 30,000 ft. and loosing high-explosive bombs over the earth, hoping that they would hit something, I should paint a halfwitted, leering, vicious face chosen from the denizens of a lunatic asylum, roaring with laughter as it just tosses out its missiles and gaping with glee at what will happen."
(Extract from a sermon by Archbishop Partridge of Portsmouth)
We bring a few portraits of German airmen by the draughtsman Wolf Willrich as the most convincing refutation of the foul calumnies on German airmen given vent to by a high dignitary of the Anglican Church

Von links nach rechts: Oberleutnant Elmar Schaefer, ein Sturzkampfflieger. — Der Flugzeugführer eines Messerschmitt-Zerstörers. — Ein Kampfflieger, der bei Scapa Flow dabei war

From left to right: Flying Officer Elmar Schaefer, pilot of a dive bomber. The pilot of a Messerschmitt destroyer. A bomber pilot, who was one of those at Scapa Flow

Ein Oberleutnant und Staffelkapitän der Kampfflieger. — Bild links: Der mit dem Ritterkreuz ausgezeichnete Fallschirmjäger Oberleutnant Schmidt

A Flying Officer and Squadron Leader of bomber pilots. Left: Flying Officer Schmidt of the parachute troops, decorated with the Knight's Cross

Fliegers

Der Kampfflieger: Major Harlinghausen Ritterkreuzträger.
— Bild rechts: Der Ritterkreuzträger Oberleutnant Schacht
war bei der Wegnahme der Brücke über den Albert-Kanal
westlich Maastricht am 10. Mai 1940 schwer verwundet
worden

The bomber-pilot: **Major Harlinghausen, decorated with
the Knight's Cross. Right: Flying Officer Schacht, decorated
with the Knight's Cross, was severely wounded at the capture
of the bridge over the Albert Canal west of Maastricht on
May 10, 1940**

Zeichnungen PK Wolf Willrich

Generalmajor v. Döring, Jagdfliegerführer im Westen, und sein Adjutant.
— Bild links: Ein Oberleutnant von den Sturzkampffliegern. — Es ist zu
hoffen, daß diese kühl entschlossenen Gesichter deutscher Flieger diesem
seltsamen englischen Geistlichen und seinen Kumpanen zu Gesicht
kommen. Sie werden dann wissen, was die Stunde für England ge-
schlagen hat

**Major-General von Döring, pursuit plane pilot, and his adjutant.—Left:
A Flying Officer of the dive bombers.—It is to be hoped that these portraits
of German airmen with their expression of cool determination will come
under the notice of the singular English minister of the gospel quoted
above and others of his kidney. They will then know what is in store for
England**

Ein „fliegen" wird übernommen

Taking Delivery of a "Flying Pencil"

Die Do 215 wird wegen ihrer langgestreckten Gestalt gern „Der fliegende Bleistift" genannt. Für eine Frontbesatzung ist es immer ein Ereignis, wenn sie beauftragt wird, auf dem Werkflugplatz eine neue Maschine zu übernehmen. Es ist ja „ihre" Maschine, mit der sie in kurzer Zeit zu einer kämpferischen Einheit verschmolzen sein wird

Owing to its elongated form, the Do 215 is widely known as the "flying pencil". It is always a great event for a front-line crew to be ordered to take over a new machine at the factory airdrome. For it is "their" machine, with which they will soon be welded into a fighting unit

Zum Bilde links: Die Frontbesatzung, die die neue Do 215 übernehmen soll, ist auf dem Werk-flugplatz eingetroffen und wird von dem Werkingenieur herzlich begrüßt

Left: The crew from the front arrives at the factory airdrome to take over the new Do 215 and is warmly welcomed by the works engineer

In seiner langgestreckten Form macht der „fliegende Bleistift" seinem Scherz-namen alle Ehre. „Funkelnagelneu" fliegt die Do 215 (Bild rechts) über die Dächer ihrer Heimat   Aufn. Hartmann-Mauritius (7)

The elongated form of the plane does all honor to its nickname of the "flying pencil". Right: Spick-and-span, the brand new Do 215 flies over the roofs of its old home

Zum Bilde unten: Die Besatzung interes-siert sich für alles, was mit der neuen Ma-schine zusammenhängt. Hier sehen wir sie an der Prüfstelle. Ein solcher Anschauungs-unterricht verdoppelt natürlich das Ver-trauen auf das zu übernehmende Flugzeug

Below: The crew are naturally keenly inter-ested in everything in connection with the new machine and appreciate an inspection of the test bench. An object lesson like that of course redoubles their confidence in the machine to be taken over

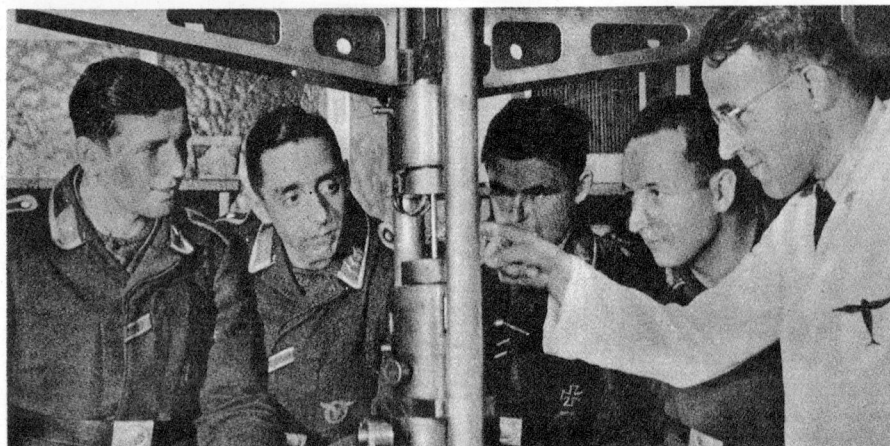

84

der Bleistift"

Ordnung muß sein! Hier werden kleine Ausrüstungsgegenstände und Zubehörteile übergeben und an Hand der Liste genau nachgeprüft

Everything proceeds in due order. Small pieces of equipment and accessories are handed over and carefully checked up with the list

Da haben wir unsere Bomben letztes Mal abgeladen!" Die Werksleute, die in der Heimat ihre Pflicht tun, hören den Erklärungen der Frontflieger vor der Englandkarte gespannt zu

"The last time, we dropped our bombs just there." The factory workers, who have their duties at the home front, listen eagerly to the tales of the pilots from the fighting front as they stand before the map of England

Zum Bilde rechts: Nun wird es Ernst! Die Formalitäten der Übergabe sind erledigt, die Do 215 ist startbereit. Gleich wird „Premiere" zum Frontflugplatz geflogen

Right: Work now begins in earnest. The formalities of acceptance have been completed, the Do 215 is ready to take off, and the first flight to the front airdrome will soon begin

Short-Distance Scouting Focke-Wulf FW 189

The New Double-Fuselage Airplane
of the German Air Corps

Das obere Bild läßt die langgestreckte schnittige Form des neuen Naherkunders FW 189 besonders deutlich erkennen, während die untere Aufnahme vor allem die interessante Doppelrumpfanordnung klar sichtbar macht. Die Vollsichtkanzel vorn und die Spitzlafette hinten bieten freie Sicht nach fast allen Seiten — eine wichtige Voraussetzung gerade für ein Aufklärungsflugzeug

Above: This photograph brings out particularly plainly the long stream-lined form of the new FW 189 short-distance reconnaissance plane, while the picture below clearly shows the interesting double fuselage arrangement. The front turret and the gun mounting at the rear permit of visibility on practically all sides—an important feature precisely for a scout plane

A new German airplane has now made its appearance on the wartime sky, such as most of us have certainly never before seen. It has a double fuselage and at first sight appears to an observer to be two airplanes fused together, like Siamese Twins of the air. This machine is the short-distance Focke-Wulf FW 189 reconnaissance airplane, which is already being turned out in series production and has often proved most efficient for its missions at the front. The arrangement of the double fuselage presents the crew with excellent sight conditions on all sides. The whole design has been directed to such an extent to ensuring good possibilities of observation that it might be called "the flying eye". The German Air Corps receives another short-distance reconnaissance plane in the shape of the Focke-Wulf FW 189 which is remarkable not only for its excellent flying performance and great manoeuvrability, but is further heavily armed for attack and defense. The designer of the double-fuselage short-distance reconnaissance plane is the well-known Wehrwirtschaftsführer Kurt Tank, Dipl.-Ing., who has already made a name for himself by his design of the successful Focke-Wulf FW 200 C long-range bomber known as the "Condor"

Das "Fliegende Auge"

The "Flying Eye"

Werkaufnahmen Focke-Wulf

Wehrwirtschaftsführer Dipl.-Ing. Kurt Tank, der Schöpfer der FW 189

Wehrwirtschaftsführer Kurt Tank, the creator of the FW 189

Das Doppelrumpfflugzeug Focke-Wulf FW 189 in der Kurve. Man sieht diesem Flugzeug geradezu an, daß es gute fliegerische Eigenschaften mit äußerster Wendigkeit verbindet

The Focke-Wulf FW 189 double-fuselage airplane banking. It is at once evident that this plane combines excellent flying qualities with extreme manœuverability

Vorderansicht der FW 189. Eben hat die Maschine, an der deutlich die Vorrichtung zum Einziehen des Fahrwerkes zu erkennen ist, die Endmontage des Werkes verlassen, und schon bald wird sie wie viele andere ihres Baumusters zu verantwortungsvollem Dienst an der Front eingesetzt werden

Front view of the FW 189, showing the device for retracting the undercarriage. The machine has just left the assembly bay and will soon, like so many others of its type, be leaving for the firing line to take up its responsible duties

Schriftleiter werden

Oben: „Lehrgang zum Unterricht angetreten"

Above: Members of the training course parade for instruction

Links: Seit Mitternacht Soldat. Gestern abend stand er noch als Rundfunksprecher am Mikrophon. Mit seinem Stellungsbefehl meldet sich nun der künftige Kriegsberichter an der Wache

Left: A soldier since midnight. Just yesterday evening he was standing as radio speaker in front of the microphone. The future war correspondent now reports himself to the guard with his order to present himself for duty

Unten: Flugzeugerkennungskunde — ein wichtiger Unterrichtsgegenstand

Below: Instruction in the recognition of aircraft—an important subject of instruction

Für alle Zwischenfälle gerüstet! Diesem Grundsatz folgend, werden auch Übungen mit dem Schlauchboot abgehalten, dessen Handhabung jedes Besatzungsmitglied kennen muß

Equipped to meet every contretemps. True to that principle, the handling of a rubber boat is also practised; every member of the crew must be familiar with it

Fliegerschützen

Journalists Become Air Gunners

Special Training of the Budding War Correspondents of the Air Corps

A war correspondent has the task of conveying as directly as possible to the home front an impression of the events of war. But that vivid directness can only result from his own actual experience. That is the reason why Germany has placed its war correspondents in the firing line as soldiers among soldiers. After having been trained in the elements of infantry drill, the budding war correspondent of the Air Corps has to undergo a further special training as air gunner. Since it is impossible to take a passenger when in action, the reporter must himself be a member of the crew as air gunner, and he has often enough had occasion to change the pen or the camera for the machine gun, to ward off enemy interceptors. The chief subject of the special training is therefore to learn how to handle a machine gun in a dependable way. Besides instruction in weapons and their use, machine-gun drill, and shooting practice, various other branches of instruction, such as tactics, aircraft recognition service, and musketry, are of great importance. They equip the future war correspondent with the necessary knowledge to enable him to fill his responsible task not only as correspondent, but also as a member of an aircraft crew

MG-Schießübung auf ein Seeziel. Nicht nur der winterlichen Kälte wegen wird die Fliegerkombination getragen, sondern um die Schüler frühzeitig an das Schießen in Fliegerausrüstung zu gewöhnen

Machine-gun shooting practice at a sea target. The air combination suit is worn not only as protection against the wintry cold, but also to accustom the pupil at an early stage to shooting in an airman's outfit

Bild oben: Alle Teile des Maschinengewehrs, aber insbesondere deren Zusammenwirken, müssen dem Schüler genau bekannt sein

Above: The pupil must be thoroughly familiar with every part of the machine-gun, but more especially with the way they work together

Aufnahmen
PK Wahner-Scherl (7), PK v. Pebal-Scherl (1)

Das große Ereignis. Zwei Lehrgangs-teilnehmer melden sich beim Lehrer zum ersten Schießen aus der Luft. Während des Fluges in der Bugkanzel liegend (unten), erhält der angehende Bordschütze die letzten Anweisungen

The great event. Two members of the training course report themselves to their instructor for the first firing practice from the air. Below: The future air gunner receives final instructions during flight, while lying in the front turret

Nicht mehr in einförmigen riesenhaften Kasernenbauten sind unsere Soldaten untergebracht,
sondern in schönen Einzelhäusern mit freiem Blick auf gepflegte Gartenanlagen

Our soldiers are no longer houses in gigantic blocks of barracks, but in handsome houses with
an open view on carefully tended gardens

So wohnen unsere Soldaten

How our soldiers are housed

Die Luftwaffe als Deutschlands jüngster Wehrmachtteil hat seit ihrer Begründung in zahlreichen Fliegerhorsten und Fliegerkasernen eine Fülle vorbildlicher Baukunst geschaffen, die in ihrer Verbindung von Schönheit und Zweckmäßigkeit wohltuend von den Kasernenanlagen früherer Zeiten absticht. Die Soldaten der deutschen Luftwaffe leben also in einer Umgebung, der schon rein äußerlich nichts mehr vom „Kaserniertsein" anhaftet

Since the creation of the Air Force as Germany's youngest Service, a series of model examples of architectural art have been erected in the form of numerous Air Force aeries and barracks which combine beauty and utility in a way that forms a most agreeable contrast to the barracks of former times. The soldiers of the German Air Force thus dwell in surroundings that even externally possess nothing more resembling confinement to barracks

Aufnahmen Dr. Wolf Strache (7)

Links: Eine Plastik von Professor Kolbe auf dem Gelände einer Fliegerkaserne. Selbstverständlich sollen Deutschlands Flieger, Funker und Kanoniere auch in unmittelbarer Nähe am Kunstschaffen unserer Zeit teilhaben

Left: A piece of sculpture by Professor Kolbe in the grounds of an Air Force barrack. Germany's pilots, wireless operators, and artillerymen naturally share in modern German art also in its immediate neighborhood

Wie anders nimmt sich dieses Haus einer kleinen Fliegerstadt bei Berlin gegenüber der „Ritterburgenpracht" früherer Kasernen aus

Right: A house of a small Air Force town near Berlin. What a contrast it presents to the splendor of former types of barracks with their imitation of a castle of romance!

Schmiedeeisernes Gitter vor dem Kasernengebäude eines Fliegerhorstes. Gerade die Eisenschmiedekunst bietet ebenso wie die Wandmalerei einem gesunden Soldatenhumor weiten Spielraum

Wrought iron railing in front of the barrack building of an aerie. Wrought iron resembles mural painting in that both arts afford wide scope for the exercise of healthy soldierly humor

Rechts: Schwimmbad in einem deutschen Fliegerhorst. Dem Soldaten der Luftwaffe stehen die modernsten Sportanlagen zur Verfügung, die fleißig benutzt werden, wie dieses Bild zeigt

Right: Swimming pool in a modern German Air Force aerie. Soldiers of the Air Force have the most modern sports equipment at disposal and it is much in use, as the illustration shows

Schöne Bauten der Deutschen Luftwaffe

Beautiful buildings of the German Air Force

Rechts: Im Unteroffizierspeiseraum eines Flakregiments. Auch hier ist durch die Kunst des Architekten ein ebenso zweckmäßiger wie anheimelnder Raum geschaffen worden

Right: The non-commissioned officers' mess of an anti-aircraft defense regiment. The art of the architect has here also created a room that is as homelike and comfortable as it is practical

Rechts: Im Waschraum eines Fliegerhorstes. Der Spruch an der Wand bringt die Kameraden morgens gleich in die richtige Stimmung

Right: The lavatory of an aerie. The legend on the wall puts the comrades in the right tune early in the morning

Der beste Ausgleich zu der rein militärischen Ausbildung ist sportliche Betätigung. Die Nachmittage und die Sonntage der künftigen Offiziere sind ausgefüllt mit Körperschulung der verschiedensten Art, Mutübungen, Boxen, Schwimmen, Segeln und dergleichen mehr

Sport and games form the best compensation for purely military training. The afternoons and Sundays of the aspirant officers are taken up with the most diversified forms of physical training, such as tests of courage, boxing, swimming, sailing, and many other branches

Zum Bilde Mitte oben: Unmittelbar aus dem Erlebnis des Fliegens heraus lernen die künftigen Offiziere im „Fliegenden Hörsaal" Taktik, Kartenlesen, Navigation und vieles andere mehr, was sie später gründlichst beherrschen müssen

Aufn. Dr. Strache (7)

Centre above: Immediately out of the experience of flying, the Cadets receive instruction in tactics, map reading, navigation, and many other subjects in the "Flying Classroom", of all of which they must command a thorough knowledge

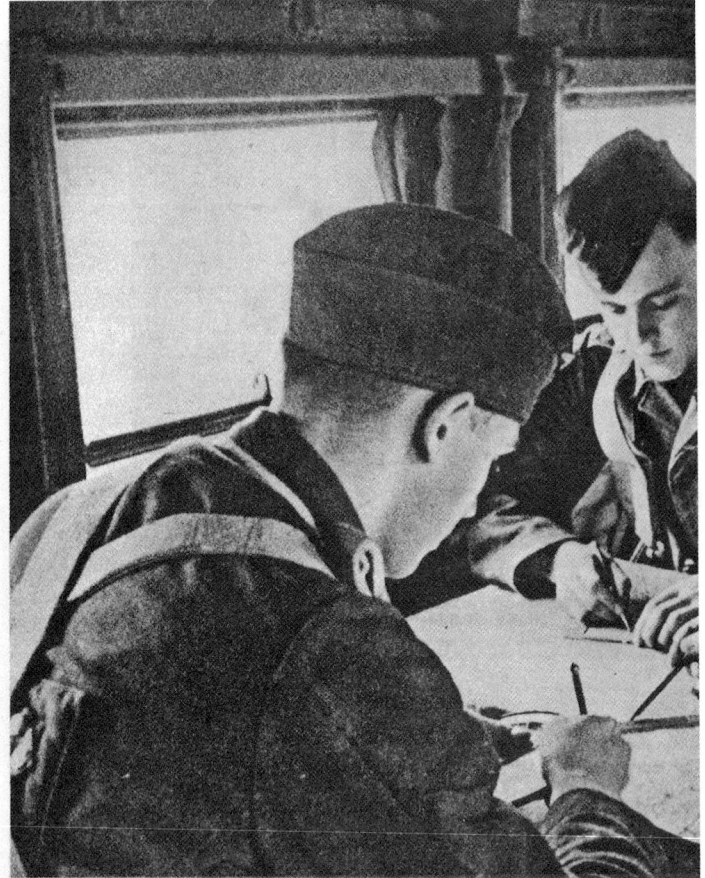

Fähnrich X wird

Fähnrich X obtains his commission

Unterricht an einem Blindfluggerät. Für die vielseitige Ausbildung ist in der Luftkriegsschule eine Fülle von Spezialapparaten und -geräten vorhanden

Learning the ins and outs of an instrument for blind flying. There is no lack of special equipment and apparatus for multifarious training in the Cadet College

Rechts: Eine Freizeitstunde im Richthofen-Zimmer der Luftkriegsschule

Right: Leisure hours in the Richthofen Room of the Cadet College. The walls are decorated with pictures of all the aces of the Great War

Wenn der Fähnrich (Bild links) die weitgesteckten Ziele seiner Laufbahn erreichen will, ist ernstes Studium selbstverständliche Notwendigkeit

Left: A Cadet must naturally diligently utilise also every spare moment for study, if he is to attain the far-flung goal of his career

Das Mittagessen nehmen die Fähnriche in fröhlicher Gemeinschaft im großen Speisesaal des Fähnrichheims ein. Daß sie nach dem straffen Dienst dem kräftigen Essen mit bestem Appetit zusprechen, braucht kaum besonders erwähnt zu werden

Aspirant officers lunch together in a merry community in the large dining hall of the Cadet's Home. It need hardly be said that they enjoy the nourishing meal with an excellent appetite after their heavy duty

Zum Bilde unten: Selbstverständlich muß der künftige Fliegeroffizier jedes Gerät, das irgendwie für die Fliegerei von Bedeutung ist, aus eigener Anschauung und Erprobung genau kennen. In unserem Bilde wird den Fähnrichen die Beschaffenheit einer Luftbildkamera erklärt

Below: The budding pilot must naturally be thoroughly familiar from his own experience and handling with every instrument of the least importance for flying. Our photo shows Cadets receiving instruction in the construction of an aerial camera

Offizier

Die Heranbildung des Offiziernachwuchses ist für die Luftwaffe eine der wichtigsten Aufgaben. Die Fahnenjunker der Fliegertruppe werden zunächst in ein Fliegerausbildungsregiment eingestellt. Dieser militärischen Grundausbildung folgen ein fliegerischer Lehrgang und die eigentliche Ausbildung zum Offizier auf einer Luftkriegsschule, von der unsere Bilder Ausschnitte zeigen. Hier legen die Fähnriche im Verlauf des Lehrganges eine Zwischenprüfung ab. Haben sie diese bestanden, so werden sie zum Oberfähnrich befördert. Den Abschluß der Luftkriegschulzeit bildet die Offizierprüfung mit anschließender Offizierwahl

One of the most important tasks of the Air Force is the training of a supply of young commissioned officers. The Fahnenjunker (aspirant officer) of the Fliegertruppe (Air Force) first enters an Air Force training regiment (Fliegerausbildungsregiment). The purely Service training received there is followed by flying instruction and the actual officer's training in an Air Force Military Academy (Luftkriegsschule), scenes from which are depicted in our photos. The Cadets (Fähnrich) have to pass an intermediate examination during this course, after which they are promoted to Oberfähnrich. The period of training at the Cadet College is closed by the examination for a commission, followed by the aspirant officer's election by officers

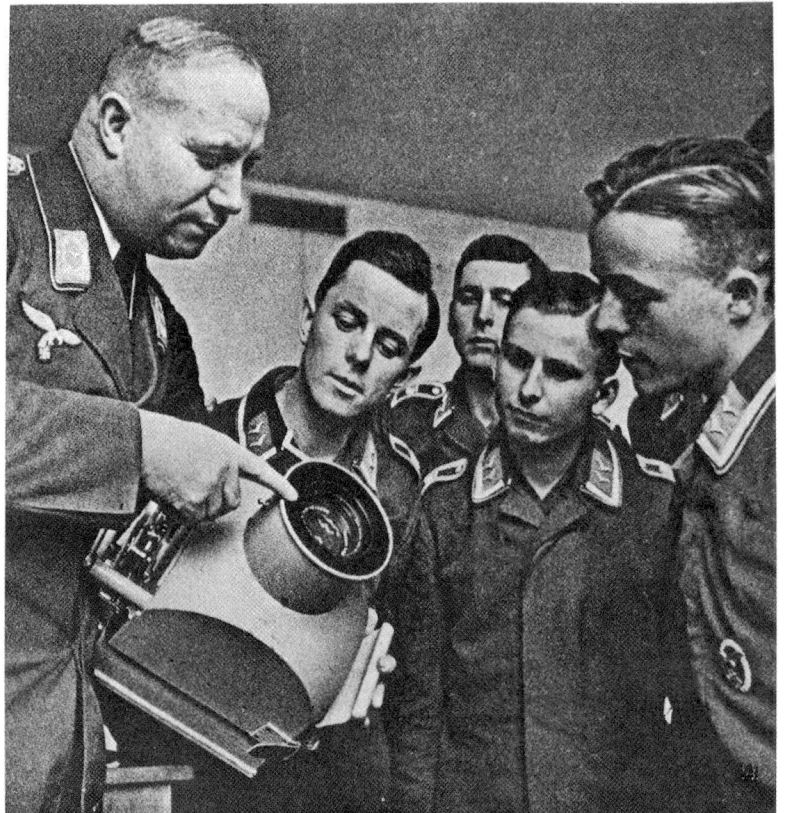

Fliegerheim PARIS

Airmen's Hostel in Paris

In quiet seclusion, behind the artistic wrought-iron railings of the Park Monceau in Paris, lies a baroque building, formerly a palace, which the General Commanding the Air Corps in Paris has had renovated and decorated by German firms according to the plans and under the supervision of the Sonderbaustab (Special Building Commission) of the German Air Corps. Our airmen in occupied territory, far from home, are here able to devote themselves to rest and recuperation after their trying duty with all its arduous requirements. Here is a spot where they can really feel themselves at home and a hostess in the person of an official of the German Red Cross provides a maternal note

Während des Mittagessens im Speisesaal des Fliegerheimes Paris, das Anfang des Jahres durch den General der Luftwaffe Paris eröffnet wurde

Lunchtime in the refectory of the Airmen's Hostel, Paris, opened at the beginning of the year by the General of the Air Corps, Paris

Rechts: Ein prächtiges schmiedeeisernes Tor bildet den Eingang zu einem ehemaligen Barockpalais, das zum Fliegerheim Paris umgestaltet wurde

Right: A splendid wrought-iron gate at the entrance to a former baroque palace, now converted into the Airmen's Hostel, Paris

Das Schreibzimmer, wie alle anderen Räume geschmackvoll und wohnlich eingerichtet

The writing room, like all the other rooms, has been tastefully and comfortably fitted up

94

Links: Einer der kultiviert und zweckmäßig eingerichteten Gesellschaftsräume, die den Fliegern zum Aufenthalt während der dienstfreien Stunden zur Verfügung stehen

Left: One of the well got-up and practically arranged public rooms at the disposal of our airmen off duty

Aufnahmen Luftwaffe

Rechts: Das Treppenhaus schmückt eine Bronzeplastik des Führerkopfes, die von der kunstvollen Schmiedearbeit des Treppengeländers umrahmt wird

Right: The staircase is ornamented by a bronze bust of the Führer, framed by the artistic wrought-iron balustrade

Pingpong-Tische im Spielzimmer, einem der beliebtesten Aufenthalträume des Fliegerheims

Ping-pong tables in the games room, one of the most popular day rooms in the Hostel

Rechts: Nach ein paar Stunden der Erholung und des kameradschaftlichen Beisammenseins geht's wieder zum Dienst

Right: Off to duty again after a few hours of recuperation among one's buddies

Unten: Kein Raum im ganzen Fliegerheim läßt leichter vergessen, daß man sich fern der Heimat im besetzten Gebiet befindet, wie dieser zünftig eingerichtete Bierkeller

Below: The beer cellar has been equipped —and stocked—by experts and there is not a room in the whole Hostel where a man can more easily forget that he's a long, long way from home

RAD

The Reich Labor Corps

The Auxiliary
of the German Air Corps

The war has left its imprint on the Reichs-arbeitsdienst (Reich Labor Corps) also. Its employment during the campaigns in Poland and France has led to intensified development of the forces latent in it, but without changing its innermost character. The formations of the Reich Labor Corps march together with the supply columns of the defense forces immediately in the rear of the fighting troops and often have to carry out their responsible tasks under hostile fire. Thus the lads of the shovel have become indispensable helpers for our Air Corps too. Laying out field airdromes and the work in connection therewith form their chief sphere of activity. The Führer has recently empha-sized the military importance of the work done by the Reich Labor Corps by the award of the First Class of the Military Service Cross to the Leader of the Corps Konstantin Hierl

Hier heißt es kräftig zufassen. Auch mittlere und leichte Bomben sind „schwere Brocken", wenn es gilt, sie zu Tausenden an die Liegeplätze der Maschinen zu schleppen, wo sie für den rollenden Einsatz der Luftwaffe bereit sind. Zum Bild unten: Männer des Spatens beim Ausheben eines Entwässerungsgrabens auf einem Flugplatz in Nordfrankreich

This job calls for plenty of muscle. Even light and medium-sized bombs are heavy enough when thousands of them have to be dragged to the places where the machines are lying ready for the continuous raids of our Air Corps. Below: The lads of the shovel at work digging a drain on an airdrome in the north of France

Unzählige Tonnen von Bomben, die täglich von unseren Kampffliegern über England abgeworfen werden, wurden von Arbeitsmännern auf den Einsatzflughäfen der Luftwaffe zu den Flugzeugen geschafft

Countless tons of bombs dropped every day by our bombers over England are transported by members of the Labor Corps to the planes on the airdromes of the Air Corps

96

Regelmäßig besucht der Reichs-arbeitsführer die im Kriegsein-satz stehenden Einheiten des RAD im besetzten Gebiet. Auf einem Feldflughafen läßt er sich an Hand einer Karte über den Fortgang der Arbeiten unterrichten

The Reichsarbeitsführer regularly visits the units of his Labor Corps at work in occupied territory. With the aid of a map, he is informing himself on an airdrome about the progress of the work

Aufn. Hans Retzlaff (7)

Bild unten: Arbeitsmänner als Boden-personal: Die schweren Kaliber wer-den mit dem Bombenheber, der gleichzeitig als Beförderungsmittel dient, zum Stapelplatz gefahren

Below: Men of the Labor Corps as ground personnel. The heavy bombs are transported to the place of storage by means of a bomb lifter

Hier wird eine „Splitterbox" gebaut — wie die Arbeitsmänner den durch Splitterschutzwände gebildeten Liegeplatz der Flugzeuge nennen. — Rechts: Bomben schweren Kalibers werden klar gemacht

They protect the machines against flying splinters, the places where they lie enclosed by low walls, known to the men of the Labor Corps as "splinter stalls". Right: Heavy bombs are being got ready

97

Weit wölbt sich der Himmel über einem Feldflugplatz in Sizilien, auf dem ein Musikzug der Luftwaffe zwischen dem Dröhnen der Motoren und dem Rattern der Transportwagen ein Unterhaltungskonzert gibt

The vault of the sky seems very high over a field airdrome in Sicily, where the band of the Air Corps is giving a concert between the roar of aero-engines and the clatter of motor lorries

The merry laugh of the clarinets mingles with the patriarchal boom of the trombine and the blare of the trumpets. The band of the Air Corps strikes up. One cannot of course be perpetually on the wing, there must be intervals between raids, which are spent by the air soldiers in rest and recuperation. Pleasant it is to stretch oneself out at ease in the warm southern sunshine and let one's thoughts fly homewards over land and sea where a loving heart is waiting. But it is a grand feeling when home melodies sound during these idle hours, when the rhythm of great times is heard in the masterly performance of a military band, when a song seems to fuse all sense of space and distance into a common world, where the palms of Sicily and the firs of the northern home, sweet-smelling meadows and glittering sands seem to blend into one

Luftwaffe spielt auf

A Band of the Air Corps Strikes up

Open air Concert under a Southern Sky

The bands of the German Air Corps have added the saxophone to the old familiar instruments of German military bands. Its lightly fluttering notes best characterize a sense of flating far from all earthly cares

Bild links: Die Musik, die unter freiem Himmel zündende Weisen spielt, ist für diese Flugzeug-besatzung ein brausender Auftakt zu neuem Kampf

Left: The band is playing rousing airs in the open air and provides this airplane crew with a thundering opening beat for fresh combat

Flug und Musik — beide haben ein überwältigendes Gefühl gemeinsam: Befreiung, Losgelöstsein, Triumph über die Alltäglichkeit. Sie alle, die da auf einem Feldflugplatz am Mittelmeer in losen Gruppen den Darbietungen der Musikkapelle lauschen, mögen von ähnlichen Gedanken beseelt sein

Flying and music have one overwhelming feeling in common: the sense of freedom, detachment, and triumph over the workaday world. All those listening there in small groups to the performance of a military band on a field airdrome on the Mediterranean may be animated by similar thoughts

Aufn. PK Petertil-Scherl (3), PK Raeder-Scherl (1), PK Onken-Scherl (1)

Auch diese fliegende Besatzung eines Kampfgeschwaders, die sich im Schutze „ihrer" He 111 recht wohlzufühlen scheint, ist ganz Ohr für die musikalische Abwechslung

The flying crew of a bomber group seem to be enjoying themselves in the protection of their He 111 and are giving the musical interlude every attentio

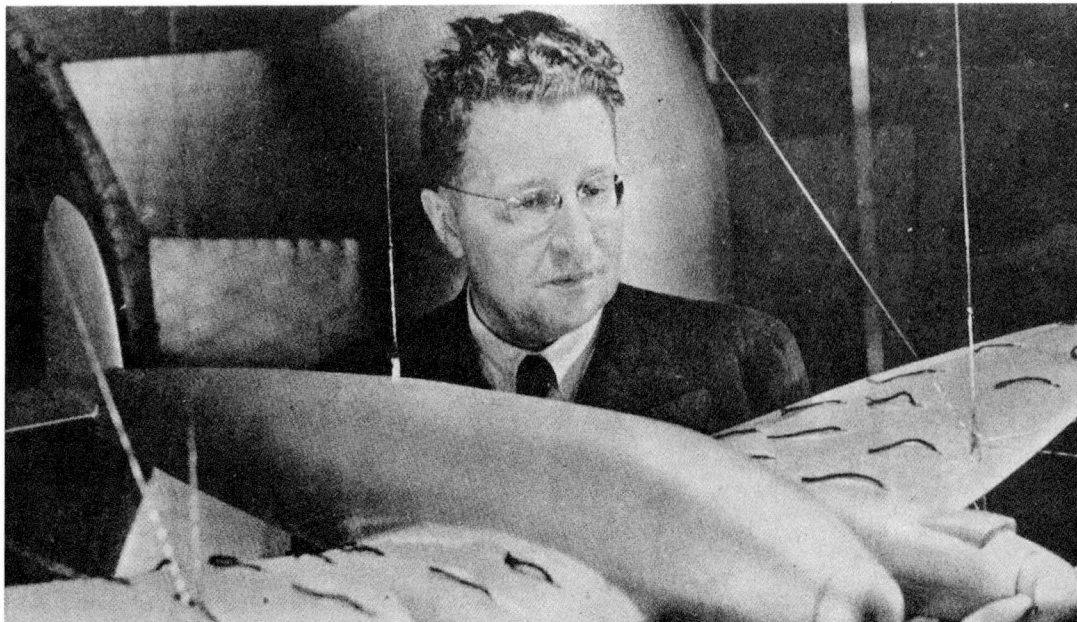

Nach durchgeführter Berechnung und Konstruktion des Kampfflugzeugs wird ein Modell der Zelle auf seine aerodynamischen Eigenschaften hin geprüft. Unser Bild zeigt den Entwurfskonstrukteur der He 111 bei der Prüfung eines Modells im Windkanal

After the necessary calculations have been completed and the design of the bomber settled upon, the aerodynamical properties of a model of the airframe are tested. Our photo shows the design engineer of the He 111 testing a model in the wind tunnel

Unten: Schweißen des Motorträgers. Einer Kraft von Tausenden von PS müssen die Schweißnähte widerstehen können, eine der zahllosen Voraussetzungen für die Sicherheit des Flugzeugs

Below: Welding the engine bearer. Welding seams must be able to withstand stresses of the order of several thousand horse-power. That is one of the countless points that go to ensure the safety of an airplane

Vom MODELL zum BOMBER

From the Model to the Finished Bomber

It is a big stretch from the drawing office or, more correctly, from the designer's brain, to the finished bomber and the final design is based upon years of development, which in turn rests upon the sum total of all the experience gained in aircraft construction. Thousands of busy hands are now set to work on large-scale series production according to methods that have been carefully planned down to the tiniest detail and finished machines roll uninterruptedly out of the assembly shops by day and by night

Beim Walzen der Motorhaube wird das Leichtmetallblech unablässig zwischen den glatten Walzen hin und hergezogen

The light-metal sheet for the engine cowling is continuously drawn backwards and forwards between the smooth rolls

Das Leichtmetallblech formt sich zur Motorhaube. Auf kleinen Hellingen wird die Form montiert und vernietet

The light-metal sheet is molded into an engine cowling, which is then mounted and riveted on small building cradles

Zum Bilde links: Aus diesem scheinbar sinnlosen, nur dem Techniker verständlichen Durcheinander von Streben entsteht bald die klargeformte Tragfläche der He 111

Left: The clearly molded wing of a He 111 soon arises out of this apparently meaningless confusion of struts, which only an engineer can pretend to understand

In der Montage, wo in zunehmendem Maße auch Frauen Verwendung finden, fügen sich die zahlreichen Einzelteile zum Ganzen. Unser Bild rechts gewährt einen Blick in den Kanzelzusammenbau

Women also are being employed to an increasing extent in the assembly bays, where numerous single parts are put together to form a whole. Right: A turret is being assembled

Aufnahmen:
PK Lysiak-Scherl (9)

Kabel und Instrumente werden in großen Rumpfbauwerkhallen eingebaut. Wie Räder eines Uhrwerkes greifen überall die Arbeitsprozesse ineinander

Cables and instruments are installed in large sheds where the fuselages are built. The various operations engage with the precision of clockwork

In der Endmontage (Bild rechts) erhält das Kampfflugzeug seine Motoren. Mit besonderer Präzision werden die Luftschrauben auf die Propellerwellen aufgesetzt

In the last assembly bay (right) the engines are installed in a bomber. The propellers are set with particular precision on the propeller shafts

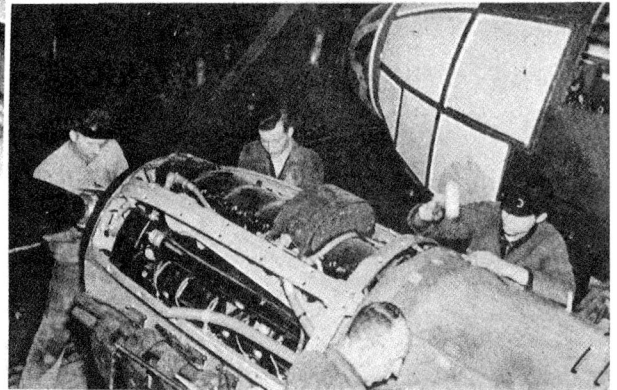

Der letzte Arbeitsgang vor der Fertigstellung. Überall — in und auf der Maschine — sind Männer in schwarzen Kitteln dabei, die letzte Hand anzulegen. In wenigen Minuten erfolgt das Signal zum Taktwechsel, und eine neue Kampfmaschine verläßt fix und fertig die Montagehalle

The last operation before completion. Men in black overalls are swarming everywhere in and on the machine, putting the finishing touches to it. The signal for change of beat will be hard in a few minutes and a new bomber will leave the assembly shop complete in every detail

Flak bastelt ihre Ziele

Der Unterstand einer Flakstellung (Bild links) ist zur Bastelwerkstatt geworden. Mit den einfachsten Mitteln hat man den engen Raum zweckentsprechend hergerichtet. Das Bett ist eine ideale Sitzgelegenheit, die Bank aber muß gleichzeitig als Hobelbank dienen

Left: The dugout has been turned into a workshop and the confined space has been suitably equipped with the help of very simple means. The bedstead provides an ideal seat, while the bench must do duty as carpenter's bench

Wohl manch einer hat sich schon Gedanken darüber gemacht, wie die Flakartillerie am weiten Himmelsraum ihr Ziel auffindet und wie sie vor allem nun feststellt, ob es sich um eigene oder feindliche Flugzeuge handelt. Wohl stehen den Beobachtungsposten die besten Ferngläser zur Verfügung. Aber unsere Flak schießt weit, und so müssen die Männer erkennen können, ob es sich um feindliche oder eigene Flugzeuge handelt. Da nun die bildlichen Wiedergaben zur Ausbildung nicht ausreichen, hat sich die Flak selbst geholfen und auf Grund vorliegender Abbildungen Modelle gebaut, die maßgerecht sind und genau mit den Originalen übereinstimmen

Zum Bilde links: Der Batteriemaler hat mit Feuereifer die Gelegenheit ergriffen, sein berufliches Können unter Beweis zu stellen

Left: The battery artist has seized the opportunity with red-hot enthusiasm to give proof of his professional skill

Anti-aircraft Gunners as Aero-Modellers

Many of us have doubtless wondered how the anti-aircraft defense is able to make out their objectives in the far depths of the sky and, more particularly, how the gunners can tell whether friendly or hostile aircraft are in view. The observation posts are of course equipped with the very best binoculars, but our anti-aircraft guns carry far, so that the crew must be able to recognize whether friendly or hostile aircraft are approaching. Since pictures are not sufficient for their training, the gunners have found a way out of the difficulty by building small models based on the photos and sketches available. These models are built to scale and tally in every detail with the originals

Der Bastlerchef der Batterie in seinem „Laboratorium". Das Handwerkszeug ist auch erst mit Mühe zusammengetragen worden

The chief modellist of the battery in his "laboratory". The tools have just been collected at great pains

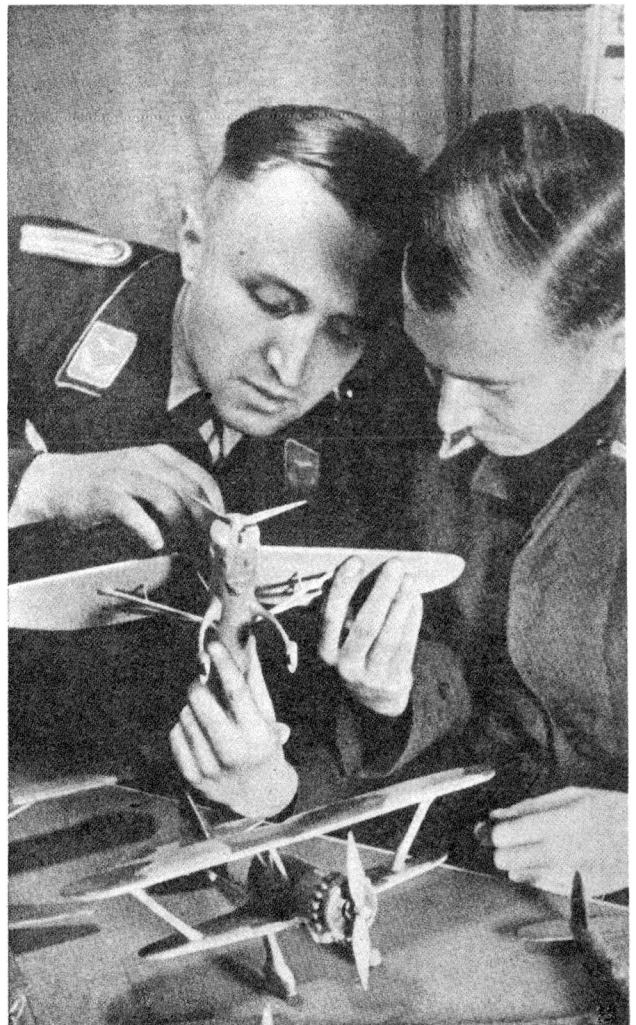

Hier entsteht das Großmodell eines Kampfabschnittes. „Landschaftsbaumeister" haben Berg und Tal geformt und auch Verteidigungswerke nicht vergessen

A large model of a battle sector is being constructed here. "Landscape architects" have moulded hill and dale, not omitting even the defense works

Zum Bilde rechts: Ein spannender Augenblick — die letzte Kontrolle. Wird das Modell vor den kritischen Augen des Herrn Leutnants bestehen?

Right: A dramatic moment—subjecting the model to a final scrutiny. Will it pass muster under the critical eye of the battery lieutenant?

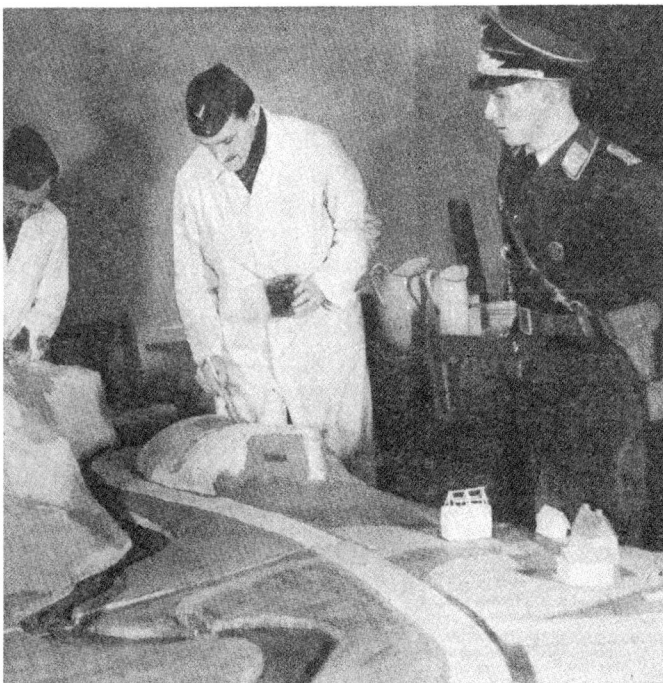

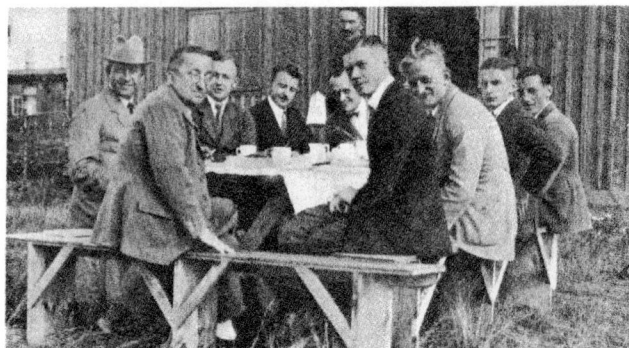

Ein seltenes Dokument aus den Anfangsjahren der Heinkel-Werke. Männer, die sich in der Geschichte der deutschen Luftfahrt einen Namen gemacht haben: Zweiter von rechts der jetzige Generalstabschef der Luftwaffe General der Flieger Jeschonnek; dritter von rechts General der Flieger Student; fünfter von rechts (sitzend) der Kanzler der Deutschen Akademie für Luftfahrtforschung Ministerialdirigent Baeumker; zweiter von links Dr. Heinkel

A rare document dating from the first years of the Heinkel-Werke, showing men who have made a name for themselves in the history of aviation in Germany. Second from the right, the present Chief of Staff of the Air Corps General der Flieger (Air Chief Marshal) Jeschonnek; third from the right, General der Flieger Student, fifth from the right (seated), the present chancellor of the Deutsche Akademie für Luftfahrtforschung (German Academy for Aviation Research) Ministerialdirigent Baeumker; second from the left, Dr. Heinkel

Dr. Heinkel überprüft mit einem seiner engsten Mitarbeiter am Modell der He 111 eine aerodynamische Vervollkommnung

Dr. Heinkel tries out an aerodynamical improvement with one of his closest co-workers on a model of the He 111

Dr. Heinkel läßt es sich nicht nehmen, eine praktische Neuerung mit einem Gefolgschaftsmitglied selbst durchzusprechen

It is a matter of course for Dr. Heinkel to discuss practical innovation with one of the staff

Flugzeugkonstrukteur in zwei Kriegen

Dr Heinkel's work for German aviation

Through the high glass walls on three sides of the large private office in the chief administration building an unimpeded view, as from a commander's bridge, is to be had of the landing ground and the buildings of the extensive factory. Seated opposite Dr. Heinkel in his sanctum, we feel at once that here is a man charged with energy and driving force, of whom there can be no doubt that he certainly did not gain his dominating position as aircraft designer simply by letting things slide. He watches his partner keenly as he talks with him, and there is no difficulty in recognizing that it is his aim to get down to brass tacks at once. Dr. Heinkel likes to call himself "a regular obstinate fellow", whereby he illuminates with a considerable dose of self-persiflage only one side of a really marvelous pertinacity and energy. Ernst Heinkel is descended from a family of handworkers domiciled for generations at Grunbach in the Rems Valley. The Suabian race seems to play a special rôle in the history of aviation in Germany, and if Wurttemberg has been justly termed the land of poets and thinkers, it may equally justifiably be called the land of pioneer aviators. The stubborn purposefulness characteristic of his race has never abandoned Dr. Heinkel throughout his eventful career. As far back as 1911, at a time when aviators were a laughing stock and regarded as being half crazy, the young student of engineering at the Stuttgart Technical College was engaged in the construction of a biplane, being unable to take any pleasure in the dry lecture routine. After laborious trials, he was finally able to induce his self-built plane to fly, but crashed over the Cannstatter Wasen by banking too steeply, with the result that he was found to be seriously injured when dragged out of the blazing debris. It is characteristic of Heinkel's unswerving tenacity of purpose that he did not abandon his plans even during the ensuing serious weeks of his stay in hospital. A wheel of the undercarriage that had been left over from the smash stood beside his bed while he lay delirious in a high fever, which may be regarded as symbolic of the defiant attitude embodied in the words "for all that!". Hardly able to hobble around with the aid of a stick, he applied himself with redoubled energy to his

Immer ist Dr. Heinkel bemüht, seine Flugzeuge technisch bis ins letzte durchzubilden und neue Typen zu entwickeln. Aufmerksam folgen die leitenden Männer des Werkes den Ausführungen ihres Chefs

It it always Dr. Heinkel's aim thoroughly to develop his aircraft down to the last detail and to design new types. The leading men of the factory follow attentively the remarks of the chief

Aufnahmen: Weltbild (4), Carl von Gerlach (2), Barbara Lüdecke (2), Heinkel-Archiv (2)

Im Kreise von luftfahrtbegeisterten Jungen ist Dr. Heinkel besonders gut gelaunt. Gern unterhält er sich mit den Lehrlingen seines Werkes, orientiert sich über ihre Ausbildung und läßt sich von ihren Wünschen und Zielen erzählen

Dr. Heinkel is in specially good humor among air-minded boys. He gladly chats with the apprentices of his factory, informs himself about their training, and gets them to confide their wishes and ambitions to him

Aircraft designer in two wars

Das weltbekannte Kampfflugzeug Heinkel He 111, das durch seine große Kampfkraft und Schnelligkeit an den Erfolgen des Luftkrieges hervorragenden Anteil hat

The world-famed Heinkel bor ber He 111, which has had a surpa sing share in the success of the German operations in the present air war owing to its great fighting power and its speed

constructional work. The young engineer first became known in the circles of aspiring aviation through his activities in the Albatros-Werke. But it was the Great War that brought the real test and Dr. Heinkel, as technical manager and chief designer of the Hansa-Brandenburgische Flugzeugwerke, contributed to no inconsiderable extent to the fact that Germany was soon able to overtake the start gained by the aero-engineers of the enemy powers. Military planes of every conceivable type, from the single-seater pursuit plane to the large bomber, have passed through his hands. Practically three fourths of all the types of aircraft employed from 1914 to 1918 in Austro-Hungary were designed by Dr. Heinkel.

The German naval pilots stationed at Zeebrügge during the Great War had at first a hard battle to fight against the Englisch pilots with their superior equipment and the present Führer of the NS-Fliegerkorps, General der Flieger (Air Chief Marshal) Christiansen, has himself once told of the enthusiasm with which they hailed the arrival of the new single-seater and two-seater pursuit planes from the Hansa-Brandenburgische Flugzeugwerke. From that day on, the superiority of the German air forces on the coast of Flanders was assured, and Kapitänleutnant (Senior Lieutenant) Christiansen, as he then was, has never forgotten to be grateful to Ernst Heinkel for the help received in the direst need.

Bad times came also for Dr. Heinkel following the collapse of Germany in 1918 and the dictated peace of Versailles. But we meet him already in 1920—moreover collaborating with the Pour-le-Mérite pilot Christiansen—as technical manager of an aircraft factory at Travemünde. But the self-willed designer longed to be free to unfold his powers within the more ambitious scope of a busin'ss of his own, with the result that the Heinkel-Flugzeugwerke were established at Warnemünde in 1922, forming the nucleus of the present world-renowned German aircraft firm. An aircraft designer in Germany met with resistance on all hands

Von seinem Arbeitszimmer in Rostock-Marienehe beobachtet Dr. Heinkel die Werkpiloten bei ihrer Arbeit. Stets liegt ein Fernglas bereit, um ihre Übungsflüge zu verfolgen

From his office at Rostock-Marienehe Dr. Heinkel watches his works pilots trying out new machines. A field-glass is always handy, so that he can follow their trial flights

Trotz unermüdlicher Arbeit für die deutsche Luftfahrt hat Dr. Heinkel noch Zeit, sich um seinen Gutsbetrieb zu kümmern. Er läßt sich von dem Inspektor und dem Gärtner Bericht erstatten

In spite of his untiring labors for German aviation, Dr. Heinkel still finds time to attend to his garden. He is listening to a report by the manager and gardener

Vater und Sohn beim gemeinsamen Spiel. Dr. Heinkel mit seinem Jungen Karl Ernst

Father and son at play. Dr. Heinkel with his boy Karl Ernst

during that period of impotence in foreign politics and the frittering away of energies by internecine struggles in domestic politics. Dr. Heinkel was very successful in establishing business relations with countries abroad, since the home market was unable to offer any sufficient scope for aircraft production, and his never slackening activity succeeded in developing a series of pioneering new designs, more particularly of hydroplanes, but also of land airplanes for the most diverse purposes, biplanes and monoplanes, commercial planes, and sport machines.

The name Heinkel had soon come to embody the conception of German skill and reliability far beyond the German frontiers. It has been the aim of Dr. Heinkel and his colleagues in the development of aircraft not so much to increase engine power, as rather to improve aerodynamic qualities. In that way the stream-'ined Heinkel airplanes took their origin. The great hit of the Heinkel-Werke, which have meanwhile removed to Marienehe near Rostock and considerably extended their plant, was the high-speed commercial plane Heinkel He 70, the so-called Heinkel "Blitz" (Lightning), which secured for itself a number of records in 1933.

Then, when the building-up of the Air Corps was being accomplished in Germany from 1935 on, after National-Socialism had taken over, Dr. Heinkel naturally again stood in the front rank of German aircraft designers. From the training plane to the world-famous bomber He 111, he has forged a weapon of the greatest striking power for the aspiring German defense forces. It was due to no small extent to these services that he was distinguished by award of the German National Prize for Art and Science in 1938.

It is difficult to find a common denominator for Heinkel's extraordinarily fruitful and multifarious activities. It is not so much his aim to carry a rigid theoretical principle into practical effect, but he rather considers it necessary to engage at a point where an important demand makes its appearance in the development of commercial or military aviation. He has consistently been very successful in that aim. The airplanes that have been taking their way into the world from the factory at Marienehe and also, for some years past, from the modern manufacturing plant at Oranienburg, bear the hall-mark of German reliability and inborn creative power. Just as the Heinkel planes proved satisfactory everywhere in air traffic and in flying sport before the present war, they have now stood the acid test of active service conditions under fire on every front.

Eine große Schafherde grast auf den weiträumigen Flächen der Heinkel - Flugzeugwerke. Die Tiere haben sich längst an die Flugzeuge gewöhnt

A large flock of sheep grazing on the extensive open spaces of the Heinkel-Flugzeugwerke. The animals have long since become accustomed to the machines

Modellflieger von heute-
Kampfflieger von morgen

Aircraft Modellers of Today Are the Bomber Pilots of Tomorrow

By Colonel von Bülow

The Reich Minister of Aviation and Commander-in-Chief of the Air Corps has instructed the Reichsjugendführer (Youth Leader) and the Korpsführer (Leader) of the National-Socialist Fliegerkorps (which might be termed an official organization for the promotion of aviation and is familiarly known in Germany as the NSFK) to arrange an air-service propaganda week from April 17 to 24, 1941. The management of the arrangements lies in the hands of the NS-Fliegerkorps in cooperation with the Hitler-Jugend (Hitler Youth). The propaganda of the week will be supported by lectures by wearers of the Ritterkreuz (the Knight's Cross to the Iron Cross), by the military bands of the Air Corps, and there will be numerous features. Colonel von Bülow, himself a veteran pilot of the Great War, who gained the distinction of the Ritterkreuz in the present war, has kindly placed the following article at the disposal of the "ADLER" in his position as Obergruppenführer and instructor to the NS-Fliegerkorps

During the few years of its reconstruction in every direction, Germany has indisputably acquired the foremost position in every branch of aviation. The enemies of Germany daily feel the weight of its superior fighting power, more particularly, the striking force of the German Air Corps. The chief guarantee that the leading position will not only be maintained, but even still further improved and extended by every means at command is the existence of an air-minded younger generation that comes up to all requirements in respect of numbers and quality. The National-Socialist Fliegerkorps places an organization at the disposal of German aviation and, more particularly, of the German air service which aims at placing the supply of such a reserve on a firm footing and regards that as being its supreme mission, on the lines already laid down in the Ordinance of April 17, 1937, by which the Führer ordered the establishment of the NSFK. The fulfilment of that mission has been steadily carried on during the four years that have since elapsed. That is chiefly the service of the man whom the Führer called to the head of the organization, Korpsführer General der Flieger (Air Chief Marshal) Fr. Christiansen, who was awarded the Pour le mérite Order during the Great War as the most successful airman of the naval air base Flanders I and has now been decorated by the Führer with the Kriegsverdienstkreuz First Class with Swords, as commanding officer of the forces in Holland. The men who wield the German sword in the sky today and aim their blows wherever the foe sets up opposition are men indeed. Men who know how to pair their actions with bravery and deliberation, who unite stubbornness with decision, relentless against themselves, and imbued with a strong esprit de corps. These characteristics, which mark out the typical soldier of the Air Corps, must also be tended in training the younger generation. The Modellfluggruppen (Model Flying Groups) of the Deutsches Jungvolk (German Youth) and moreover the Air Units of the Hitler Jugend must be dominated by the team spirit among airmen that became the germ cell of a new German aviation during a period of political downfall and the foundation for the reconstruction of the German Air Corps, and which today, as twenty-

five years ago, presents the most dependable guarantee for the successful employment of man and machine in the struggle with England. Aeronautical enthusiasm is inseparably connected with the esprit de corps of airmen, and with that enthusiasm further the struggle to make Germany air-minded, to create an appreciation of the necessity of aviation from the point of view of defense policy and the policy of the State, and to secure recognition of the fact that the position of Germany as a world power will be decided by the strength of its air force.

Although the first mission that the NS-Fliegerkorps has to fulfil within the framework of the preliminary training of the reserve for the air service entrusted to

Air Chief Marshal Fr. Christiansen

Korpsführer of the NS-Fliegerkorps, recently received from the hands of the Reich Marshal himself the Kriegsverdienstkreut First Class with Swords awarded to him by the Führer. He has rendered signal service to the German Air Corps by the training of the air-minded younger generation, creating the foundations of the immediate future Photo Scherl

it by the Führer is thus shown to be a task of educating the spirit of aviation, yet it cannot be separated from the actual task of training, because no model flying can be pursued for its own sake, no gliding flight could be prosecuted for the sake of flying alone. On the contrary, a boy should learn and make the experience that his personal performance finds its highest fulfilment in the performance of the community to which he belongs, thereby creating a team spirit that never dies. Model flying is of fundamental importance as part of

the preliminary aeronautical training, such as the younger generation experiences on the part of the NS-Fliegerkorps in very close cooperation with the Reichsjugendführer. The reason is that it presents the best possibility of directing the attention of the largest numbers of the very youngest boys of the Deutsches Jungvolk to aviation, bringing close to them the idea of German aviation, arousing genuine aeronautical enthusiasm in them, and providing them by suitable means with a theoretical knowledge and air mechanical skill that is not to be underestimated.

Training in model flying further makes it possible to make a first selection, which in turn is for the benefit of the following training in gliding flight. Thus the rising generation of the Air Corps grows up already in the model flight groups of the Deutsches Jungvolk. The aero-modellers of today become the bomber pilots of tomorrow and are the foundations of the immediate future. Gliding instruction is preceded by training as air mechanic, which familiarizes the boys in the aviation section of the Hitler Jugend with the tools and materials required for the building and maintenance of aircraft components and parts. First build, then fly! But mechanical training also fulfils a higher mission, by leading a boy to recognize the fact that the value of his own performance is decided by its importance for the performance of the whole building group. After the boy has acquired in shop service the requisite proficiency in air mechanical manipulations, he proceeds to the gliding locality, where he soon makes his first real gliding flight and gains his own aeronautical experience after a series of slides and hops. The chief importance of gliding training lies in the acquisition of aeronautical experience and therewith in the aeronautical enthusiasm, as here imparted to the lads. Apart from that, it is an excellent means of physical, mental, and character training and of self-training, which represent the embodiment of eagerness for service, readiness to make sacrifices, courage, and strength of mind. Finally, training in gliding further makes it possible to determine in a reliable way the especial aeronautical or air-mechanical talent of the boys and therewith to select those who come into consideration as being best adapted for service as pilot. To these important tasks of aeronautical and air-mechanical training must be added the special tasks of the training of radio operators and parachute attendants. It is due not least to the way in which the honorary instructors of the NS-Fliegerkorps have unreservedly devoted their services to the cause that all these important tasks are being in every respect fulfilled.

To these instructors we owe a special debt of gratitude. The present war has naturally greatly depleted their ranks. Many are out in the fighting line, many have earned high, even the highest distinctions, and many have sacrificed their lives to the struggle of the German nation for its destiny. Their sacrifice imposes a duty upon us, and everyone who can today be active as instructor in the workshops and on the airdromes of the NS-Fliegerkorps is aware of that duty. His work is done under the device:—The best reserve for the best air service in the world.

107

Da stehen sie in ihren Fliegeruniformen mit grünen Spiegeln auf dem Kragen und lassen die Flugzeuge starten oder nicht und beaufsichtigen das An- und Abrollen der Maschinen. So regeln sie den Verkehr zwischen Himmel und Erde. Die Männer vom Reichsluftaufsichtsdienst sind im besten Sinne des Wortes die Verkehrspolizisten des Luftraumes, die Hüter der Ordnung, die überhaupt erst die Durchführung eines geregelten Luftverkehrs auf den großen Flughäfen ermöglicht. Der Dienst auf dem Rollfeld ist nur ein Teil der Aufgaben. Die Überwachung des Luftraums erfordert genau soviel Sorgfalt wie die Beratung der Flugzeugführer über die verschiedenen Sperrgebiete und Gefahrenbezirke. Hier erweist sich der Angehörige des Reichsluftaufsichtsdienstes im besonderen Maße als Freund des Fliegers, indem er ihm nicht nur sagt, was verboten ist, sondern auch praktische Vorschläge für die Durchführung des geplanten Fluges macht

There they stand in their Air Force uniforms with green tabs and allow the machines to start—or not—and superintend their arrival and departure, regulating the traffic between the sky and the earth. The men of the Reich Air Police Service are traffic police of the air in the best sense of the term, the keepers of order, but for whom it would be impossible to ensure regular air traffic at the large air-ports. Their duty on the runway is only part of their work. Supervision of the air-space demands just as much care as advising pilots about the various prohibited zones and danger areas. The air police are in that respect the friends of the pilot to an unusual degree; for they can not only inform him of what is prohibited ground, but also give him useful practical hints for the intended journey

The "Traffic Cops" of the air

Auf dem Kommandoturm des Weltflughafens Berlin-Tempelhof. Von hier aus haben die Beamten der Reichsluftaufsicht einen unbehinderten Rundblick au den gesamten Flugbetrieb

On the traffic control tower of the international airport Berlin-Tempelhof, from which the air police have an uninterrupted view of the whole traffic of the airdrome

Zu den Pflichten der Reichsluftaufsicht gehört auch die sorgfältige Prüfung der Flugzeuge. Selbstverständlich darf keine Maschine starten, die nicht völlig in einwandfreiem Zustand ist

Among their duties is also the careful inspection of aircraft. Of course no machine is allowed to start unless it is in perfect trim

Von den Verkehrswächtern des Luftraums

Dieser hohe Turm, der wie ein Riesenthermometer aussieht, ist der weithin sichtbare Windgeschwindigkeitsanzeiger

Above: This tall tower, looking like a gigantic thermometer and visible at a great distance, is the wind velocity indicator

Der Beamte im Bilde rechts gibt einem zur Landung anschwebenden Flugzeug mit Leuchtkugeln Landeverbot

Right: A machine is just manœuvering to land, but the official is firing Very lights, forbidding it to do so

Ein Großflugzeug vom Baumuster Fw 200 „Condor" (Bild links) erhält das Zeichen für die Freigabe des Starts

Left: A large "Condor" airplane of the type Fw 200 is given start permission

Das ist der Motor JUMO 211, das Herz der Ju 87.
Ein Elektriker stellt gerade die Anschlüsse her

**This is the JUMO 211 engine, the soul of the Ju 87. An
electrician is just making the connections**

Hier

Das deutsche Sturzkampfflugzeug vom Baumuster „Ju 87" hat längst seine Feuertaufe bestanden und gehört zu den vom Feind am meisten gefürchteten Waffen unserer Wehrmacht. Schon im polnischen Feldzug haben die deutschen Stuka-Angriffe den Gegner in kürzester Zeit zerschmettert, in Norwegen haben unsere Sturzkampfflieger dem in unwegsamstem Gelände vorrückenden deutschen Heer immer wieder erfolgreiche Hilfe geleistet, und die englische Flotte hat die ver-

The German dive-bomber of the Ju 87 type has long since received its baptism of fire and is one of the weapons of our forces most dreaded by the enemy. The German dive-bomber raids smashed the adversary in a very short time in the campaign in Poland; our dive-bombers in Norway again and again successfully rendered assistance to the German army on its advance in the most impassable ground; the British fleet has felt the destructive

In der Fertigmontage. Noch werden Leitungen und Kabel verlegt und angeschlossen, und bald kann wieder ein Sturzkampfflugzeug „Ju 87", von den geschickten Händen tüchtiger Facharbeiter betreut, das Werk verlassen

**In the assembly shop. Leads and cables are still being laid and connected. Another Ju 87 dive-bomber can soon leave
the works tended by the skilled hands of capable experts**

Ein Stuka-Flügel geht seiner Vollendung entgegen.
Für die Herstellung eines Flugzeuges kommt nur
die Arbeit allererster Fachkräfte in Frage

**The wing of a dive-bomber is nearing completion. Only
specialists of the very front rank are engaged on the
construction of aircraft**

Links: Selbstverständlich entstehen auch die Stukas
in einem bis ins letzte durchorganisierten Serienbau

Left: Dive-bombers are of course built in series construction carefully organized down to the smallest detail

Aufsetzen der oberen Rumpfhälfte auf die Unterschale. So sehen wir die Gestalt des Stukas durch Zusammenarbeit vieler Hände sich vollenden

Setting the upper half of the fuselage on the lower shell. The form of the dive-bomber is thus seen nearing completion by the cooperation of many hands

Über dem Vordersitz wird die Bedachung angebracht, die aus einem außerordentlich widerstandsfähigen und splitterfreien Werkstoff besteht

The roof is attached above the front seat. It is composed of an extremely strong, non-splintering material

entstehen unsere Stukas

Where our dive-bombers are built

Aufnahmen JFM (8)

nichtende Gewalt deutscher Stuka-Bomben zu spüren bekommen. Auf den Schlachtfeldern des Westens haben die Sturzkampfflieger mit ihren machtvollen Schlägen wesentlich zu einer schnellen Entscheidung beigetragen. Der Sieg an den Fronten dieses Krieges ist nicht zuletzt auch den Männern zu verdanken, die in den Waffenschmieden des Großdeutschen Reiches unermüdlich auf ihrem Posten standen

force of German bombs dropped by the "Stukas". Dive-bomber pilots with their smashing blows have largely contributed to a speedy decision on the battlefields of the West. Victory on the fronts of this war is due in no small degree to those men also who are untiringly at work in the armories of the greater German Reich

Natürlich darf auch die „Kriegsbemalung" nicht fehlen. Zum Schluß werden Rumpf und Tragflächen mit dem Balkenkreuz versehen

Naturally, the war-paint must not be omitted. Fuselage and wings are finally provided with the beam cross

Rechts: So leicht wie ein Spielzeug hängt die fertige „Ju 87" an den Stahltrossen des Krans

Right: The finished Ju 87 hangs as lightly as a toy from the steel cables of the crane

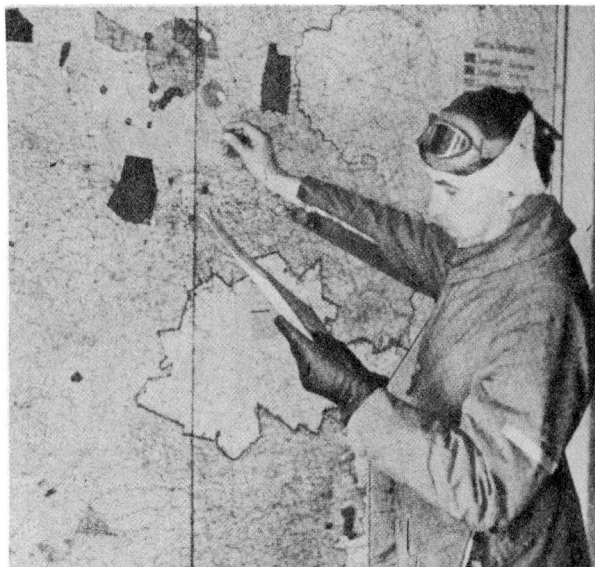

Vor jedem Start hat sich der Flugzeugführer nicht nur über die Wetterverhältnisse zu vergewissern, er muß auch genau die Sperrgebiete in seinem Flugbereich kennen. Die Karte der Luftaufsicht ist ihm ein zuverlässiger Ratgeber

Every pilot must not only inform himself to the weather cond'tions before he starts, but must also be thoroughly familiar with the prohibited zones in his flight area. The air police map gives him valuable advice

E in schnellbewegliches Funkfernsprechgerät, mit dem der Beamte der Startaufsicht sich jederzeit mit dem Kommandoturm, dem Hauptquartier des Flughafenbe riebes, in Verbindung setzen kann. Dieses Gerät ist fahrbar, weil sich je nach Windrichtun oft mehrmals am Tage der Startplatz ändert   *Aufnahmen Dr. Wolf Strache — 1939*

A mobile wireless telephone apparatus which enables the police supervising the starts to communicate at any moment with the traffic control tower and headquarters of the airport traffic. The equipment has to be portable, because it may have to shift its position several times a day, according to the direction of the wind

V on der Brücke des Kommandoturms beobachten die Beamten der Reichsluftaufsicht (unteres Bild) die Bewegungen der zur Landung hereinschwebenden und der sich zum Start begebenden Flugzeuge. Noch ist der Start nicht frei. Ein Druck auf den Knopf, das rote Blinklicht leuchtet auf, und der Beamte draußen am Startplatz muß so lange mit dem Flaggenzeichen zur Freigabe warten, bis ihm durch grünes Lichtzeichen der entsprechende Befehl erteilt worden ist

Below: The air police on the bridge of the traffic control tower watch the movements of the aircraft manoeuvering for a landing or just taking off. The starting signal has not yet been given; at the pressure of a button the red signal lamp flashes up and the official at the starting point must wait for a green light before flagging start permission

Der Kommandoturm
des Flughafens
The traffic control tower
of the air-port

Ein Flugzeugträger

The aircraft carrier is the latest type of ship to be placed in the service of the navies of the great maritime powers. The idea of allowing aircraft to take off from shipboard is about as old as aviation itself. It may be of interest to learn that the U.S. navy, and not the British navy, was the first to carry out trials with that aim in view and an American pilot was the first to take off from a warship. A few months later he even succeeded in the more difficult task of alighting on deck. The trials were carried out on the battle cruiser "Pennsylvania", which was fitted with a makeshift flying-off deck for the purpose. The Great War naturally lent an impetus to these efforts and it was of course mainly the belligerent powers that devoted their energies to the problem. But it was only shortly before the end of the war that the British navy succeeded in placing in commission the first aircraft carrier deserving of the name. It should be remarked at this point, in order to clear up a widespread misapprehension, that an aircraft carrier must be distinguished from an aircraft depot ship. To put it briefly, an aircraft carrier is a floating airdrome, from which, as a rule, only landplanes with wheel undercarriage take off, while an aircraft depot ship operates only seaplanes. Every capital ship and every cruiser is nowadays an aircraft depot ship, since they all carry one to four airplanes. They are accommodated in hangars on deck and are started by catapult, being hoisted on board again by cranes after alighting on the water.

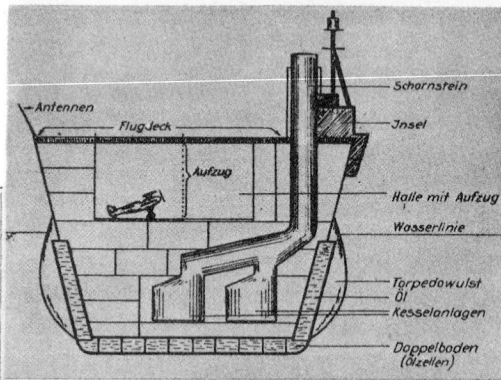

The air photo of an aircraft carrier shows the same ship represented in the drawing below. The diagrammatic section of an aircraft carrier shown at the left represents in bold outlines the same equipment

Photos and drawings, courtesy of the Archiv Luftfahrtministerium

An aircraft carrier

A further peculiarity is to be seen in this picture, which illustrates the gigantic size of the flying deck of a modern aircraft carrier. Brake hawsers (arrester gear) are stretched across the flying deck which hook into a device beneath the airplane as it alights and very considerably shorten the run-out, because a landing plane requires a longer run-out than the length of the deck

It was not until 1925 that Japan and England commissioned the first aircraft carriers really adapted for first-line service, and the other great powers followed suit. The first aircraft carriers, most of which are still on the active list, naturally do not possess the same fighting value as those constructed within the last few years, because they are really nothing but converted battleships or cruisers with all the drawbacks that such a solution by compromise brings with it. Although the mission of an aircraft carrier is mainly offensive, it may also be entrusted with defensive operations, in particular, with the repulse of enemy air raids on convoys or naval formations, as well as supplying pursuit plane escorts for the bomber formations of their own side. With the exception of heavy bombers, an aircraft carrier generally carries every type of war plane, including pursuit planes, general-purpose aircraft (simultaneously torpedo carriers), light bombers, and spotter-reconnaissance planes.

The most important part of an aircraft carrier is the flying deck, the floating airdrome. It may be constructed of wood or even of steel, as in the British aircraft carriers. The number of aircraft operated apiece varies between 40 and 80 and naturally depends on the size of the ship. Aircraft are moved by means of elevators from the hangar deck to the flying deck above. Several British aircraft carriers are further equipped with catapult launching gear from which the aircraft can be started when the flying deck is covered with too many planes, so as to be able to take off in more rapid succession. Aircraft carriers are fitted with a superstructure, known as the "island", at the side of the flying deck, which incorporates the navigating and control positions on an elevated bridge, as well as the funnel. The numerous anti-aircraft weapons for use against sea and air targets are also located there. Guns and multiple machine-guns are accommodated in annexes on the deck.

Ship planes are mostly designed so that the wings can fold back along the fuselage, in order to be able to accommodate as many as possible on board. They are serviced and refueled in the hangars beneath the flying deck. Fireproof curtains subdivide the hangars into small compartments and are intended to banish the fire hazard thereby involved, which is further enhanced by the storage and conveyance of the fuel. hangars beneath deck must produce large quantities that must not be underestimated.

An aircraft carrier operating 60 planes must also carry about 350 tons of gasoline. Such an accumulation of readily inflammable fuel makes an aircraft carrier very vulnerable to attack, whether from the air or from the sea. For that reason and also in view of the fact that an aircraft carrier must be able rapidly to change its position, modern vessels of that type have been given a very high speed of up to 30 knots. An aircraft carrier itself is not intended to fight, but should, as far as possible, evade attack by naval forces, more especially as it is not armed with heavy artillery, in spite of its size.

Wir fliegen bewaffnete Aufklärung

Noch ist es Zeit bis zum Start, aber das Küken der Besatzung, ein junger Gefreiter, macht sich bereits fertig. Er hat die Ruhe noch nicht so weg . . .

There is still time and to spare before the machine starts, but the greenhorn of the crew, a young leading aircraftman, is busy getting ready. He is not yet as hardboiled as . . .

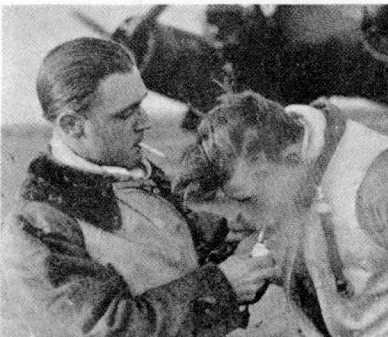

. . . wie seine älteren Kameraden, die sich gemächlich eine Zigarette bewilligen; denn zehn Minuten sind für „ausgewachsene Lufthasen" eine lange Zeit

. . . his older comrades, who have time for a cigarette. Ten minutes is a long spell for an old hand like them

Die Zielunterlagen in der Aktenmappe, steigen die Besatzungsmitglieder, mit Fallschirmen und Schwimmwesten ausgerüstet, in ihre Ju 88

The crew clamber into their Ju 88. They are equipped with parachutes and life jackets, and carry the data for their objective in their attaché cases

Ein Arm wird aus dem Kabinenfenster gestreckt. Das heißt in der kurzen Zeichensprache der Flieger: „Latten frei! Wir lassen die Motoren an!"

An arm is poked out of the window, meaning "Propeller free! We're starting the engines!"

Sekunden später rollt die Ju 88 zum Start. Gleichzeitig mit ihr ein anderer Fernaufklärer vom selben Baumuster

A few seconds later the Ju 88 taxies to the take-off, simultaneously with another long-distance scout plane of the same type

Aufn. PK Stempka-PBZ (11)
PK Martin-Scherl (1)

Noch einmal schauen Flugzeugführer und Beobachter zurück auf ihren Flughafen, der bereits winzig, wie ein Spielzeug, unter ihnen liegt

Pilot and observer look back once more at the airdrome, lying no bigger than a toy far below them

We fly with an armed reconnaissance plane

The camera accompanies a Ju88 on a flight over the enemy

No bomber formation ever starts on a raid before the objective has been reconnoitred as thoroughly as possible. The long-distance reconnaissance pilots are responsible for collecting these important data for a raid, so that they may be called the eyes of the Air Corps. But they can only be successful when they are able to transmit their reports with the utmost celerity, so that the chiefs of the horizontal and dive-bomber formations have their radio messages before them within a few minutes after the observer has made out his objective. Each bomber pilot has with him a dependable air-photograph map of his target, which his comrades of the long-distance scout service have brought back in their cameras. These scouts are thrown entirely upon their own resources during their flights, which often occupy many hours and cover hundreds of miles. Besides being protected by their armament, the planes also carry bombs, so that the scouts are in a position to carry out independent operations. These daring scouts have successfully carried out many a coup de main

Mehrere Stunden schon ist das Flugzeug, das unsere Kamera begleitet, über England. Jetzt liegt die Ju 88 auf Heimatkurs; da entdeckt der Beobachter tief unter sich Flugzeughallen, ein Rollfeld, Kampfmaschinen. Im Sturzflug geht es hinunter, die Bomben werden ausgelöst. Verheerend ist ihre Wirkung

The airplane that our camera is accompanying has been over England for several hours and is now homeward bound. Suddenly the observer spies hangars, a landing ground, and bombers far below. The pilot attacks in a nose dive and the bombs are released with devastating effect

117

Mit wütendem Flakfeuer beantworten die Engländer den kühnen Angriff. Gefährliche weiße Wölkchen — vorn — rechts, plötzlich eine heftige Erschütterung. Verdammt! Öl läuft aus dem rechten Motor. Also ein Treffer — aber die Männer der Ju 88 lassen sich dadurch nicht aus der Ruhe bringen. Der kranke Motor wird abgestellt. Seltsam genug sieht es aus, wie die Latte rechts vor ihnen unbeweglich im Raum steht

The British reply to the bold attack with a furious antiaircraft defense fire. Dangerous little white clouds appear in front and at the right. Suddenly a violent shock is felt. Oil begins to trickle from the right-hand engine, which has been hit. But the crew of the Ju 88 do not let that worry them and cut out the engine. It is a curious sensation to see the propeller at the right standing quite still

Sofort nach der Landung geht das Bodenpersonal an „seine" Maschine, um den Schaden genau zu besehen und traditionsgemäß die Treffer zu zählen. Für die Besatzung heißt es aber, Kombinationen 'runter und hin zum Kommandeur zur Meldung

Immediately after landing, the ground personnel give "their" machine a careful look over to note the damage done and count the hits in the traditional way, while the crew struggle out of their combination suits and hurry off to report to the commander

Trotz ausgefallenen Motors bringt der Flugzeugführer die Maschine gut zurück. Die Kameraden eilen ihnen entgegen. „So ein Ding war das, Jungs", ruft der Beobachter schon von weitem

The pilot brings the machine safely home, although one engine has fallen out. The observer cries to his comrades hurrying up that it was "as big as all that"

118

Eine Go 242 im Schlepp auf einem Transportflug nach der Ostfront

Auf dem Rückflug nimmt der Lastensegler Schwerverwundete mit, nachdem er auf dem Hinflug Motoren und Ersatzteile geladen hatte

Die Go 242 wird ausgewogen, damit festgestellt werden kann, ob das Ladegewicht auch im Schwerpunkt liegt. Charakteristisch ist die Bauart mit dem hochstehenden Doppel-Leitwerk, das die ungehinderte Heranführung der Transportgüter unmittelbar an die durch das Herabklappen des Hecks entstehende Laderampe gestattet

Der „Bauch" des Lastenseglers kann eine Unmenge von Material fassen. Hier wird ihm ein ganzes Ersatzteillager für Flugzeuge „einverleibt"

Rechts: Ein Kraftfahrzeug wird verladen, das bequem im Lastensegler Platz hat

GO 242

Ein neuer Lastensegler der deutschen Luftwaffe

Neben dem Lastensegler, über den im letzten Heft des ADLER ein Bildbericht veröffentlicht wurde, verfügt die deutsche Luftwaffe seit längerem noch in der Go 242 über ein größeres Flugzeug dieser Gattung, das sich ebenfalls überall im Fronteinsatz außerordentlich bewährt hat. Die besondere Bauform mit dem doppelten Leitwerk hat einen großen Laderaum mit einer weiten Ladeluke ermöglicht, die durch Abklappen des Hecks entsteht. Ein weiterer Vorteil für den Transport selbst größerer Lasten ist die niedrige Ladehöhe des dicht über dem Boden befindlichen Rumpfes

PK-Aufnahmen
Kriegsberichter Wanderer (PBZ)

Rechts: Am Führersitz der Go 242. Das eigenartige Staffelabzeichen des Schleppzugs leuchtet von der Bordwand

119

Eine Kette
Kampf-
flugzeuge vom
Baumuster
Heinkel He 111

A group of combat-
ant planes of the
Heinkel He III type

Gerüstet
für die
Luftwaffe

Die Aufgaben des NS-Fliegerkorps

Equipped for the Air Force

The Tasks of the NS Fliegerkorps

Die Auslese der deutschen Jugend auf den Dienst in der Luftwaffe vorzubereiten, ist die vornehmste Aufgabe des NS-Fliegerkorps, eine Aufgabe, deren Erfüllung zumal während des Krieges von entscheidender Bedeutung ist: ist doch ein tüchtiger fliegerischer Nachwuchs das wertvollste Unterpfand für die dauernde Erhaltung der Kampfkraft der deutschen Luftwaffe. Darüber hinaus ist es die Aufgabe des NS-Fliegerkorps, dem deutschen Luftfahrtgedanken die breiteste Basis zu schaffen, denn jeder Deutsche ist zum Träger deutscher Luftmachtpolitik, deutscher Weltmachtpolitik berufen

The chief mission of the NS Fliegerkorps (NS Aviation Corps) is the selection of German youth for service in the Air Force, a task of decisive importance more particularly at present during the War. For a rising generation of capable airmen is the most valuable guarantee that the fighting power of the German Air Force will be permanently maintained. The NS Fliegerkorps has the further mission of widely popularizing airmindedness, because every German is called upon to be the supporter of German air-power policy and German world-power policy

Aufnahmen NS-Fliegerkorps (Riehme)

Der Korpsführer des NS-Fliegerkorps, General der Flieger Friedrich Christiansen, sitzt heute noch selbst am Knüppel seiner Messerschmitt-,,Taifun'' und ist der Jugend ein leuchtendes Vorbild deutschen Fliegergeistes

General der Flieger (Air Vice Marshal) Friedrich Christiansen, still takes his seat at the joy-stick of his Messerschmitt "Taifun" and presents a brilliant example of German flying spirit to the youth of the country

Modellflug im NS-Fliegerkorps. Der Bau von Segelflugmodellen ist die erste Ausbildungsstufe des Flieger-Hitlerjungen. Hier wird ein Motorflugmodell gestartet

Model flying in the NS Fliegerkorps. The construction of model gliders is the first stage in the training of the Aviation Section of the Hitler Jugend. The illustration shows a power-driven model being started

Die erhabene Schönheit des Wolkenmeeres offenbart sich dem Segelflieger, der frei wie der Vogel durch die Lüfte fliegt (Bild oben)

Above: The sublime beauty of the ocean of clouds reveals itself to the glider pilot as he flies through the air free as a bird

Zum Bilde links: Flieger-Hitlerjungen erhalten Bordfunkerausbildung durch Funklehrer des NS-Fliegerkorps

Left: Lads belonging to the Aviation section of the Hitler Jugend (Flieger-Hitlerjungen) are being trained as board wireless operators by radio instructors of the NS Fliegerkorps

Rechts: Praktischer Unterricht am Motor auf einer Reichsschule für Motorflugsport des NS-Fliegerkorps. Viele begeisterte Flieger, die sich im NS-Fliegerkorps den Motorflugschein erworben haben, werden in jedem Jahre der Luftwaffe zugeführt

Right: Practical instruction at the engine in a Reich school of the NS Fliegerkorps for powered flight sport. Many enthusiastic airmen who have acquired the engine certifcate of the NS Fliegerkorps join the Air Force every year

In den Flugmodellbau-Werkstätten des NS-Fliegerkorps entstehen naturgetreue Nachbildungen
deutscher und feindlicher Kriegsflugzeuge, die als Anschauungsmaterial dienen

Scale models of Germany and enemy aircraft are built in the model aircraft workshops of the
NS Fliegerkorps. They serve as material for instruction

Rechts: Wehrsport im NS-Fliegerkorps. Das Kleinkaliberschießen spielt in der wehrsport-
lichen Ausbildung im NS-Fliegerkorps eine bedeutende Rolle

Right: Military sport in the NS Fliegerkorps. Small-bore shooting plays an important rôle in the
training of the NS Fliegerkorps in military sports

Geschütz feuerbereit!

Gun Ready to Fire!

Anti-aircraft defense has scored an unusual number of successes during the last few months, in which not only the heavy artillery, but also lighter weapons, chiefly rapid-firing machine guns of small calibre, have shared. These immediate calibre weapons do not shoot with the aid of fire as control apparatus, as do the heavy artillery, but each gun fires by itself according to independent aircraft ranging and automatic determination of the speed allowance by the aiming mechanism of the gun. The high firing speed of 200 shots a minute ensure an extremely high effect; at the very least, the enemy plane is immediately compelled to turn aside. A visit to such a battery during firing practice shows the extreme mobility of the heavy caterpillar vehicles and the rapidity and precision with which the crews manipulate their gun on the vehicle and train it on the target

Aufnahmen Weltbild (8)

Der E-Meßmann auf dem Bild links stellt die sich stets ändernde Entfernung des anfliegenden Feindes fest und gibt die gewonnenen Schußwerte laufend dem vor ihm postierten Geschütz weiter

The soldier at the left measures the constantly changing range of the approaching airplane and immedialety passes on the firing data to the gun in front of him

Das motorisierte Geschütz ist in die befohlene Richtung gebracht, der Rahmen mit den Geschossen wird eingesetzt. Um die Leichten Flakgeschütze besonders beweglich zu machen, sind sie auf Raupenfahrzeuge montiert

The motorized gun has been brought into the direction ordered and the frame with the ammunition is inserted. The light anti-aircraft guns are mounted on caterpillar vehicles, so as to be particularly mobile

„Geschütz geht dort, 100 Meter halbrechts in Stellung!" mag hier der Befehl des Leutnants für die Stellung des Leichten motorisierten Flakgeschützes lauten

The lieutenant orders the light motorized anti-aircraft gun to incline to the right and move to another position 100 yards off

Schnelligkeit in jeder Handlung und Bewegung ist bei der Flakartillerie alles. Im Bilde rechts wird eben dem Ladekanonier in Windeseile der Rahmen mit der Munition zugereicht, die für den Nahbeschuß bestimmt ist

Speed in every manipulation and every movement counts for everything in anti-aircraft defense. A frame with ammunition for short-range shooting is just being handed with lightning speed to the charger at the right

125

Mit angestrengter Aufmerksamkeit beobachtet der
Geschützführer den seinem Geschütz zugewiesenen
Abschnitt im Luftraum

**The gun captain watches with strained attention the
sector in the air space assigned to him**

Bild unten: Solche Fahnen zeichnen die Leichten Flakgeschütze mit
ihren Leuchtspurgeschossen bei einem nächtlichen Fliegerangriff in
den Himmel

**Below: These are the streamers drawn in the sky by the light anti-
aircraft guns with their tracer ammunition during a nocturnal raid**

Das Geschütz ist feuerbereit! Sekunden später schon jagen in kurzer Folge hinter-
einander ganze Feuerstöße aus dem langen schlanken Rohr der Leichten Flakartillerie

**The gunner is ready to fire and a few seconds later the long slender barrel of the light
anti-aircraft gun will be spewing bursts of fire in rapid succession**

Die Leichte Flakartillerie ist äußerst beweglich. Sie eröffnet ihr Feuer meist dann,
wenn das feindliche Flugzeug tiefer herunter kommt, um ein Ziel anfliegen zu können

**Light anti-aircraft guns are extremely mobile and mostly open fire as the hostile pilot
flies down to approach his target**

Drei Generationen deutscher Fliegerei

Der Weltkriegsflieger, der junge Offizier der neuen
deutschen Luftwaffe und zwei Jungen der Flieger-HJ
Aufn. Münchener Bildbericht (Buchecker)

Three Generations of German Aviation

The World War airman, the young officer of the
new German Air Force, and two lads of the Flieger-
Hitler-Jugend (Aviation Section of the Hitler Youth)

Ein Bordfunker bei der Durchgabe einer Meldung. Auf den japanischen Luftwaffenschulen werden die Soldaten für die verschiedenen Aufgaben der Flugzeugbesatzung ausgebildet

A radio operator is putting through a message. The soldiers are trained at the Japanese air service schools for the diverse duties of an aircraft crew

Japans Luftwaffe gerüstet

Wie Nippons Söhne zu Fliegern ausgebildet werden

The close cooperation of our Far-East partner of the Three-Power Pact is specially emphasized by the visit of Matsuoka, the Japanese Minister of Foreign Affairs, to the Axis Powers. Japan desires peace, but is standing at the order, and its military power is prepared for all eventualities that might threaten its just claims on existence. The Japanese air service has an important rôle assigned to it in the situation. That young service has long since attained maturity and has undergone its baptism of fire in the war with China. Any antagonist of Japan would have to reckon with it as an important factor of power. Japan naturally devotes special attention to the training of its air reserves and has for that purpose equipped a number of training schools for airmen on European lines. A continuous stream of young, well-trained airmen flows to the air service from these schools

Auch Jagdflieger werden hier ausgebildet. Ein Übungsjäger dreht nach erfolgtem Beschuß eines links unten sichtbaren Schleppsackes ab, um zu neuem Angriff anzusetzen

Pursuit pilots are trained here. A pilot practising has successfully shot down a towed-sleeve target (to be seen below at the left) and is banking to renew the attack

Wie hoch fliegt das Flugzeug? Jeder Soldat der japanischen Luftwaffe muß mit bloßem Auge ausreichend sicher die Flughöhe einer Maschine schätzen können

How high is the airplane flying? Every soldier of the Japanese air service must be able to estimate with the naked eye the approximate flying altitude of a plane

Japan's air service is prepared

How Nippon's sons are trained as airmen

Aufn. Japan-Foto-Library (7)

Hart gegen sich selbst, zäh, entschlossen und opferbereit, bringt der Japaner viele Voraussetzungen für den guten Fliegersoldaten mit

Severe to themselves, stubborn, decided, and ready to make sacrifices, the Japanese bring with them many of the qualities required for good air soldiers

Energiegeladene Ruhe spricht aus dem Gesicht dieses Fliegerschützen, dem man zutraut, daß er den mit scharfem Auge einmal erfaßten Gegner nicht mehr aus dem Visier läßt

The face of this air gunner tells of calm decision charged with energy. The antagonist that he has once seized over the sight with his keen eye will not readily evade him

Gute Mechaniker sind ebenso notwendig wie tüchtige Flugzeugführer. Angehende Bordmechaniker werden an einem Sternmotor in ihre künftigen Aufgaben eingeweiht

Good mechanics are as essential as skilful pilots. Mechanics in training are being initiated at a radial engine into their future tasks

Angetreten zum ersten Alleinflug. Vor Beendigung des Lehrgangs macht die Schülerbesatzung eine Reihe von selbständigen Flügen

Paraded for their first solo flight. Before passing out, each cadet crew has to make a number of solo flights

129

Das Gesicht des deutschen Zerstörers Fw 187. Deutlich ist die Anordnung des MGs zu beiden Seiten des Führersitzes zu erkennen

Front view of the Fw 187 destroyer, showing the arrangement of the machine-guns at each side of the pilot's seat

Der deutsche Zerstörer

Fw 187

The German Destroyer Fw 187

Bei der Fw 187 handelt es sich um einen Zerstörer der Focke-Wulf-Flugzeugwerke, der durch außerordentliche Schnelligkeit und Wendigkeit in Verbindung mit einer starken Bewaffnung eine Kampfkraft besitzt, die fast unwiderstehlich ist. Vielfach erprobt, ist dieser „schwere Jäger" ein wichtiges Glied der deutschen Luftwaffe geworden

The Fw 187 is a type of destroyer or heavy fighter plane built by the Focke-Wulf-Flugzeugwerke. Its extremely high speed and great manoeuverability in conjunction with its powerful armament give it a fighting power that makes it practically irresistible. It has repeatedly proved itself to be a valuable addition to the German Air Force

Aufnahmen Alex Stöcker (4)

Die Fw 187 im Rückenflug. Man sieht es der schnittigen Form dieses modernen Zerstörers an, daß er es an Schnelligkeit und Wendigkeit mit jedem Gegner aufnehmen kann

The Fw 87 flying upside-down. The clean-cut lines of this modern destroyer plane show that it can compete with any antagonist in speed and manoeuverability

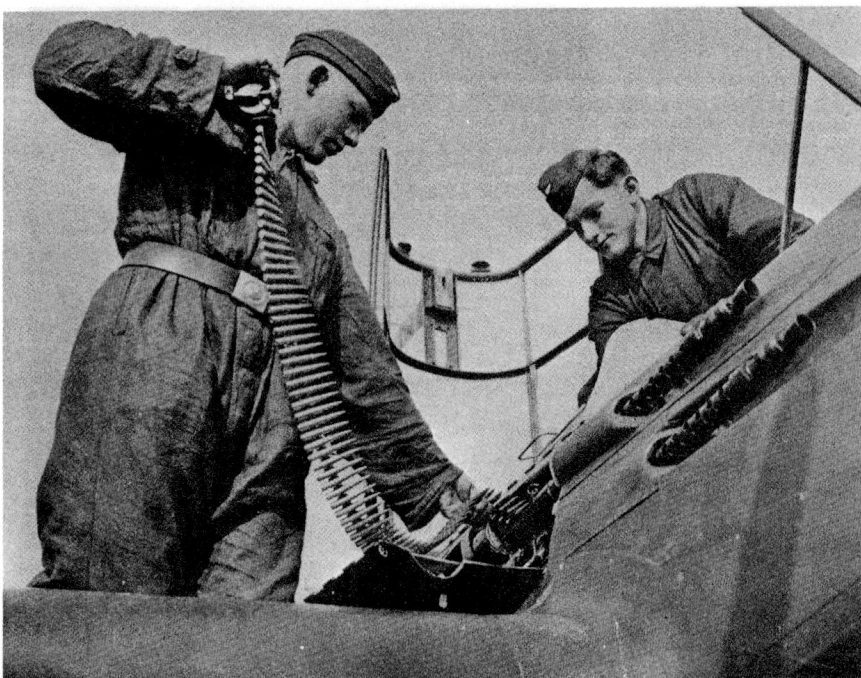

Ein Blick von oben läßt den schlanken Rumpf des Flugzeuges besonders eindringlich hervortreten

Viewed from above, the slim lines of the fuselage are emphasized in an impressive way

Links: Vorbereitung für den nächsten Start. Die Waffenwarte beim Einführen der Munitionsgurte in die MG-Trommeln

Left: Preparations for the next take-off; the armorer is fitting ammunition belts into the machine-gun drums

Max Schmeling
in REIH und GLIED

Ein großer Sportsmann wird Fallschirmjäger

A Famous Pugilist

Turns Parachutist

The great German pugilist, Max Schmeling, "our Max", as he is known to youthful admirers, volunteered for active service with the parachute troops. After a thorough course of training, he is now waiting orders for the front. Stringently disciplined in body and mind, courage and tenacity, paired with an unyielding determination, have marked his career as a pugilist from the start and the "good sport" has proved himself to be a good soldier too. Max is enthusiastic about his new rôle and all who known him are loud in their praises of an exemplary comrade who is always ready to help. Without losing a word, he places himself with all his energy and decision at disposal for a new commission that calls for the qualities of a real man. He is a fighter by nature and it was a matter of course for him to take his stand in the very front line in Greater Germany's struggle for existence. When questioned about his training as parachutist Max replied that the only thing to it was to avoid getting "cold feet" at the first time of baling out. "Once that stage has been got over, parachute jumping is a fine sport that only needs a little courage and good nerves. I enjoy it quite as much as boxing", he said. Max Schmeling has proved as a pugilist that he knows how to hit hard and he will be ready when the gong goes

Fallschirmjäger angetreten! Max Schmeling in Reih und Glied; er überragt seine Kameraden noch um Haupteslänge. — Unten: Fertigmachen zum Start! Max Schmeling hilft einem Kameraden beim Anlegen des Fallschirms

Parachutists fall in. Max Schmeling in the ranks; he is a good head taller than his comrades. Below: Making ready for the start. Max helps a comrade to adjust his parachute

Frühmorgens marschieren die Fallschirmjäger zur Übung. Das Transportflugzeug steht startbereit

Parachute troops march off to practice in the early morning. The transport plane is ready to take off

131

Rechts: Mit pendelnden Bewegungen schwebt der Fallschirmjäger Max Schmeling zur Erde

Right: Max Schmeling floats with swaying movements to earth

Ruhig trifft Max Schmeling die letzten Vorbereitungen ... Dann (Bild unten) besteigt er, den treuen Fallschirm auf dem Rücken, das Flugzeug, das ihn und seine Kameraden an den Absetzplatz bringen wird

Max Schmeling quietly makes his final preparations. Below: Then he climbs into the plane with his faithful parachute on his back to be carried with his comrades to the point of deplaning

Vor dem Absprung! Gebückt, energiegeladen, den Blick geradeaus auf den Gegner gerichtet, so haben wir „unseren Maxe" einst im Boxring gesehen. Jetzt gilt es einen anderen, größeren Einsatz

Before baling out. Crouching, charged with energy, his eye fixed right on his opponent—that is how we have seen Max in the ring. Now the purse is of a different kind and bigger

Der große Augenblick!. Max Schmeling „steigt aus". Gleich wird sich der Fallschirm öffnen

The great moment has arrived! Max bales out. The parachute will open in the next few seconds

Aufnahmen Bruno Waske (10)

Rechts: Kameradschaft nach dem Sprung. Einer hilft dem anderen beim Einrollen des Schirmes

Right: Comradeship after the descent. Mutual help in packing the parachute

Spaniens

Young Spain Learns to Fly

Das mit dem Zeichen der Falange geschmückte Tor der spanischen Flugzeugführerschule. Rechts: An einem der Flugzeuge, einem „Bücker Jungmeister", erklärt der Lehrer die Grundbegriffe des Motorfluges

The gate of the Spanish aviation school ornamented with the sign of the Falange. Right: The lecturer is explaining the ABC of powered flight by means of a Bücker-Jungmeister airplane

Nicht nur auf die fliegerische Ausbildung allein, sondern auch auf die körperliche Ertüchtigung wird in der spanischen Flugzeugführerschule großer Wert gelegt

Great importance is attached not only to training in aviation but also to physical training to keep the cadets thoroughly fit

Aufnahmen: ℋ-PK Roth

Rechts: Zur Kontrolle über die Maschinen und die ausgeführten Flüge wird jeder Start genau aufgezeichnet

Right: Each take-off is carefully recorded to keep tab on the machines and the flights carried out

Jugend lernt fliegen

Ein Bericht von der spanischen Flugzeugführerschule in Sevilla

The Spanish Aviation School at Seville

Following the example of other countries, the Spain of General Franco now gives the youth of the country an opportunity of testing their flying capabilities. An aviation school has been opened near Seville, where the rising generation receives a thorough grounding in aviation. Entrants are fed, housed, and clothed in the school and must be Spanish nationals of 18 to 22 years of age. If they prove satisfactory, they may be passed out to a permanent commission in the Spanish Air Force. A number of German sporting planes of the Bücker-Jungmeister type are available for training purposes

Er ist seiner Sache sicher. Die zukunftsfreudige Jugend lacht uns aus dem Gesicht dieses spanischen Flugschülers entgegen, der wenige Augenblicke später (links) zu seinem ersten Alleinflug startet

This boy is sure of himself. The joy of youth in the future to be seen in the face of this young Spaniard greets us laughingly. In a few minutes (left) he will be taking off on his first solo flight

Mit gespannter Erwartung verfolgen sie den ersten Alleinflug ihres Kameraden und lernen aus der Kritik des Lehrers

With tense expectation the cadets follow the first solo flight of one of their comrades and learn much from the criticism of their instructor

Startbereit stehen die Schulflugzeuge auf dem Rollfeld der Escuela de Pilotos bei Sevilla

The training planes are standing ready to take off from the landing ground of the Escuela de Pilotos near Seville

135

Wie ein urweltliches Ungeheuer zieht das sechsmotorige Großtransportflugzeug „Gigant" vom Baumuster Me 323 mit der riesigen Spannweite von 55 m seine Bahn Deutlich ist das Fahrwerk zu erkennen, das aus 10 Rädern besteht und so angelegt ist, daß es, ähnlich einem Raupenrollwerk, Bodenhindernisse überwinden kann. Eine besonders starke Bewaffnung sichert den Großtransporter vor überraschenden Feindangriffen. Trotz ihrer Größe kommt die Me 323 mit einer Besatzung von nur 5 Mann aus

DER «GIGANT»

Me 323, das größte
Landflugzeug der Welt

Als erste Zeitschrift veröffentlicht der ADLER Aufnahmen von dem seit einiger Zeit bei der deutschen Luftwaffe eingesetzten Großraumflugzeug Me 323, das wegen seiner riesigen Ausmaße den Beinamen „Gigant" erhalten hat. Deutsche Konstrukteure haben mit diesem sechsmotorigen Flugzeug der Messerschmitt-Werke, dem größten Landflugzeug der Welt, einen Transporter geschaffen, der sich bei den militärischen Operationen der jüngsten Vergangenheit über weite Strecken außerordentlich bewährt hat

Fast unerschöpflich ist der Bauch des „Gigant" mit seinem Laderaum von 100 cbm. Munition, Verpflegung, Mannschaften mit voller Ausrüstung bis zu 130 Köpfen, ja sogar Geschütze, Panzer und vollbeladene Lastkraftwagen nimmt der Rumpf auf (unten)

Startklar! Die sechs Motoren sind dröhnend angelaufen, gleich wird der „Gigant" über die Startbahn rollen und sich trotz seiner großen Belastung leicht in die Lüfte erheben

PK-Aufnahmen
Kriegsberichter Seeger (Atl)

Rechts: Behutsam werden die Verwundeten vom Sanitätspersonal aus der Me 323 herausgetragen. Ihre weit über dem Durchschnitt liegenden Ausmaße lassen auch Transporte bis zu 60 Verwundete in Betten ohne Schwierigkeiten zu

HEFT 5 / BERLIN, 11. MÄRZ 1941

Der **Adler**

USA
8 Cents

HERAUSGEGEBEN UNTER
MITWIRKUNG DES REICHS-
LUFTFAHRTMINISTERIUMS

Der Schöpfer der deutschen Luftwaffe, die am 1. März auf ein ruhm-
reiches sechsjähriges Bestehen zu-
rückblicken kann, im Gespräch mit
einem jungen Fliegeroffizier an der
Westfront   Aufn. PK Eitel Lange

The creator of the German Air Corps
in conversation with a young officer
of the Air Corps at the western front.
On March 1, 1941, the German Air
Corps can look back on a glorious
existence of six years

137

Zerstörer am südlichen Himmel

Über der sizilianischen Stadt Palermo zieht ein Messerschmitt-Zerstörer Me 110 seine Kreise

A Messerschmitt destroyer of the Me 110 type circles over Palermo, the Sicilian city

Auch unter südlich blauem Himmel wird der Fußdienst nicht vernachlässigt. Damit die alten Knochen nicht einrosten, wird ab und zu ein wenig exerziert

Drill is not neglected even under the blue of the southern skies. A little gentle exercise now and again keeps the old bones from getting rusty

Links: Auf einem Flugplatz in Süditalien. In der Luft scheint allerlei los zu sein. Im Hintergrund ein Messerschmitt - Zerstörer

Left: On an airdrome in the south of Italy. Something seems to be going on in the sky! A Messerschmitt destroyer can be seen in the background

Zum Bilde links: Zehn Flaschen Orangeade warten auf die zurückkommenden Zerstörerbesatzungen

Left: Ten bottles of orangeade are waiting on the return of the crews of the destroyers

Aufnahme Luftwaffe (3)
PK Heinemann (1)
PK Göricke (3)

Die vorzüglichen Sichtverhältnisse für die Besatzung veranschaulicht dieses im Innern der Kabine aufgenommene Bild (rechts)

Right: This exposure, which was made in the interior of the cabin, vividly demonstrates the excellent visibility conditions for the crew

Destroyers in the Southern sky

Me 110 in action over the Mediterranean

For quite some time past the roar of German aeroengines over the Mediterranean has been throbbing unpleasantly in British ears. Not only bombers of the German Air Corps are at work in the south of Italy, but also destroyer planes spread their wings over the Mediterranean. They are entrusted with special commissions

Die Aufnahme oben gibt ein deutliches Bild vom Aufbau des Zerstörers. Vorn sitzt der Flugzeugführer, mit dem Rücken zu ihm der Fliegerschütze, der Jagdfliegerangriffe von hinten abzuwehren hat. — Bild unten: Zerstörerrotte im Fluge. Die starken Motoren, verbunden mit einer großen Kraftstoffreserve, verleihen diesem Flugzeugmuster eine große Eindringungstiefe

The illustration above clearly shows the design of a destroyer. Pilot and gunner are seated back to back, the latter has to ward off attack by pursuit planes from the rear. Below: Destroyer formation on the wing. The powerful engines and a copious supply of fuel give this type of airplane a wide radius of action

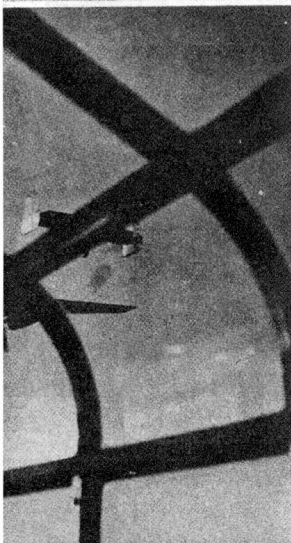

Bewaffnete Aufklärung im Seeraum „Planquadrat XY —“ Der Kommandant des Fernaufklärers bespricht den bevorstehenden Einsatz

"Armed reconnaissance over the sea in map square XY." The commandant of the long-range reconnaissance plane discusses the coming mission

Our present pictorial report tells of the close comradeship on board a naval long-distance reconnaissance plane. The lower row of photos shows the four members of the crew. None of the four knew anything about the others before the fateful days of September 1939. One was a mechanic in an aircraft factory, the second was a clerk in an office, the third was an engineman, and only the commandant had been on the active list. One came from Berlin, another from Hamburg, the third from Stuttgart, and the fourth from the Rhineland. The war threw, or rather welded them together. They form the crew of an airplane and are a homogeneous unit in life and death. From left to right:—The pilot, the commandant and observer, the radio operator and flight mechanic

Vier auf Leben und Tod

Unterdes lassen die Motorenwarte die Motoren anlaufen, während der
Funkwart eine letzte Überprüfung der Antennenanlage vornimmt

The engine mechanics meanwhile start the engines, while the radio
operator gives the antenna a final scrutiny

Bei einer gut eingespielten Besatzung ist die Einsatzbesprechung von lakonischer Kürze. Meist
genügt die Bekanntgabe des Auftrags, dann begibt sich die Besatzung zu ihrer Maschine

When every detail has been so well coordinated, the discussion of the mission can be brief. As
a rule, the crew go straight away to their machine, after having received their orders

Four men united in life and death

So sitzen Flugzeugführer (links) und Beobachter nebeneinander. Sie fliegen das bewährte Flugzeug Do 18, eine Weiterentwicklung der berühmten Dornier-Wale

Pilot (left) and observer sit side by side. They are flying the well-tried Do 18, a further development of the famous Dornier "Whale"

Aufn. A. Schultze (Mauritius)

Bild rechts: Für die Vier aber wird jede Rückkehr vom Feindflug neu zum Erlebnis. Das schnittige Flugboot im abendlichen Frieden über den Buchten der heimatlichen Gewässer

Right: Every return from a flight over the enemy is a new experience for the four. The flying boat with its graceful lines over the bays of the home waters in the peace of the evening

Bild links: Der Begriff „Bewaffnete Aufklärung" verbindet mit der Aufgabe des Aufklärers die Waffenwirkung. Neue Bomben für den nächsten Einsatz!

Left: The conception of "armed reconnaissance" unites the work of scouts with the action of weapons. A fresh load of bombs for the next mission

Das untere Bild zeigt die treue Freundin der Besatzung, „Bessie", den Bordhund

Below: "Bessie", the flying dog, the faithful friend of the crew

Kommt es zum Angriff auf feindliche Schiffseinheiten oder zum Luftkampf, bedient der Beobachter das MG

The observer has to serve the machine gun when attacking hostile ships or in air combat

Kaum ist der Fernaufklärer vom Feindflug zurück, schon wird aufgetankt

The machine is refueled immediately upon returning from a mission

142

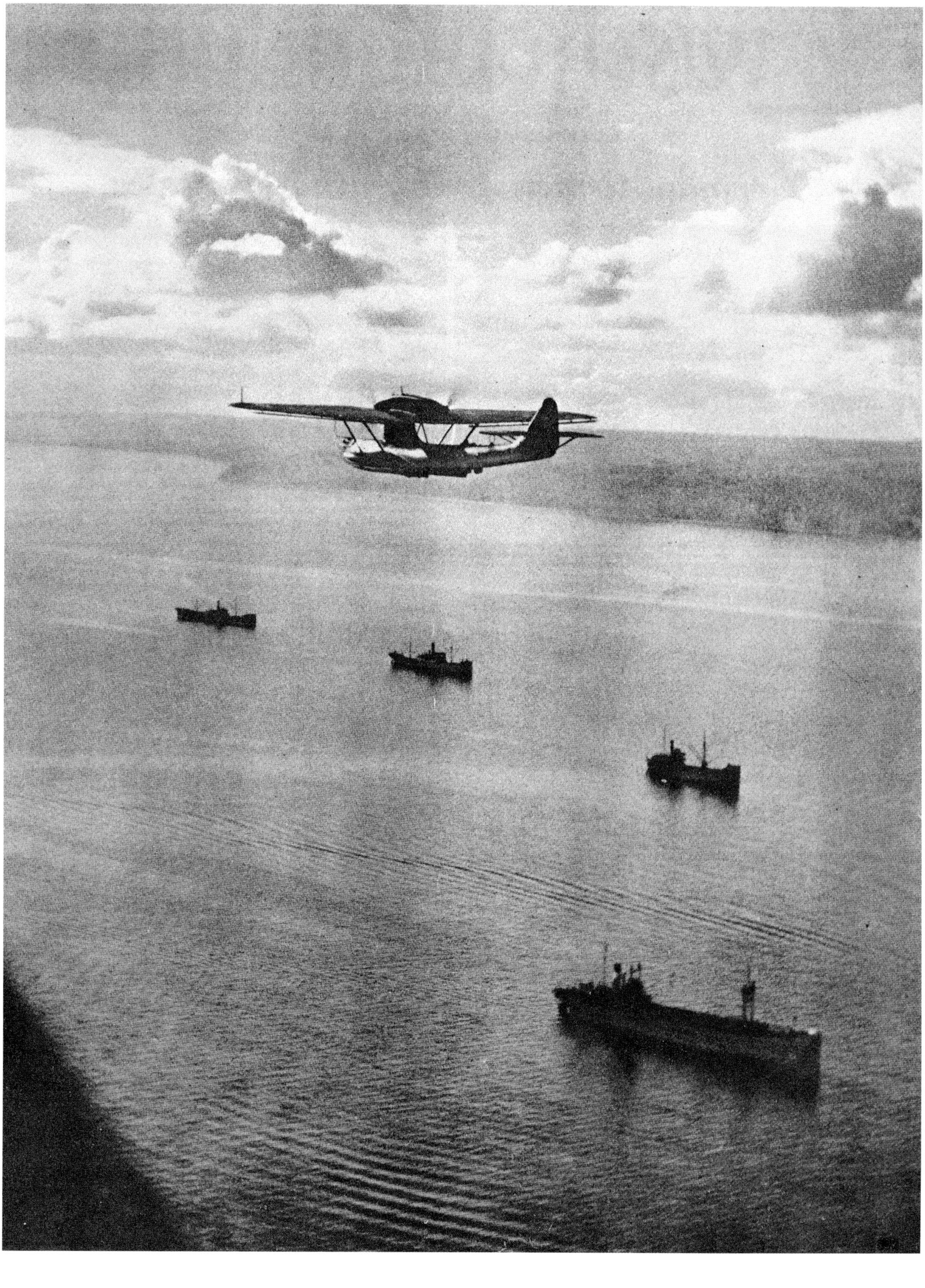

Zwischenlandung
in Libyen

Intermediate landing in Libya
German Airmen are fighting in Africa

Einer kleinen Festung gleicht das durch ein Drahtverhau geschützte Unterkunftgebäude eines italienischen Flughafens in Libyen, auf dem nach einem Feindeinsatz mehrere deutsche Zerstörer eine Zwischenlandung vorgenommen haben. Die Besatzungen werden vom Rollfeld mit dem Kraftwagen zur Unterkunft gebracht

Zwei Welten begegnen sich: Beduinen mit Reitkamelen, die heute wie vor Jahrhunderten das einzige Verkehrsmittel der Eingeborenen durch die Wüste darstellen, vor einem modernen Messerschmitt-Zerstörer mit einer deutschen Besatzung. Unten: Mit Interesse folgen die eingeborenen Soldaten den Erklärungen eines deutschen Fliegers

The quarters of an Italian airdrome in Libya with their wire entanglement protection resemble a small fortress. Several German destroyers made an intermediate landing here on their return from a raid. The crews are taken by car from the landing ground to the quarters

Two worlds meet. Bedouins with riding camels, even today as centuries ago their sole means of communication through the desert, standing in front of a German Messerschmitt destroyer with a German crew. Below: Native soldiers follow interestedly the explanations of a German airman

Aufnahmen: PK Rechenberg-Scherl (1), PK Kaiser - Welt-bild (4), PK Sturm-PBZ (2)

The keen sword of our Air Corps has vanquished the enemy wherever it struck. It dominates today a gigantic area stretching from the North Cape far over the continent of Europe out to the west over the Atlantic, and covers the whole of the Mediterranean. To that area has been added North Africa, where the power of our Air Corps is steadily making itself more and more intensively felt. German horizontal and dive bombers and pursuit planes have already undergone their baptism of fire in the Libyan desert also and have become a frequent and dreaded assailant on the British troops there

Ein einsames Zeltlager inmitten der sich fast endlos dehnenden Wüste. Nach erfolgreichem Einsatz in Nordafrika suchen unsere Flugzeugbesatzungen häufig dieses Lager bei ihren Zwischenlandungen auf. Unten: Ein deutscher Fliegeroffizier beim Fertigmachen zum Start. In wenigen Minuten wird ihn seine Maschine zu neuem Kampf dem Feind entgegentragen

A strange tent encampment in the endless desert. After a successful raid in North Africa, our airplane crews fr quently visit this camp on an intermediate landing. Below: A German air officer preparing to take off. In a few minutes his machine will be carrying him to a fresh struggle with the foe

„Schönheitspflege" unter afrikanischem Himmel. Unten: Beduinen, die täglichen Besucher eines Stukaverbandes

"Beauty culture" under the African sky. Below: Bedouins, daily visitors to a dive-bomber formation

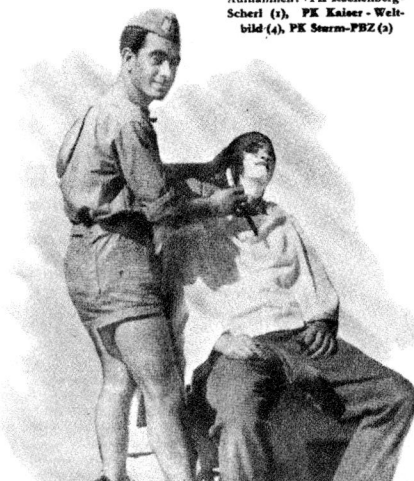

„Flügel des Krieges"

"The Wings of War" — Italy's War in the Air

Italiens Luftwaffe im Kampf

Der Kriegseintritt Italiens hat die Waage des Sieges zugunsten der befreundeten Achsenmächte tief gesenkt. Wo er bisher unbehelligt seine verbrecherischen Unternehmungen starten konnte, im Mittelmeer, da treffen den Briten jetzt, wo er auch auftreten mag, die vernichtenden Schläge der siegesgewohnten Luftmacht des Italienischen Imperiums

Italy's entrance into the war has weighted the scales of victory heavily in favour of the Axis partners. In the Mediterranean, where Britain was hitherto able to set out unhampered on her criminal undertakings, she now falls a prey to the crushing blows dealt out by the superb Air Force of the Italian Empire

Einsitzige Jagdflugzeuge vom Baumuster Fiat CR 32 im Verbandsflug, in dem die italienische Luftwaffe es zu Höchst-

Single-seater Fiat pursuit planes of the type CR 32 flying in formation, in the art of which the Italian Air Force excels and has reached

Luftmarschall Balbo am Steuer seines Flugzeuges über Libyen, das sich unter seiner Hand in wenigen Jahren zu hoher Blüte entwickelte. Italo Balbo, einer der ältesten Mitkämpfer des Duce und der Organisator der faschistischen Luftwaffe, fand vor kurzem im Luftkampf mit Engländern den Heldentod

Air-Marshal Balbo steers his machine himself over the Italian province of Libya, which has developed enormously in a few years under his ægis and is now in a most flourishing condition. Italo Balbo, one of the oldest comrades of the Duce and organiser of the Fascist Air Force, was recently killed on active service in an air combat with British airmen

Bombenübernahme bei einem dreimotorigen Kampfflugzeug der italienischen Luftwaffe kurz vor dem Angriff auf einen englischen Stützpunkt in Afrika. Die schweren Bomber

A three-engined bomber of the Italian Air Force is loading bombs just before a raid on an English base in Africa. Uniting flying

leistungen gebracht hat. Wie eine eindringliche Verkörperung der Luftmacht des siegreichen Italiens wirkt dieses Bild

a wonderful pitch of skill and dexterity. This picture arouses an impressive feeling of the embodiment of the Italian Air Force

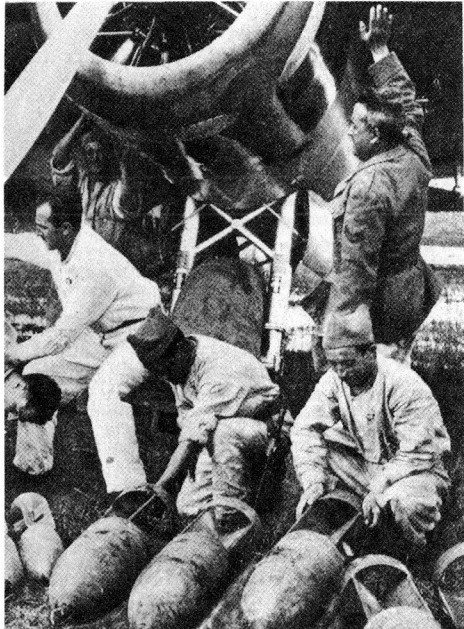

Italiens sind in ihrer Verbindung von fliegerischer Tüchtigkeit und großer Tragfähigkeit eine ebenso wirkungsvolle wie gefürchtete Waffe der faschistischen Luftmacht

capacity and great carrying power, these Italian bombers form an arm of the Fascist air power which is as effective as it is dreaded

General Pricolo, der Generalstabschef der italienischen Luftwaffe, nimmt auf einem Einsatzhafen die Meldung eines Offiziers entgegen, der kurz danach zum Feindflug gegen Malta, den britischen Stützpunkt im Mittelmeer, startet   Aufn. Luftfahrtministerium Rom (2), Schwabik (1), Witzleben (1)

An officer, just about to start on an air raid on Malta, the British naval base in the Mediterranean, reports for duty to General Pricolo, Chief of Staff of the Italian Air Force, at an Italian aerodrome

147

Mit Bomben
dem Briten

The German Air Corps bears a great share in the hard struggle that Germans and Italians in faithful comradeship in arms are waging in the east of Cyrenaica on the Egyptian frontier against the common foe. The Air Corps formations in North Africa are at work practically every day with the mission of hitting the British wherever encountered. Horizontal and dive bombers inflict their blows on British ships in the Mediterranean and on the fortified supporting positions of the British. Our pages show pictures of these attacks

Links oben: Im Tiefflug braust ein Messerschmitt-Zerstörer Me 110 über die Libysche Wüste. Das Flugzeug hat mit mehreren anderen die Aufgabe, an einem bestimmten Treffpunkt den Schutz einer Kampfgruppe gegen feindliche Jäger zu übernehmen. Links im Hintergrund ein arabisches Gehöft

Left above: A Me 110 destroyer is thundering at a low altitude over the Libyan desert. With a number of other machines, the plane has the mission of meeting a bomber wing at a certain point and protecting them against hostile pursuit planes. An Arab farm can be seen in the background and beneath the airplane runs the road, which consists of the tracks of the motor trucks and caterpillar tractors that have left their mark in the sand

Trostlose Wüste, Sanddünen, die ein kärglicher Strauchwuchs kaum unterbricht, breiten sich unter den deutschen Flugzeugen aus, deren Schatten ihnen vorauswandert

German airplanes cast their shadows over a dreary expanse of desert and sand dunes, hardly interrupted by scanty brush and scrub

Dankbar begrüßen es die Flieger, wenn das ewige Einerlei der Wüste durch eine Palmenoase unterbrochen wird. Im Tiefflug rasen sie über die gefiederten Bäume hinweg

The airmen are grateful when an oasis of palms interrupts the monotony of the desert, and thunder at a low altitude over the feathery crests of the trees

Die Küste des Mittelmeeres kommt in Sicht und, unmittelbar am Ufer gelegen, eine schwere Flakbatterie der italienischen Waffengefährten. In ihren von gemauerten Steinwällen umgebenen Ständen drei festeingebaute Geschütze, dazu (links oben) das Kommandogerät. Die im Tiefflug gemachte Aufnahme läßt jede Einzelheit der Batterie hervortreten. Bei jedem Geschütz liegen, auf der Umwallung sauber aufgereiht, die acht Stahlhelme der Bedienung

The coast of the Mediterranean comes into view. A heavy Italian anti-aircraft battery is located directly on the shore with three gun emplacements surrounded by walls of masonry; the position indicator can be seen above at the left. The exposure was made at a low altitude and reveals every detail of the battery. The eight steel helmets of the crew have been neatly laid out on the wall beside each gun

und MGs
auf den Fersen

On the Heels of the British with Bombs

and Machine Guns

In den Schutz des deutschen Feldflugplatzes teilen sich kameradschaftlich deutsche und italienische Abwehr. Ein Bersagliere am schweren Fliegerabwehr-MG. Malerisch schmückt den Tropenhelm das Kennzeichen seiner Waffe, der Hahnenfederbusch

German and Italian anti-aircraft defense share in the protection of the German field airdrome. A Bersagliere can be seen beside the heavy anti-aircraft machine gun, his tropical helmet picturesquely adorned by the tuft of cock's feathers

Schwarze Schwarzen

The Black Gang in

Ground Personnel of the German Air Corps at Work on the Libyan Front

Der Bordmechaniker hilft seinen Kameraden vom Bodenpersonal. Eine Ju 88 ist vom Feindflug zurückgekehrt. Sofort machen sich die „Schwarzen Jungens" daran, sie wieder aufzutanken und zu neuem Einsatz bereitzumachen

The air mechanic helps the ground personnel. A Ju 88 has returned from a raid and the mechanics immediately start to refuel it and service it for the next raid

Aufnahmen: PK Boecker (Scherl)

Deutsche Luftwaffensoldaten im Tropenhelm. Auf dem Einsatzflughafen in Libyen, den unser Bildbericht schildert, herrscht Hochbetrieb. Eben fällt ein vom Feindflug zurückgekommener Verband ein, und schon warten große Mengen neuen Brennstoffs auf ihre Verwendung

German soldiers of the air service in tropical helmet. A busy hour on an airdrome in Libya. A formation has just returned from a raid and large quantities of fresh power fuel are already waiting for them

Eine Transportmaschine ist auf einem Einsatzflughafen in Nordafrika gelandet. Kaum stehen die Motoren, da öffnen sich auch schon die Luken, und das Ausladen beginnt

A transporter has landed at an airdrome in North Africa. Hardly have the engines stopped, before the hatches are opened and unloading begins

Flugzeuge, Brennstofffässer und Bomben aller Kaliber in endlosen Reihen: das ist die Umgebung, in der unsere Männer vom Bodenpersonal ihre schwere Arbeit verrichten

Endless rows of aircraft, gasoline drums, and bombs of every calibre; such are the surroundings where the ground personnel do their heavy work

Jungens im Erdteil

the Dark Continent

Wherever German horizontal and dive bombers are engaged, there is no need to look far for their auxiliaries, who always follow hard on their heels. Thus the "black gang", as they are affectionately termed on account of their black overalls, have arrived in Libya with the air formations. Here, however, they mostly wear light suits and tropical helmets, instead of the airman's service cap, as being better suited to the climate. The ground personnel steadfastly look after the weapons and instruments of their comrades, in particular, the machines themselves, which must always be kept ready for action. The loading of the bombers with bombs, the unloading of material from the transport planes, and the refueling of the machines when they return from a raid make a full day's work here also in the dark continent

Sandsturm auf dem Flughafen. Glücklicherweise dauert er nur wenige Sekunden, denn es ist der Propellerwind eines startenden Flugzeuges, der den Wüstensand aufwirbelt

Sandstorm on the airdrome. Fortunately it lasts only for a few seconds, being caused by the propeller of a machine just taking off, which whirls about the sand of the desert

Rechts: Zwischen Zelten und Kraftstoffbehältern entwickelt sich in der Freizeit ein zünftiges Lagerleben

Right: During duty off, the customary camp life develops between tents and power fuel containers

151

Drehscheibe zwischen 3 Kontinenten

A Turntable between Three Continents

WILL THE NEAR EAST
BE THE SCENE OF MOMENTOUS?

BY Dr. W. SCHEUNEMANN

Located at the crossroads of the ancient world where the three continents of Europe, Asia, and Africa intersect, the near east is nowadays of great political and strategic importance, as it has ever been in the course of its stormy history, in conformity with the rôle assigned to it by nature. Numerous wars have been fought for the domination of the space stretching from the Dardanelles to the Bab el Mandeb (the Gate of Tears), and from the Libyan-Egyptian frontier to Iran. At the present day, as during the Great War, the near east exerts a great power of attraction, more especially as it is of vital importance for the communications between England and its important colonial possessions, India and the other territories fringing the Indian Ocean. Besides that, its soil conceals great mineral wealth, in particular, war-essential petroleum, as well as iron ores and rare metals, while Mesopotamia, the land between the Euphrates and the Tigris, presents enormous agricultural possibilities. The near east therefore occupies the focus of interest now as always, not only inherently, as it were, on account of the forces and possibilities for the future dwelling in it, but also owing to its position as a bridge between the three continents of the ancient world.

*

Geopolitically regarded, the near east may be said to comprise not only Turkey and the lands of Syria and Arabia, but also, for a diversity of reasons, Egypt and Iran. It covers 30 degrees of latitude and 35 degrees of longitude, or an area not much less than Europe (excluding the Soviet Union), which extends from the 36th to the 72nd parallel of latitude and from the 10th degree west longitude to the 30th degree east longitude. But it counts barely 60 million inhabitants on its area of approximately 5.5 million square kilometres (about equal to the whole of Europe excluding the Soviet Union), because far more than half of the ground is occupied by deserts of sand or stone and inhospitable mountain ranges. Of the one million square kilometres belonging to Egyptian territory (which is about twice the size of Germany in 1914), only 35,000 square kilometres (an area about equal to that of the province of Brandenburg) are under cultivation. A population of some 16 million souls is thus confined within that area, which is made extremely fruitful by irrigation and yields large crops. It has even been estimated that the country lying between the two rivers Euphrates and Tigris in present-day Iraq, the Mesopotamia of the early kingdoms of Assyria and Babylonia, could even support a population of 100 million, as compared with its present population of about three million. There is here a complete lack of the artificial irrigation

and drainage works which in ancient times made the present-day areas of desert and march centers of prosperity and civilization,the monuments of which still testify to the greatness and power of the states of those early days. Similar scanty population and the unsuitability of very extensive regions for settlement, while dense masses of people are crowded together in small areas, are a phenomenon to be observed everywhere in the near east. As a matter of course, it exerts mostly a negative effect on the power of the space to form states, no less than on the importance of its policy with regard to means of communication and transport, and finally also on the strategic situation. Another geopolitical peculiarity is that the most important arteries of communication, the Suez Canal, the Bab el Mandeb, and the Dardanelles, all lie at the edges of the space. The Suez Canal is the most important of these three maritime routes, and the results of the recent campaign in Greece have brought it many hundreds of miles closer to the range of the German Air Corps. A glance at the map shows the great extent to which its safety of communication and its importance, already lowered apart from that, must further be reduced. The connection between the western and the eastern parts of the British Empire is thereby interrupted and the value of the British naval bases built up by many years of work with the support of diplomatic intrigues is imperilled by a single blow. Cyprus and Palestine, forming the direct northern flank protection of the Suez Canal, lie, as it is, within effective range of the German Air Corps, but have further lost their real strategic meaning, now that the object to be protected, the Suez Canal, canal so be directly attacked or raided. The situation is fundamentally the same in respect of Malta and Gibraltar, Aden, and the islands of Perim and Socotra, and therewith for the whole network of British dominion that has been cast for the last century, more particularly since the Great War, over the Arab nations and states of the near east. British near-east policy, as far as it is determined by the policy of communications and strategic considerations, has stood under the necessity of providing flank protection for the sea-route to India. In that connection it has nowadays to a great extent already lost its meaning. But the near east has become of problematic value, being associated with too much

risk for Great Britain considered from the viewpoint of air traffic. As a matter of fact, no inconsiderable part of the value that the lands of the near east possess for British imperial policy is based also on the fact that Palestine, Transjordania, and, in particular, Iraq offer suitable sites for airports on the air routes between England and India, Singapore, and Australia, from which branch off their air traffic routes to Cairo and therewith the Cairo to Cape Town route running through Africa from north to south. During the second and third decades of the present century, the value of Iraq and Transjordania rose with the growing intensity of Empire air traffic, in particular, for the Imperial Airways and for British traffic policy in general. But that has also now come to an end. The consequence are all the more serious for imperial policy, as the maritime connections with the territories of the British Empire in the far east, southern Asia, and Australia have moreover been interrupted, and can only be maintained on the much longer route round the Cape of Good Hope, which is also no longer to be considered safe.

The near east, as bridge of the British Empire, has now been eliminated to a considerable extent both by air and by sea, and that supporting pillar of the Empire structure will be completely removed, should the exasperation of the Arabs, repressed for twenty years and more, be inflamed by the example of Iraq and break out openly. Regarded from that angle, the great thorough-fare route and the scene of important decisions represented by this link between the continents of Europa, Asia, and Africa since the early days of human history, might acquire fresh historical importance and

Schwarzes Meer

TIFLIS — ÖL-LEITUNG — BAKU

BATUM

U.D.S.S.R.

Kaspisches Meer

US

TRAPEZUNT

SAFRANBOLU SAMSUN

UDAR EREGLI

TOKAT

ANKARA SIWAS

ESKISEHIR

TÜRKEI MALATYA

KAYSERI

KONIA

ADANA

EGIRDIR

ERZERUM

VAN-S

TABRIS

URMIA-S

TEHERAN

SENDJAN

IRAN

MARDIN

MOSUL KIRKUK

SAMARRA

BAGDAD

DISFUL

SCHUSCHTER

ALEPPO

Euphrat

SYRIEN

HAMA ÖL-LEITUNG

HOMS

STRASSE

Tigris

Tripolis

CYPERN (brit.)

BEIRUT

DAMASKUS

KERBELA

HILLE

IRAK

KUT-el-AMARA

AMARA

NASRY

SAMAWA

POST

ÖL-LEITUNG

BASRA

KOWEIT

Persischer Golf

es Meer

HAIFA

TELAVIV JERUSALEM

JAFFA

ANDRIEN PORTSAID

PAL. TRANS-JORDANIEN

AKABA

SAUDI-ARABIEN

NEU-TRAL

ERDÖLGEBIETE

KM

0   100   200

HAMMAM KAIRO SUES KANALI SUES

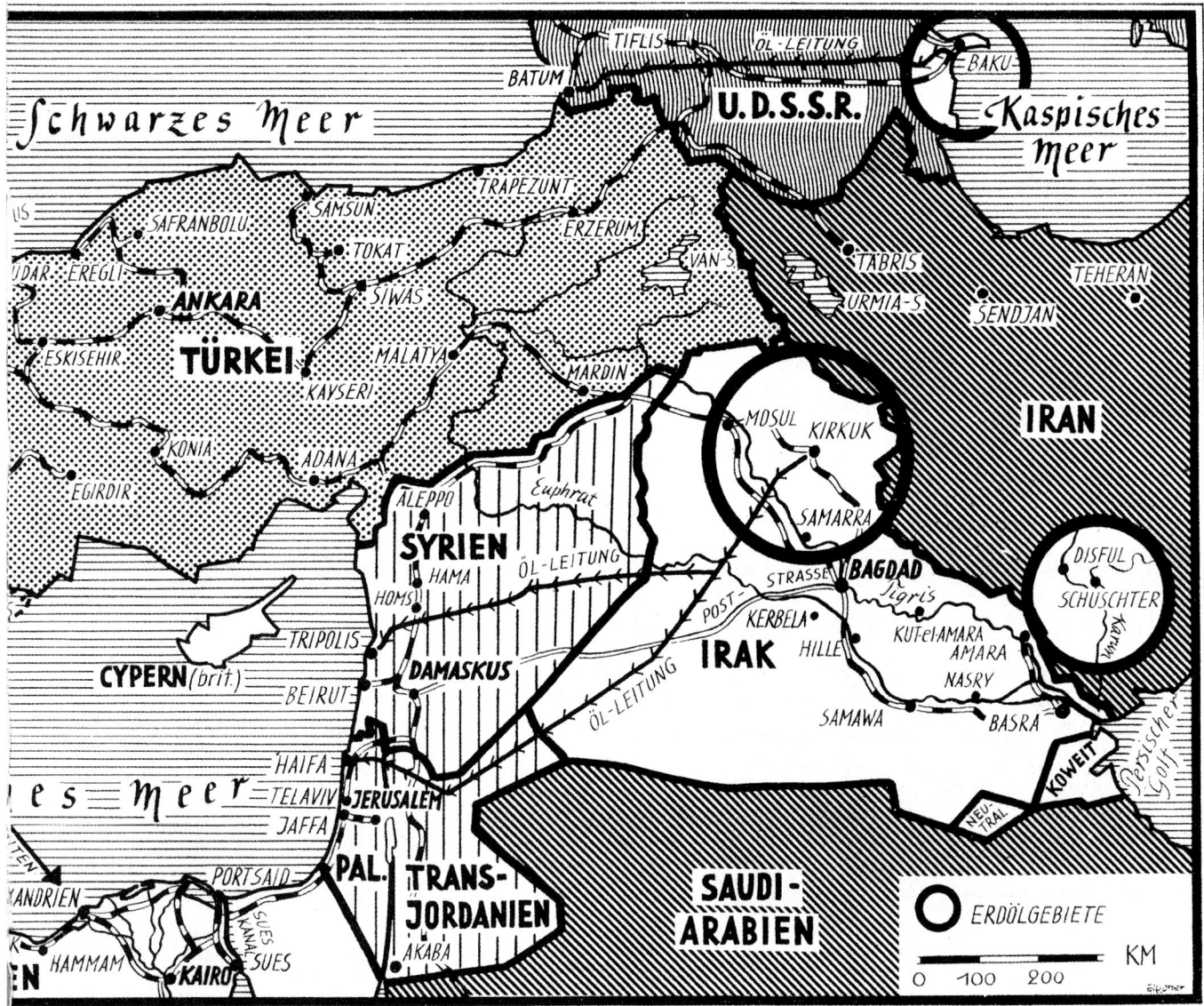

simultaneously great actuality. As a matter of fact the lands between the Black Sea and the Red Sea, between the Mediterranean and the Persian Golf have been the scene of numerous warlike expeditions, beginning with the Egyptian conquest as far as Mesopotamia, the Assyrian invasions of Egypt, the conquering expeditions of the Persians under Cyrus, the Macedonians and Greeks under Alexander the Great, the wars of the Romans and Parthians, the invasions and wanderings of the Saracens and Seljuk Turks, the expansion of Islam, the Christian crusades of the Middle Ages, the Mongol invasions, and, at a later date, Napoleon's expedition to Egypt with the unattained goal of India in view, and finally the battles of the Great War fought in Armenia and sou thern Arabia, on the Suez Canal front and the Dardanelles, in Mesopotamia and on the frontier of Iran.

That important region was rich, although it was to a great extent unexploited, or had sunk back into oblivion and backwardness, so that it stood in the focus of political and economic interest at times when it was not within the field of forces of the armies crossing it. The French and Italians were the powers interested in the Mediterranean and the Levant; there were further the Russians with their dreams of the Dardanelles and, for a time, their urge through Persia to the open Indian Ocean, the English, interested in the land bridge between their African and Indian colonial empire, the pan-British fringing of the Indian Ocean, and finally the Germans following up their ideas of economic expansion in the south-east by the projected Baghdad railway—all these nations took an

interest in the region, whereby the interest of Germany, as in so many parts of the world, was mainly, if not exclusively, of an economic nature. Germany was actually the sole great power that made a really concrete and positive contribution in the shape of the Baghdad railway to opening up part of these countries in the interests of their inhabitants themselves. In consequence of recent events, the near east has once more acquired enhanced international importance and actuality. It is for that reason useful to be reminded that it has therewith again assumed an age-old function.

Its value as source of raw materials is of much more recent origin, but its mineral wealth certainly has made it doubly interesting and worth coveting. Under that head falls not only the cotton of Egypt, which would doubtless find equally favorable cultivation conditions in Mesopotamia, but also valuable minerals which, together with iron ores, are to be found distributed everywhere in these extensive regions in deposits which would repay exploitation. At the present time petroleum is being chiefly worked in the Mosul-Kirkuk area, to the east of Basrah in southern Iran, and on the Bahrein Islands in the Persian Gulf, while there can be no doubt that it occurs elsewhere also and only awaits discovery. A reckless and stubborn struggle has been waged for that petroleum since the beginning of the century. Details cannot be given here, but the conflict ended with the ascendency of England, which ousted the other nations concerned, chiefly France, its ally in the Great War, from the circle of beneficiaries. The war between Greece and Turkey engineered by London in 1921/22 offered the welcome opportunity

of occupying the petroleum area of Mosul, which was formally annexed by Iraq, to which country England allowed the appearance of independent sovereignty. In reality, however, British policy has not only always striven against any abandonment of its influence in this part of the near east also, but has made every effort to strengthen it as much as possible. The Bahrein Islands in the Persian Gulf are a second petroleum area of importance. It is exploited, it is true, by American firms, but the oil flows to the English, like that of the oil wells in Iraq, which are worked by the Anglo-Iranian Oil Company. Apart from that, the near east is rich in oil wells at other places also, such as the whole of the western and southern shores of the Caspian Sea, where the exploitation is concentrated in the Russian oil center Baku.

The oil wells of Mosul, Kirkuk, southern Iran, and the Bahrein Islands are of great importance both for the fuel supply of the British Mediterranean fleet, as well as for civil air communications along the route London, Baghdad, Karachi, and Bombay. Pipelines were laid a few years ago at great expense through the desert to the Mediterranean ports of Tripolis and Haifa. The present interruption of these oil lines means a heavy blow to the supply and therewith to the fighting power of the British Mediterranean fleet.

Any shock to British power in the near east, or even complete loss of the command of the oil wells and the most important communication routes would hit the Empire at its most vulnerable point, and the effects would be noticed far beyond the confines of the near east throughout the whole Arab and Mohammedan world.

Köche im Süden

Von Kriegsberichter Horst Kanitz * Aufnahmen PK Lossnitzer (Atlantic)

Cooks in Southern Climes

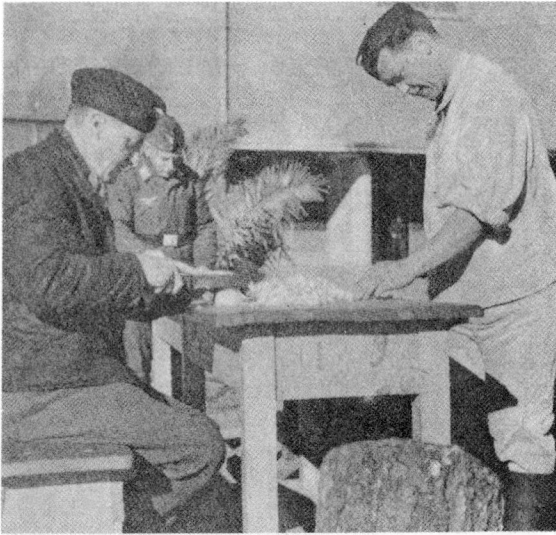

Unter der warmen Sonne des Südens ist das Zerkleinern von Früchten ein wahrhaftes Vergnügen

Breaking up fruit is a real pleasure under the warm southern sky

Da sitzen dann die Soldaten auf Bänken oder Lavablöcken, erzählen, lachen und lassen es sich gut schmecken

The men then sit around on benches or blocks of lava, chatting, laughing, and enjoying their meal

Even in Italy one cannot always be eating nothing but "spaghetti al pomodoro", otherwise known as macaroni with tomatoes, or even cuttlefish with olives, washed down with sparkling red Chianti. No sir. Now and again the stomach of the second reserve man calls for a hearty chunk of barrack bread and for the midday meal potatoes and gravy with an outsize in cutlets as mother used to make it. If it be true that love takes its way through the stomach, it is equally true of the happy good-humor of the soldier which always shows a marked rise at the approach of the steaming army kitchens or of the comrades with their ration carriers filled to the brim.

The southern climate generates a hearty appetite. The heat is not yet overpowering, and oranges, mandarines, or olives provide the necessary stimulus. Above all, we must not forget that there is work and toil every day and to spare. Even those who cannot accompany raiding expeditions, but have their allotted duties among the ground personnel, are often very heavily worked. We need only think of the men in the spare-parts store and the repair shops, the gas-pit attendants, the radio men, and many others, who are frequently all alone at their posts and do their duty in a wonderful matter-of-course way. There is no one around to admire them, no one to crack them up, and yet they are an important for the success of the great achievements of our airmen as the pilot or the bomb aimer themselves. Everyone is looked after. Trains or our faithful Ju 52, the transport plane that has everywhere proved its

worth, bring up supplies, spares, and food, the quality of which after the long journey is carefully examined before being issued. Then somewhere or other, on the coast of Sicily or in the lonely desert, hidden in the shade of palms, the cooks set up their tents and prepare a good square meal for their comrades, while an army kitchen sends its appetizing vapors into the pale blue of the sky.

Things liven up about midday. The cook is surrounded by his comrades who laughingly hold out their mess tins and insists on his filling in a substantial helping, perishing of hunger as they are.

And then they sit around in the warm sunshine on benches or on blocks of lava that Mt. Etna, which now looks so friendly, once spewed out to devastate the landscape. Others rest a while in some godforsaken oasis in the desert, but everywhere chatting, joking, laughing, and not forgetting to tuck in heartily.

Noch einen Schlag! — Der „Küchenbulle" hat ja nichts dagegen

Another helping! The cook has no objection

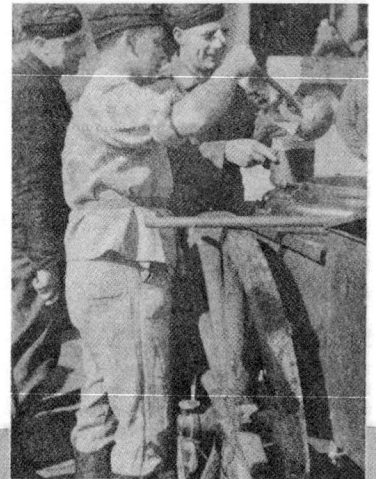

Feldküchen dampfen in das Azurblau des südlichen Himmels, und freundlich grüßt der sonst so drohende Ätna herüber

Army kitchens send up their steam into the azure blue of the southern sky. Mt. Etna, otherwise of threatening aspect, greets the men across the country in a friendly way

VORSTOSS in die

The American commercial airplane Boeing "Stratoliner" enjoys itself most at 20,000 ft. up. The passengers sit in a pressure-tight cabin in which a pressure corresponding to a flying height of about 10,000 ft. is automatically maintained. Altitude-planes of that type with pressure cabin are a paying proposition only on very long routes

STRATOSPHÄRE

The Advance to the Stratosphere

Engineers Struggle to Reach the Limits of Altitude Flight

By Gerhard Meyer

The alarm is raised. Pursuit planes scurry over the ground and climb away at a steep angle, shooting into the sky like gigantic projectiles. Within a few minutes, the machines just thundering over the tents have become tiny flickering specks in the clear sky. The Me 109 can climb 19,700 ft. in five minutes, whereby the raging pistons of the 1,000 h.p. engine raise 50 cwt. at a rate of more than 43 m.p.h., which is faster than aircraft were able to fly at all in the early days of aviation.

The vision of the fluttering dance of the pistons, the brilliant whirl of flame that ceaselessly snorts through the cylinders is one of the most fascinating pictures that engineering presents us with. A primitive element has been aroused and thunders against the confining walls. The bridling of that power-charged volcano, ready at any moment to rend the walls of its prison, calls for the exercise of the highest powers of the human intelligence, which have been applied to make the fiery stream surge still more powerfully and still more mightily.

Thus was developed the engine that lifts airplanes into the stratosphere. The human organism has been compared with an engine and the comparison has been reversed and the engine has been likened to the human organism, and the comparison is very plausible when one thinks of an ascent to great heights where cosmic cold seeks to grasp man and machine, while the air becomes increasingly rarefied. Man needs oxygen to feed the combustion process in his cells, and the fiery stream in the engine also needs oxygen to discharge its power with full force through the pistons, crankshaft, and propeller; for no flame can burn, unless nourished by oxygen.

The fiery stream roaring through the cylinders of the engine slackens and comes to a stop in the air beyond the cloud limits with its deficiency of oxygen, just as the vital processes in the human tissues also flag.

But the pursuit plane must climb still higher to be able to pounce from aloft upon the enemy. And the bomber must also feel as much at home at the icy heights of 6,000 or 8,000 metres (19,700 to 26,200 ft.),

The hermetically sealed test cabin for one man, which was tried out in Italy for altitude flight, clings closely to the shape of the body. The pilot is snugly encased in it, like the chrysalis of an insect. Pressure cabins for several persons, such as are needed especially by commercial aviation, are naturally differently designed

as it does near the earth. It must flit through the clouds in the same ghostly way in which it thunders close above meadows, fields, and hedges. Indeed, it would even have to fly more and still more rapidly the higher that it rises, because the rarefied air at these altitudes opposes much less resistance to its flight than the dense atmospheric envelope in the neighborhood of the ground.

But that must all remain a pious wish, as long as the engine with its hunger for oxygen at that altitude gets

increasingly meagre rations of the gas that nourishes the flames in its cylinders and releases power. It pants for air and does not get enough, the flame in its cylinders demands nourishment, and receives none. The 1,000 h.p. engine at ground level becomes a 500 h.p. engine, and the output finally drops to 300 h.p. only. No altitude flight can be undertaken with such an engine.

The engine also might defend itself against the collapse of its powers, just as man can do, by means of an oxygen apparatus, but it would be an extravagant curative treatment to feed an engine with oxygen for any length of time, so that it must be helped in another way. The rarefied air is simply recompressed before entering the cylinders to the same density as at the ground level. A vane wheel, a blower, can be allowed to run before the cylinders; it draws in the air and whirls it in any quantity, according to the rate at which the wheel rotates, to the intake openings of the engine. A supercharger of that kind is identical with the compressor that presses more air into the cylinders of the engines of racing cars than they can take in unaided.

The crankshaft of an aero-engine rotates two thousand times in the minute, but the vane wheel of the supercharger whirls round 18,000 to 20,000 times in a minute and would have to run at a still higher speed, the further that the engine penetrated into the thin air aloft; it would therefore have to be made larger or proportionately more wheels would have to be run one behind the other.

But that droning circle of vanes consumes power, which must be supplied by the stream of fire in the cylinders. The blower-fed engine must therewith rotate, as it were, two propellers —the actual driving propeller and the blower vanes, so that the power fed to one is lost to the other. The power consumption of a simple supercharger, it is true, is not high, but a simple supercharger is not very efficient and would be too weak, even at a few thousand feet. Above a definite limit, however, the complicated multistage and multipassage superchargers are too extravagant in engine power consumption, compared with the useful effect. How can the supercharger be driven, without robbing the engine of too much power? A research engineer had a hunch one day. The tongues of the fiery current in the cylinders are continually lapping into the open air through the exhaust pipes and the yellow flames of the exhaust can often be seen flaring out below or alongside the engine. These exhaust gases represent so much power lost. They shoot out of the exhaust pipes at a speed of more than 600 m.p.h.; if they could be led into a turbine, they would cause it to rotate at a very high speed, without in the least impairing the rotation of the crankshaft or the propeller. The vane wheel of the supercharger could be mounted on the turbine shaft, so that the supercharger would be driven without loss of power.

However, childishly simple that problem may appear to be at first sight, its solution is actually extraordinarily difficult, as may be gaged from the fact that aviation engineers in every country with any interest in flying have been struggling for twenty years to find a solution. It is only now that the exhaust-gas turbo-supercharger is approaching maturity, so as to fit it for practical operation. The blower-fed engine is a source of power that usually gives the same performance at 16,400 or 19,700 ft. as at ground level, and it is hoped to preserve that output of 1,000

The Italian altitude-record pilot Pezzi gives his mechanic his final instructions before the start. The metal helmet is bolted to the collar of the suit a few minutes later and the pilot is separated from the outer world. The start to the solitude of the stratosphere can now begin

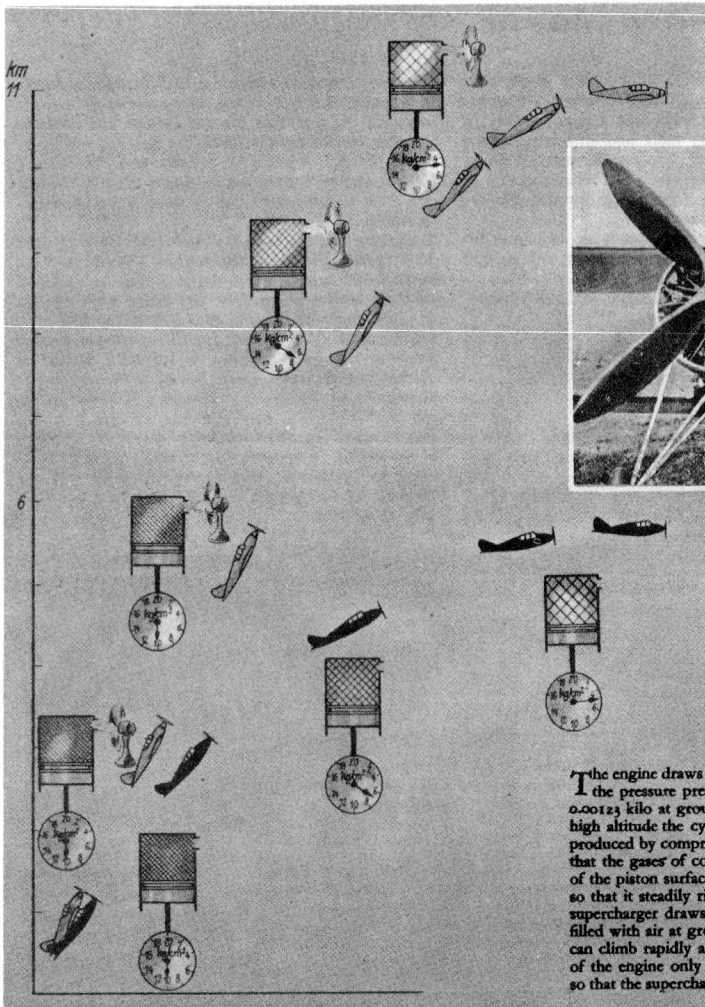

This tremendous four-blade propeller drew the Caproni altitude plane 161 with Pezzi at the wheel to an altitude of 51,362 ft., the world-record of that time. The blades are unusually broad and long, in order to grip sufficiently large masses of air

h.p., let us say, even at 53,000 ft. by means of the blower-fed engine.

But altitude flight brings up an unending number of other burning problems, all of them connected with the low density of the air, the deficiency of oxygen, or the cold at great altitudes. Just think of the propeller. Its operating conditions are completely changed, as are those of all other parts that have to arouse living powers out of air currents, when the agent that they work with, that is, the air itself, is changed.

The propeller also is thus faced by fresh difficulties at great altitudes, which may be simply expressed as follows. The propeller blades beat the air obliquely, seizing a definite mass of air and throwing it backwards. They naturally seize less of the rarefied air at great altitudes, so that the force of reaction produced, the thrust, is smaller. It may therefore occur that an engine is still supplying 1,000 h.p. at 16,400 ft. up, while the thrusting force with which the airplane is dragged along, which, in the last resort, is after all the main factor, is very much less than at ground level.

Now the propeller might be rotated more rapidly, because it would then seize more air, but unfortunately the temperature of the air also sinks to about —52. C as the altitude increases. But the speed of sound in air also drops as the temperature falls and the laws of flow are revolutionized at the speed of sound to such a sweeping extent, that they can only be hinted at here. All the laws of flow are practically turned topsyturvy, which means that the propeller must not be allowed to rotate so rapidly that parts of the blade,

The engine draws oxygen with the air into the cylinders. While on the ground, ech cylinder is filled with air at the pressure prevailing there. Assuming that the cylinder has a capacity of one litre, the air will weigh 0.00123 kilo at ground level, but only half as much at about 21,300 ft., because the air becomes rarefied. At a high altitude the cylinder thus actually contains less air, combustion becomes weaker, and the working pressure produced by compression and combustion, which represents the actual power of the engine, drops. Assuming that the gases of combustion, for example, at ground level exert a pressure of 10 kilos per square centimetre of the piston surface, that pressure will fall to 8, 6, 4 kilos and still less, as the plane climbs to greater heights, so that it steadily rises more slowly, until the power of the pistons is too weak to raise it any further.—The supercharger draws in the rarefied air and compresses it, so that the cylinders of blower-fed engines remain filled with air at ground-level pressure up to rated altitude. The engine output does not fall off and the plane can climb rapidly and uniformly up to the rated altitude, which is generally 16,400 to 20,000 ft. The power of the engine only then begins to fall off, and the supercharger can no longer compress the air sufficiently, so that the supercharger airplane now climbs more flatly, until it reaches its ceiling, which lies at about 36,000 to 39,500 ft. for modern pursuit planes

Die „grünen Teufel" von Cassino — so hat die anglo-amerikanische Presse in einem unfreiwilligen Lob unsere heldenhaften Verteidiger von Cassino genannt. Eine Bombenlast von vielen tausend Tonnen und tagelanges Artillerietrommelfeuer haben die Kampfkraft der Fallschirmjäger und Grenadiere nicht zermürben können. Hinter Mauerresten und in zerborstenen Kellern haben sie ihre MG-Nester und Kampfstände eingerichtet, immer bereit, jeden Versuch des Feindes, sie daraus zu vertreiben, blutig zu vereiteln

Die „grünen Teufel" von Cassino

In den zerstörten Häusern und Gängen der Stadt und des Klosters Cassino jagen die Granatwerfergruppen der Fallschirmjäger ihre Salven auf kürzeste Entfernung in die Stellungen des Feindes und weichen keinen Schritt zurück, auch wenn der feindliche Geschoßhagel sie fast einzudecken droht

Ein Hauptmann der Fallschirmtruppe hat seinen Gefechtsstand mit primitiven Mitteln im Keller eines zerstörten Hauses aufgeschlagen. Ein Sturmgeschütz ist in Deckung gegangen; es wird Minuten später einen Gegenstoß der „grünen Teufel" wirkungsvoll unterstützen

PK-Aufnahmen
Kriegsberichter Zscheile
(Atl 2, HH 1), Wahner (Atl 1)

Jeder Angriff kostet die Anglo - Amerikaner Ströme von Blut. In einigermaßen gesicherten Höhlen und Unterständen haben sich die Fallschirmjäger ihre Verbandplätze eingerichtet. Auch der Feind wird hier versorgt, bevor er in die deutsche Gefangenschaft wandert

157

Bombs on Belgrade

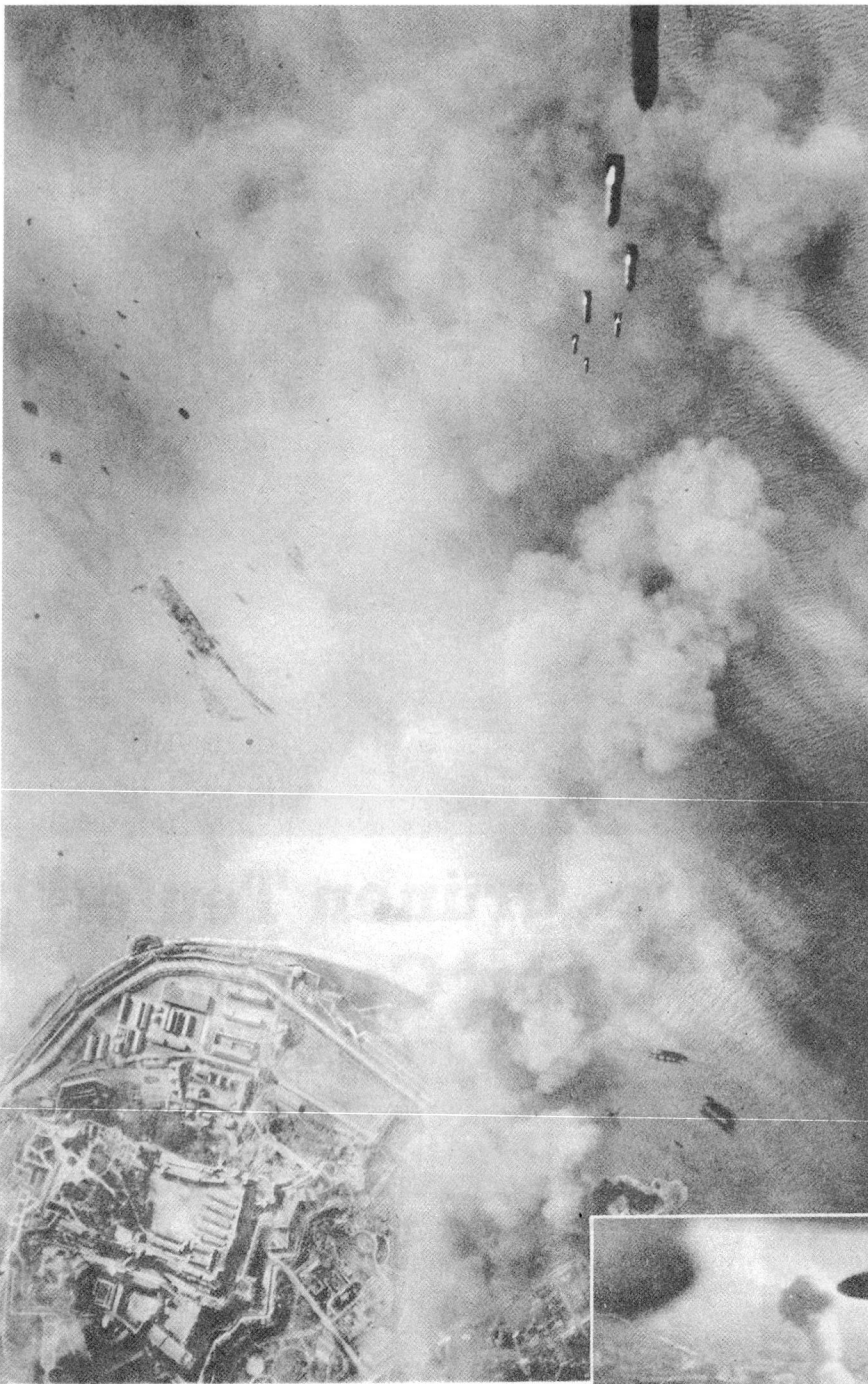

Following the challenge to Germany by the Servian insurgent government under General Simovich, the conspirators were rudely awakened in the early hours of April 6 in a way that they had not expected so speedily. German horizontal and dive bombers appeared over the capital of former Yugoslavia and bombed the numerous military objectives of the fortress of Belgrade. The photos on this page show how successful they were. The picture above covers the citadel on the foreland over the Danube; thick clouds of smoke are rising from it and bombs are still dropping on the target. The small photo at the right was taken by a bomber wing during an attack on a large hut camp. The smoke of the explosion of the bombs just dropped is ascending skywards. The large air photo at the right was taken at a great altitude and presents a bird's-eye view of part of the fortress of Belgrade. The railroad depot is ablaze; the flames can be plainly seen at the point where the clouds of smoke are rising and further fires are smoldering close by. The confluence of Save and Danube can be seen in the upper part of the photograph. The shadow cast by the big bridge over the Danube brings it out in wonderful relief

Photos: Air Corps (3)

Bomben auf Belgrad

The Bulgarian Air Force has been in existence only for a few years, after having freed itself from the shackles of the Treaty of Neuilly, following the example of Germany. The work of reconstruction effected in the short space of less than three years is astonishing, when one sees the large, fine-looking airdromes, erected on German lines, the numerous field airdromes, the large numbers of modern machines, and the training of flying crews and ground personnel. Everyone who has had an opportunity of visiting the Bulgarian airdromes and has experienced the spirit that animates these splendid airmen feels that he is among the Prussians of the Balkans, in the finest sense of the term

Eine Flugzeugbesatzung ist mit ihrem Bodenpersonal angetreten. Der Leutnant gibt den Flugauftrag

Auf einem Feldflughafen bewacht der Posten während der Mittagsruhe die getarnten Flugzeuge

A sentry watches the camouflaged planes on a field airdrome during the midday interval

Flugbetrieb! Ein Martin-Bomber, wie sie in Bulgarien zahlreich zur Umschulung auf zweimotorige Flugzeuge verwendet werden, ist soeben gelandet und rollt zu neuem Aufstieg an den Start. Der Flugleiter überwacht die Schulung

A busy airdrome. A Martin bomber, a type of which large numbers are used in Bulgaria for training pilots for the twin-engined type of plane, has just landed and is taxiing to the take-off for another flight. The flying instructor is supervising the training

160

Bulgariens Flieger

Bulgaria's Airmen

Ein Kampfflugzeug wird enttarnt und zum Start fertiggemacht

The camouflaging is just being removed from a bomber, which is being got ready to take off

Der Leutnant Georgieff „fliegt die Zweimotorige schon sehr ordentlich", meint sehr befriedigt der Flugleiter

The flying instructor remarks with satisfaction that Lieutenant Georgieff is already flying the twin-engined plane very smartly

Das rechte Bild zeigt (links) den Kommandeur eines bulgarischen Fliegerregiments, Oberstleutnant Stoikoff. Rechts (mit Lederjacke) der Ausbildungsleiter des Regiments, Leutnant Simeonoff

Right: Lieutenant-Colonel Stotkoff, commander of a Bulgarian air regiment (at the left) and Lieutenant Simeonoff, regimental flying instructor (at the right, wearing a leather jacket)

Die vier Porträte links unten zeigen Flugzeugführer, Beobachter, Funker und Bordwart eines Do-17-Kampfflugzeuges deutscher Herkunft. Diese vier Flieger bekleiden den Rang von Offizier-Stellvertretern, den höchsten Dienstgrad, der für Unteroffiziere erreichbar ist

The four portraits at the left below are those of pilot, observer, wireless operator, and flight mechanic respectively of a Do 17 bomber of German origin. These four airmen rank as Offizier-Stellvertreter (temporary lieutenant), the highest rank attainable by non-commissioned officers

Ein deutscher Fliegeroffizier ist als Vorkommando soeben gelandet und meldet sich bei dem bulgarischen Fliegerhorstkommandanten

A German air officer has just landed as advance party and reports himself to the Bulgarian commandant of the airdrome

Aufnahmen PK-Grabler (9)

Leichte Flakartillerie ist auf einer Anhöhe in Stellung gegangen, um die Sicherung des Flugplatzes gegen etwaige Luftangriffe zu übernehmen

Light anti-aircraft defense artillery have taken up a position on an eminence for the protection of the airdrome against air-raids

Auf Bulgarischen Flugplätzen

On Bulgarian Airdromes

Für das gegenseitige Grußverhältnis ist die Kenntnis der Rangabzeichen notwendig. Ein bulgarischer Dolmetscher erläutert die Abzeichen eines deutschen Fliegerleutnants. — Das Bild rechts zeigt einen Feldflugplatz bei einem bulgarischen Dorf. — Das untere Bild zeigt Soldaten der Flakartillerie, die einen Ausflug nach Burgas gemacht haben

Familiarity with the badges of rank is necessary for the mutual saluting. A Bulgarian interpreter is explaining the badges of a German pilot officer. Right: A field airdrome near a Bulgarian village. Below: Men of the anti-aircraft defense pay a visit to Burgas

In kameradschaftlichem Einvernehmen wird die Frage der Brennstoffversorgung geregelt

The fuel problem is settled in comradely agreement

Er wollte sich nur einmal das große Flugzeug der „Germanskis" ansehen

He wanted just once to see the big airplane of the "Germanskis"

Waffenbrüder von einst - Kameraden von heute

Brothers-in-arms in Days Past - Comrades of Today

General der Flieger von Richthofen, Kommandierender General eines Fliegerkorps, verabschiedet sich vor dem Start mit dem Fieseler-„Storch" von bulgarischen Offizieren

General der Flieger (Air Vice-Marshal) von Richthofen. General commanding an air-service corps, says goodby to Bulgarian officers before leaving in a Fieseler "Stork"

Die erste Zigarette wird ausgetauscht. Die anfänglich befürchteten sprachlichen Schwierigkeiten sind nicht eingetreten, da alle bulgarischen Offiziere recht gut Deutsch sprechen. Auch im Unteroffizierkorps finden sich viele Männer, die genügend Deutsch sprechen, um eine einwandfreie Verständigung zu gewährleisten

The first cigarette is exchanged. The language difficulties at first feared did not mature, because all the Bulgarian officers speak German quite well. Many of the non-coms too speak enough German to ensure perfect understanding